THE BRITISH CARIBBEAN

ELISABETH WALLACE

The British
Caribbean

From the decline of colonialism
to the end of Federation

UNIVERSITY OF TORONTO PRESS
TORONTO AND BUFFALO

© University of Toronto Press 1977
Toronto and Buffalo
Printed in Canada

Library of Congress Cataloging in Publication Data

Wallace, Elisabeth.
    The British Caribbean: From the decline of colonialism to the end of Federation.

    Bibliography: p.
    Includes index.
    1. West Indies, British — Constitutional history.
    2. West Indies, British — Politics and government.
    3. West Indies, British — Economic conditions.
    I. Title
    JL602.W34   320.9'729'73   76-48191
    ISBN 0-8020-5351-3

This book has been published during the
Sesquicentennial year of the University of Toronto.

Contents

Preface

This study's main concern is to examine constitutional developments in twelve British Caribbean territories during the first sixty years of the twentieth century, when they were evolving from colonialism to self-government. Ten eventually joined to form a short-lived federation. The book discusses the growth of trade unions and parties, the causes and results of the strikes and riots of the 1930s, the advent of adult suffrage, the federal movement, and the rise and fall of the ill-fated West Indies Federation.

Caribbean scholars have tended to concentrate more on the economics, history, and sociology of their region than on its politics, sometimes dismissed as simple manifestations of imperialism or neo-colonialism. There seems room for a political analysis based neither on hypothetical models nor on the protracted debate about cultural pluralism.

West Indians are understandably impatient of the numerous studies by expatriates of their manifold problems, analyses which have seldom led to significant reform. In extenuation for adding to these the writer can only plead long-standing interest in the area, warm liking for its peoples, and concern for good relations between the Commonwealth Caribbean and Canada. Although with the best will in the world no foreigner can hope to rival the intimate knowledge of a country possessed by its own citizens, he enjoys the modest advantage of being able to stand back from his canvas. The writer hopes that distance will lend objectivity as well as enchantment and that an outsider's desire to understand will partially compensate for occasions when she appears to see through a glass darkly.

Professor Alexander Brady, Dr David Lowenthal, the late Mr Earle Maynier, and Mr Robert Reford were all good enough to read the manuscript and to give me much valuable advice and perceptive criticism. I am particularly grateful for the kindly interest in my work shown by numerous West Indians in many territories and various walks of life, who generously spared time to discuss with me the intricacies of Caribbean politics.

I am also much indebted to the Canadian Institute of International Affairs, which commissioned this study, for encouragement and financial aid; to the University of Toronto for contributions towards travelling and clerical expenses; and to the Canada Council for two grants which enabled me to complete it. This work has been published with the help of grants from the Social Science Research Council of Canada, using funds provided by the Canada Council, and the Publications Fund of University of Toronto Press. To them I am much indebted.

E.W.
Department of Political Economy, University of Toronto
June 1976

THE BRITISH CARIBBEAN

1

Prologue

This book examines political developments in the former British Caribbean colonies from the beginning of the twentieth century to the collapse of the West Indies Federation in 1962. The Commonwealth Caribbean territories curve in a sickle-shaped arc across the Caribbean Sea from Jamaica, far to the west among the Greater Antilles, 90 miles south of Cuba and 665 miles from British Honduras, to Trinidad, a thousand miles southeast. Apart from Canada, Bermuda and the Bahamas in the Atlantic (which are not part of the West Indies), and Belize and Guyana in Central and South America respectively, these territories, covering 104,000 square miles, are the only Commonwealth countries in the hemisphere. Without Jamaica, a natural geographic unit is formed by the archipelago of the Eastern Caribbean islands: the British Virgins (not discussed here because they never considered joining the Federation); the Leewards (Antigua, with its dependencies Redonda and Barbuda, St Kitts-Nevis, Anguilla, and Montserrat); the Windwards (Dominica, St Lucia, St Vincent, Grenada with Carriacou, and the little Grenadines divided between Grenada and St Vincent); the Dutch and French territories; Barbados; and Trinidad and Tobago. The British islands vary in size from the 1980 square miles of Trinidad and Tobago to the 32 square miles of Montserrat.

To the West Indies, as to North America, and later to Australia and New Zealand, early English settlers brought the ideas and practices of their homeland: the rule of law, civil and political liberties, and constitutions modelled on that of Britain. Although these were for centuries the monopoly of a handful of whites, in the 1960s, when the British West Indies began to attain independence, in Barbados, the Leewards, and Jamaica parliamentary institutions were more than three hundred years old. Seventeenth-century Caribbean legislatures usually had an appointed upper house and an elected lower one. Barbados alone has retained unbroken the self-government thus early granted. With the exception of the

Bermuda House (founded in 1620), the Barbados Assembly, formed in 1639 of burgesses chosen to represent the freeholders, is the oldest in the overseas Commonwealth.

SUGAR, SLAVERY, AND EMANCIPATION

Past politics, said Lord Acton, is present history. To understand the twentieth-century British West Indies requires some knowledge of their history, especially since emancipation in the 1830s.

The slave trade long established in Africa began in the Caribbean at the end of the fifteenth century, when Christopher Columbus transported Amerindians as slaves to Spain. In 1501 a reverse movement began when the king of Spain authorized the export to the Spanish West Indies of slaves from Africa. Sixty years later his example was followed by an Englishman, Sir John Hawkins, who introduced slavery to the British islands in order to provide labour, especially on sugar estates. From the outset of European colonization slavery and sugar were inextricably connected.

For some two hundred and fifty years this trade in human beings continued. In the first three-quarters of the eighteenth century alone almost 500,000 Africans were transported as slaves to the British West Indies. During this period, when sugar plantations flourished on slave labour, the United Kingdom's Caribbean colonies were major contributors to her wealth, power, and prestige. Yet from the beginning of the eighteenth century, when sugar profits were still spectacular, the iniquities of slavery were attacked by such Englishmen as John Locke, Daniel Defoe, and Samuel Johnson, and later by John Wesley, Thomas Paine, Adam Smith, William Wilberforce, and Thomas Fowell Buxton.

The United Kingdom abolished the slave trade in 1807 and the anti-slavery movement finally triumphed in 1833, when Britain's newly reformed parliament passed an act to abolish slavery throughout the empire on 1 August 1834. In the West Indies alone this measure freed some 700,000 people, or nine-tenths of the population, at a cost of £20 million to British taxpayers.

After emancipation most former slaves continued to view estate labour as a species of serfdom and manual work in general as degrading: attitudes still widely prevalent. In British Guiana, Jamaica, and many of the Windwards, where unoccupied land could easily be obtained, the majority of freedmen refused to work as paid employees on plantations where they had once been slaves. Their great desire, like that of country folk everywhere, was and has remained to own a patch of ground, no matter how small. In Trinidad, Tobago, Grenada, Dominica, and Montserrat large estates practically disappeared, as most land was bought, in small plots, by black farmers. In Barbados, St Kitts, and Antigua, however, where almost all cultivable land was owned by estates, little was for sale. Their peoples shared the widespread distaste for plantation labour, which as late as the 1860s paid less than a shilling a day. Yet since no other work was available, the majority of freedmen continued to serve their former masters as hired labourers. Hence in these three islands emancipation produced few major economic changes and did little to alter the traditional attitudes of employers and employees.[1] Everywhere, however, estate owners faced a shortage of labour, many plantations were abandoned or broken up, and in most territories a class of black peasant proprietors began to develop.

While the problems of the sugar industry were diverse, the primary difficulty was to obtain workers. Various attempts were made to solve it. During the first few decades after emancipation and especially in 1848-9 more than 11,000 free Africans voluntarily migrated to the British West Indies. Since, however, sugar estates required far more labourers, largely unsuccessful efforts were made to import Scots, Irish, and Germans. Of the 36,000 who emigrated, one-third later returned home. Portuguese from Madeira and a few Maltese were brought in as indentured workers. Small numbers of Chinese were introduced in 1806, but the majority came between 1852 and 1862 as contract labourers on Trinidadian sugar plantations, where they were later joined by others not indentured. A few Chinese went to Jamaica, as did some Syrians and Lebanese. When in 1866 the importation of Chinese was finally abandoned, about 1200 had settled in Trinidad. Most Chinese and Lebanese proved less interested in working on the land than in market-gardening and shopkeeping, occupations in which many of their descendants are still prominent. Their success in these fields was perhaps partly responsible for Anthony Trollope's opinion in 1859 that the liveliness of Port-of-Spain contrasted sharply with the sleepiness of Jamaica and the apathy of the smaller islands.

Much the largest number of imported workers came from India and were commonly, if confusingly, described as East Indians, to differentiate them from West Indians and Amerindians. This influx, begun in 1838, was temporarily suspended by the Indian government from 1839 to 1844 and again from 1848 to 1851, because of a high mortality rate among indentured labourers and allegations that their working conditions were nearly as bad as under slavery. The system was finally discontinued in 1917, when public opinion in both India and the West Indies had become hostile to it.

Of over 500,000 East Indians who migrated to the Caribbean, almost 239,000 went to British Guiana, some 150,000 to Trinidad, and another 36,000 to Jamaica. They now form the largest ethnic group in Guyana and about 40 per cent of the population of Trinidad. Their advent permanently altered the racial structure and economy of these two territories. With the East Indians' arrival rice became first an important crop and eventually a common staple of diet throughout the region. In Guyana rice is grown by East Indians, and in Trinidad most agriculture is in their hands although there some Africans work in sugar factories.

On the conditions of indentured labourers a British public servant commented that he had seen enough of the system 'to dislike extremely the task of enforcing its draconic laws.'[2] East Indian indentured workers were entitled to free housing, clothing, food, and medical care. Those who decided to remain after their contracts expired were also entitled, in lieu of a return passage to India, in Trinidad from 1868 to 1882 and sometimes in British Guiana, to free land, the size of which was based on their length of service. Many chose this alternative. Free blacks, however, were given no such opportunity, but had to buy land they wanted to own. Their resentment of what they considered preferential treatment for latecomers was understandable. They tended, moreover, to look down on East Indians willing to work on plantations, as Africans who could avoid doing so would not. Furthermore, by providing a pool of labour East Indians limited Africans' bargaining power.

In both territories this situation led to East Indian dominance in agriculture and to racial antagonism. Many East Indians, especially in British Guiana, settled in isolated and relatively self-contained villages, often composed of only this racial group. There they clung to their religion, language, and customs, and showed little disposition to marry Africans, with whom their social relations were minimal. These circumstances fostered between the two peoples an originally accidental separation which almost amounted to unplanned segregation. With few contacts at school, at work, or in leisure hours, distrust and hostility were more common than understanding and fellow-feeling. Over the years this cleavage widened. In the twentieth century the racial gulf has become a cardinal characteristic of both Guyana and Trinidad and a major obstacle to their development as genuinely united communities – a goal which most West Indian territories have found difficulty in achieving.

Opinions differ as to whether it was the loss of unpaid workers which dealt the *coup de grâce* to the sugar industry. A former Speaker of the Antigua Assembly considered free labour cheaper than slavery. Intelligent planters there said as much in 1837 to the Quaker travellers Sturge and Harvey. This was also the view of E.B. Underhill, secretary of the Baptist Missionary Society, who visited the West Indies in the 1860s. In the same decade an American, W.C. Sewell, commented that free labourers worked more profitably and more willingly than slaves. He attributed the abandonment of numerous estates more to owners' debts and lack of capital than to want of labour.[3]

The prevalence of absentee proprietors undoubtedly played a part. Many large planters seldom visited their Caribbean holdings, but entrusted their management to agents apt to be incompetent or worse. The evils of absentee landlordism, notorious in Ireland, were multiplied in the West Indies. In 1835 some 70 per cent of Jamaican owners were non-resident. Trinidad, where two-thirds lived on their estates, was a conspicuous exception to the usual practice throughout the British Caribbean.

In 1783 the French island of St Domingo produced almost as much sugar as all the British West Indian territories combined. Much of France's advantage stemmed from the fact that in most of its other Caribbean colonies small resident proprietors raised sugar more profitably than large British estates with absentee owners. When the United Kingdom abolished the slave trade in 1807, the cost of raising sugar in Jamaica, which produced over half the quantity exported to Britain, was already twice as high as in Cuba. From 1832 to 1852 Jamaica's output fell from 71,000 to 25,000 tons, while from 1840 to 1846 sugar prices dropped from £49 to £23 a ton. On most estates expenses tended to rise after emancipation, when both crops and prices were declining. From 1824 to 1846 production throughout the British West Indies fell by 75,000 tons or 36 per cent.

When in 1840 Britain allowed sugar to be imported from India and Mauritius, the Caribbean lost its former monopoly. Six years later the United Kingdom abolished the Corn Laws and under the Sugar Duties Act reduced the preference it had previously accorded British-grown sugar. By 1854 Britain had adopted free trade and abolished preferences for West Indian sugar. This meant immediate competition with slave-grown Cuban and Brazilian sugar and later with the protected beet sugar industry of Europe, whose development played a major role in the decline of the Caribbean sugar territories.

The economic depression, which in the British West Indies prevailed throughout most of the nineteenth century after emancipation, was largely caused by uncertain markets and fluctuating prices for sugar. The drawbacks of concentration on one crop, which in the seventeenth and eighteenth centuries had brought vast wealth to plantation owners, were becoming apparent. Even without abolition many sugar proprietors must inevitably have been ruined. Yet the industry's decline was relative, not absolute. In the twentieth century the West Indies produced more sugar than during its hey-day in the eighteenth.[4]

Two decades after emancipation Anthony Trollope considered the British Caribbean territories among the most poverty-stricken spots on earth. Half the sugar estates in Jamaica and more than half the coffee plantations had reverted to bush and tropical wilderness. His opinion that local enterprise in the West

Indies was conspicuous by its absence was scarcely surprising. Every territory desperately needed better water supplies, more roads, skilled workers, agricultural research, foreign investment, and above all more adequate health and educational facilities. Trollope considered that the prosperity of Jamaica, as of 'the old-fashioned Jamaican planter, the pure-blooded white owner of the soil,' was over. He approved the abolition of slavery and the advent of free trade, but believed that 'the negro in the West Indies will never work so long as he can eat and sleep without it': his 'idea of emancipation was and is emancipation not from slavery but from work. To lie in the sun and eat breadfruit and yams is his idea of being free.'[5]

This observation came with ill grace from a white man. Beside it may be cited the comment of John Waller, an English ship's surgeon stationed in the Caribbean from 1807 to 1810, that white people brought up with slaves to wait on them had no notion of doing anything for themselves. Waller's views were advanced for his day. 'It is unfortunate, both for the negroes and their masters,' he wrote, 'that any human being, whether philosopher or idiot, should have started the notion that the Africans are by nature inferior in intellect to Europeans, and consequently incapable of cultivating those arts and sciences by which we are distinguished. This absurd opinion ... will one day prove dangerous to our colonies; for, if ever education should extend its blessings to these unfortunate people, nothing will sink so deep into the mind and rankle there, as the idea of being considered an inferior order of beings. Half the hardships these people endure may be traced to that source alone.'[6] In 1825 Samuel Taylor Coleridge's nephew considered the poor whites of Barbados 'without exception the most degraded, worthless, hopeless race I have ever met with in my life.'[7] From the beginning of slavery black and white alike were degraded by the myth of white superiority.

By 1896 the price of sugar was only half what it had been in 1881 and there were serious outbreaks of cane disease. Large numbers of plantations had been deserted, while many owners who clung to their estates were bankrupt. From 1880 to 1915 sugar production declined from 184,000 to 147,000 tons a year, in contrast with almost 208,000 tons during the last decade of slavery. During these thirty-five years the sugar industry in Nevis, Montserrat, Dominica, St Vincent, and Grenada was either abandoned or produced merely enough for local consumption. Only the introduction of a central factory system saved Antigua, St Kitts, and St Lucia from a similar fate. The tide turned in the first half of the twentieth century, and from 1910 to 1945 the output of the British Caribbean islands almost trebled. Unfortunately production costs and competition from other countries also increased, while prices fluctuated wildly, until the revived imperial preference alone saved the West Indian sugar industry from collapse.

If after emancipation many planters were impoverished, the lot of ordinary people was far worse. To the stagnation of trade produced by the decline of estates were added the hardships of drought and hurricanes and, during the American Civil War, high prices for food. Freedom was well worth its cost, yet the upheaval produced by the abolition of slavery in communities based on it for two centuries took its toll of all sections of the population and all aspects of life. 'A race has been freed,' said the Governor of Trinidad, Lord Harris, fourteen years after abolition, 'but a society has not been formed.' Two decades later Charles Kingsley wondered 'what might the West Indies have been by now, had it not been for slavery, rum, and sugar?'[8]

POLITICAL INSTITUTIONS

Despite all the implications of a slave-owning society the ruling white minority took pride in possessing civil liberties and representative institutions. After abolition many of the dark-skinned majority, hitherto excluded from traditional British freedoms, came to share this pride, although throughout the nineteenth century only a few of these had the right to vote and universal suffrage was delayed until the middle of the twentieth. In the difficult period after emancipation the white, black, and coloured (of mixed African and white ancestry) peoples of the Caribbean, uneasily adjusting to new relationships, at least had behind them two centuries of living together in one community. To this day the political outlook of West Indians, long accustomed to the framework of democratic government, is usually closer to that of former settlement colonies like Canada, Australia, and New Zealand than to that of African countries from which most of their forebears came.

It was nevertheless inevitable that sugar and slavery should profoundly influence, not only the economies of the British West Indies, but also their social structure and politics. The economic and social changes produced by emancipation were paralleled in the political sphere. The old representative system consisted of a governor appointed by Britain to represent the Crown and head the administration, a legislative council nominated and usually controlled by him, and an assembly elected by freeholders which granted local revenues. The Crown could neither impose taxes nor enforce payment of public officials. Buffers between colonists and British authorities, Caribbean governors were fortunate to avoid trouble with both at once, since local and imperial interests frequently conflicted. Governors' despatches to the Council of Trade and Plantations in London were filled with complaints about colonists' efforts to transfer effective power from the executive to the legislature and on occasion even to obtain complete independence.

Nineteenth-century government in the West Indies was likely to be that of a selfish and narrow obligarchy. The assemblies, elected and dominated by a few wealthy planters and merchants or their representatives, attempted through their power to withhold supply to manipulate the governors. Three times within three months in 1755 the Governor of Jamaica dissolved an unco-operative House which refused to grant supply. Neither executive nor legislature was responsible to or could control the other. In most islands wrangles between them dated from the establishment of representative institutions. Often corrupt Caribbean politics were characterized by recurring quarrels and reconciliations between two opposing authorities, while compromises were frequently made at the expense of the public. This system, which placed a premium on obstruction, produced at best friction, at worst deadlock.

From the early days of British rule each small West Indian colony was equipped with a jealously guarded, elaborate, and expensive panoply of government, widely viewed as a symbol of status. 'Not one of these communities, not even the tiniest of the Antilles,' a British military historian wrote of Dominica and the Leewards, 'but possessed its little legislature on the English model, and consequently not one but enjoyed facilities for the excessive indulgence of local feeling, local faction, and local folly, to the obstruction of all broad measures of Imperial policy.[9]

As Trollope noted in the mid-nineteenth century, 'all have Queen, Lords, and Commons in one shape or another' – a type of constitution which struck him as singularly unsuitable for tiny islands. 'What,' he demanded, 'could Lords and Commons do in Malta or Jersey? ... And, alas! what have they done in Jamaica? ... Kingston as a town is the most deplorable that man ever visited, unless it be that Spanish Town is worse.' To his mind the best ruled was British Guiana, whose quasi-crown colony government he described as 'a mild despotism, tempered by sugar.'[10] To a conspicuously liberal British civil servant, Sir William Des Voeux, it appeared rather 'a despotism of sugar – and a sugar which in this, as in some human conditions, is apt to turn acid.'[11] This multiplication of separate governments encouraged rivalry and accentuated the natural isolation and parochialism of scattered islands, able to trade only with Britain and to communicate with each other only at intervals determined by the sailing dates of occasional vessels. Thus a firm foundation was laid for the local particularism destined consistently to thwart efforts towards greater unity.

REVERSION TO CROWN COLONY RULE

In the British Caribbean elective legislatures were no earnest for liberal views. Their members mainly represented the tiny minority of white landowners whose livelihood depended on sugar. Maintenance of existing conditions was obviously to their advantage. With little real interest in the well-being of their communities, they bitterly resented losing their slaves. There was truth in Adam Smith's contention that slavery was more tolerable under an autocratic than a free constitution, because in the latter slave owners helped to make the laws and sharply criticized government restraints on their authority.

The usual attitude of West Indian legislatures was illustrated by the Jamaican Assembly's so-called 'humble petition' of 1823. This pointed out that the people of this island had taken no oath of allegiance to the imperial Parliament and would not submit to the degradation of having their internal affairs governed by the British House of Commons, whose powers in the United Kingdom were not superior to those of Jamaica's Assembly. The petition was supported by a unanimous resolution deploring the fact that 'the inhabitants of this once valuable colony (hitherto esteemed the brightest jewel in the British Crown) are destined to be offered [as] a propitiatory sacrifice at the altar of fanaticism.' Shortly after emancipation a discouraged governor observed that the Jamaican legislature of the day would not permit any governor to do justice to the black population.[12]

In Barbados freedmen could not vote unless they owned land. In Jamaica, where payment of taxes gave the right to vote, there were coloured members of the Assembly even before emancipation. When slavery ended in 1834, in all the territories most of the population, including whites, were illiterate.

Conditions in the West Indies should be viewed in their historical context. Abolition came only a year after the First Reform Act enfranchised half the British middle class. Working people in the United Kingdom had to wait another four decades for the first public education act and an additional fourteen years for manhood suffrage. If, however, the British Reform Acts of the nineteenth century had been paralleled in the West Indies, an early foundation would have been laid for the self-government postponed for more than a century in the Caribbean.

The consequences of abolition, scarcely appreciated in advance, were in fact momentous. Representative institutions had been promptly established in England's first West Indian territories because their white settlers were considered as much entitled to self-government as American colonists. Yet when slavery finally ended, whites formed only a tiny minority in comparison with the black population, transformed at one stroke from chattels to citizens and fellow-countrymen. The prevalent view of West Indian whites and free coloureds was that newly emancipated blacks were unready for self-government. But British colonial policy had long been based on the principle that the imperial power could not withdraw representative institutions once granted. Solution of this dilemma was difficult.

Emancipation created a middle class which had not been able to develop under slavery. As early as 1823 the free people of colour in Trinidad and Barbados (many themselves slave owners) asked in vain for full civil rights, while in Jamaica a Coloured Party was founded to campaign for this cause. Freedmen's legal disabilities on grounds of colour were abolished in all the crown colonies by a British order-in-council of 1828. The legislatures of Jamaica, Barbados, and Tobago enacted similar measures in 1830 and 1831, although the franchise was based on a low property qualification. By 1836 the majority of voters in Jamaica were coloured and in the following year eight coloured members were returned to its Assembly, then among the most reactionary of British West Indian legislatures. There the coloured members tended to vote with the whites and to dissociate themselves from the black majority of the population. A Canadian who visited the House in 1849 noted that its members ranged from jet black to white.[13] A century later only some 66,000, or less than one-twelfth of the Jamaican people, earned enough to vote, although the qualification was annual payment of ten shillings in any form of taxes.

The British Colonial Office was undecided as to what, under the circumstances, was the most liberal policy. Henry Taylor believed that former slaves needed education and experience before they could operate representative political institutions and that meanwhile administration should be carried on by the Colonial Office. His friend and colleague James Stephen argued in 1841 that 'popular franchises in the hands of the masters of a great body of slaves' were 'the worst instruments of tyranny ... ever yet forged for the oppression of mankind.'[14] After emancipation, however, Stephen put his trust in representative institutions as likely to produce maximum benefits for all sections of the community. This view prevailed when in 1836 he became Under-Secretary of State for the Colonies.[15]

On the other hand Henry Taylor, in a famous Colonial Office memorandum of 1839, recommended abolishing the representative system and reverting to crown colony government, on the ground that in multi-racial communities just emerging from slavery every attempt at elective institutions must result in oligarchy. 'Such the Assembly of Jamaica always has been,' he contended, 'now is, and will continue to be until the mass of the population shall have been educated and raised in the scale of society.' With such bodies he saw no prospect that a Colonial Office four thousand miles away could hope to secure just treatment for the black majority. 'The West Indian legislatures,' he declared, 'have neither the will nor the skill to make such laws as you want made ... they cannot be converted on the point of willingness and they will not be instructed.' Yet if there was to be an elective system, it was the interests of ordinary people which he believed should be mainly represented. So far was this from being the case that most Caribbean assemblies were largely composed of agents and attorneys, seldom even of estate owners.

The attitude of these legislatures was indicated by their prolonged struggle against the abolition of slavery. It must surely be acknowledged, Taylor observed of the Jamaican Assembly, 'in every quarter, except amongst the resident West India planters, that such a body as this, unfit to exist in any state of society, is eminently disqualified for the great task of educating and improving a people newly born into freedom.'[16] He believed, moreover, that if in due course a black oligarchy arose, it would similarly oppress the white minority without doing what no irresponsible oligarchy, whatever its colour, could be expected to do, protecting the real interests of the people.

Taylor's fundamental distrust of representative institutions in such a society was not shared by Lord Elgin, Governor of Jamaica from 1842 to 1846, before his appointment to the same post in Canada. Although Lord Durham's future son-in-law regarded the island's constitution as a *fait accompli* which he had neither desire nor mandate to change, he yet considered a popular representative system probably the best possible means of forming one harmonious whole from a multi-racial community. In colonies like Trinidad, where there was no elective assembly, he pointed out, 'aspiring intellects have not the same opportunity of finding their level, and pent up ambitions lack a vent.'[17]

Another distinguished Under-Secretary of State, Herman Merivale, writing in 1841 of the British settlement colonies, suggested that a people's temperament was more important than its institutions. Certain balancing qualities, he argued, were needed to prevent misuse of political freedom. He considered these to be 'moderation in success: self-denial in the exercise of power: habitual considera-tion for the opinions and feelings of others: readiness to compromise ... : love of justice and fair play: reluctance to push principles to extremes: the moral courage which will dare to stand up against a majority: the habit of constantly and, as it were, instinctively postponing self to the public interest, ... whether from moral choice or from the constraint imposed by public opinion.'[18] Without such qualities he believed that autonomy could lead only to anarchy.

West Indian legislatures could boast few such virtues. At the beginning of the 1860s colour prejudice between the brown and black peoples of Trinidad struck an English observer as more acute than that between black and white. When a black was elected to the legislature, several coloured members threatened to resign and government intervention was required to silence their protests.

British colonial officials were not always distinguished. 'Half our troubles in Jamaica,' wrote its Governor, Sir Henry Norman, in 1866, 'have arisen from unjust appointments of Englishmen to the prejudice of perfectly qualified Jamaicans.'[19] Yet some with dark skins rose to high office. In 1873 a black

Dominican became Chief Justice of his island. He later served as Solicitor General and Attorney General of the Leewards, and from 1886 to 1891 as Registrar and Provost Marshall of Dominica.

Lord Harris, one of Trinidad's ablest governors, urged unsuccessfully in 1850 that the right to vote should be extended and some seats in the Legislative Council be made elective. Almost three decades later, in 1877, five thousand-odd Trinidadians petitioned for constitutional reform to give taxpayers a voice in their government. Although a royal commission of enquiry was appointed, no changes were made. Not until 1921 was the franchise widened, and seventeen years later only 6 per cent of the population was entitled to vote.

The Jamaican Constitution Act of 1854 established a four-member Executive Committee chosen by the Governor, three from the Assembly and one from the Council. This body was purely advisory. Ultimate authority continued to be vested in the Governor, who could dismiss committee members if they failed to obtain the legislature's support. The act also created a Legislative Council, nominated for life by the Crown, to serve without executive functions as a second chamber. During the 1850s this system was tried in Antigua, Tobago, Grenada, and St Lucia, but in each proved unsatisfactory and was soon discontinued. As it provided neither responsible government nor completely autocratic rule, it did not avoid conflict between the legislature and the executive.

When the Morant Bay rising occurred in 1865, of the less than one in every two hundred Jamaicans with the right to vote all but a handful were white. Twenty-one of the forty-seven members of the Assembly (ten coloured and thirty-seven white) were estate owners. Riots caused mainly by agrarian distress were put down by Governor Eyre with such severity that he was recalled. He was sharply censured by an English commission of investigation and not reinstated. At his direction Paul Bogle, a Baptist preacher, was hanged, as was George Gordon, a member of the Jamaican House of Assembly, whose suspected involvement in the uprisings was not proved. Almost 600 people were killed and as many more flogged.

In England the Jamaica Committee was formed to arouse British public opinion against such oppression in the colonies. To it much time and energy were devoted by public men like John Stuart Mill, John Bright, Herbert Spencer, and Goldwin Smith. As Mill observed, they did what they could to redeem the character of their country. Goldwin Smith hoped they had at least taught officialdom that if a black were unjustly put to death in Jamaica there were those 'in a distant country and of another race who will call for an account of his blood.'[20]

The Jamaican Assembly, thoroughly alarmed by the riots and under pressure from the Colonial Office, decided to vote for its own abolition. In 1866, by a

British order-in-council, the island's 200-year-old representative system was replaced by crown colony government.[21] This involved abolition both of elective members and of bicameralism. The Governor, who ruled with the aid of a Legislative Council composed of *ex officio* and nominated members, alone had the right to introduce legislation and the Colonial Office retained ultimate power. At the turn of the century this system had been applied to every British Caribbean island except Barbados which, like Bermuda and the Bahamas, retained a wholly elective Assembly. By 1878 elected members had vanished from all British West Indian legislatures except these three and those of Antigua and Dominica, which had single chambers with a nominated majority until 1898 when they became wholly nominated. In British Guiana the Dutch semi-representative system was retained until 1928.

One reason for the apparently retrograde reversion to crown colony rule was the United Kingdom's desire to secure for its West Indian colonies, and in particular for the black majority of their people, better and fairer government than that provided by a small oligarchy of wealthy white men more concerned with their own interests than with those of the community. The so-called old representative system, under which a partially or wholly elected legislature was divorced from a nominated executive, was in fact so unrepresentative as to put Old Sarum to shame. At a St Kitts election in 1857 twenty-two legislators were returned by forty-seven electors. Another constituency could not return its two members because its single voter had departed to Europe for a holiday. In a Tobago election five years later one illiterate voter returned two members. During the 1870s only one per cent of the population of Barbados was entitled to vote, while qualifications for members of the Assembly were even more restricted.[22] Such conditions produced neither good government nor respect for nominally representative institutions.

British governors ranged from completely unsuitable place hunters (fortunately less common in the nineteenth than in the eighteenth century) to able and enlightened public servants who did what they could for the colonies and were often frustrated by their inability to do more. The best, for all their authoritarian powers, were genuinely benevolent despots and a distinct improvement on most of the corrupt and inefficient assemblies.[23] Under the representative system, for example, when liberal governors urged increased expenditures on education, health, and public works, the coloured middle class often joined whites in successfully opposing progressive policies designed to improve living conditions but necessitating higher taxes.

Crown colony rule had the practical advantage of giving some protection from the privileged few to the disadvantaged bulk of the population, who at first welcomed this change. In Jamaica, for instance, Sir John Grant, who succeeded Eyre as Governor, reformed taxation and the administration of justice, inaugurated a unified police force and an island-wide medical service, built hospitals, initiated public irrigation schemes, and in 1869 disestablished the Church of England, using the money formerly devoted to its endowment for education.

The representative system was nevertheless abandoned at an unfortunate time. Slavery had been abolished, a black and brown middle class was beginning to emerge, and the franchise was no longer based on colour but on a property qualification. A portion of the black majority at last had some prospect of a voice in government. With the elimination of elected legislatures this hope vanished. The situation was made no more palatable by knowledge that the British Caribbean assemblies approved their own abolition primarily because they considered this a lesser evil than domination by black members. In some islands discontent led to riots and protests, mainly from whites not placated by the fact that crown colony rule provided more equitable administration than the theoretically representative system it replaced.

In Jamaica such protests led during 1879 to formation of a body dedicated to securing a return to representative government. The island's desire for more autonomy was not dismissed by the United Kingdom. Lord Derby, then Secretary of State for the Colonies, declared forthrightly: 'You cannot long govern a colony like Jamaica without representative institutions in some shape.' While Derby thought full responsible government, as in Canada or Australia, unsuitable for the West Indies, he considered the autocratic crown colony system equally inappropriate. 'I do not think,' he wrote to Gladstone in 1883, 'that a population of 800,000 now fairly prosperous and living close to the United States, can be permanently governed without some admixture of an elective process.'[24] Gladstone himself favoured restoration of representative institutions in Jamaica and Irish members at Westminster supported liberal views which eventually prevailed.

The handwriting might already be seen on the wall. 'Today we lead,' wrote a white Jamaican in 1899, 'tomorrow we advise; and on the day following we are co-workers together with our black countrymen. It is as our actions or opinions relate to them that they will stand applauded or condemned by the future historian.'[25]

On the advice of a royal commission a new constitution restored a minimum of nine elective members to the Jamaican Legislative Council in 1884. The literacy requirement for voting was abolished (but reimposed in 1894) and the property qualification lowered. Parish boards, replaced in 1866 by nominated bodies, were reintroduced, with an equal number of elected and appointed members, and empowered to levy taxes. The term of office of the custodes of these councils, who acted as chairmen and were usually the largest landowners in the district, was reduced from life to seven years. All Jamaicans, regardless of colour, were entitled to write competitive examinations introduced in 1885 for the civil service. By 1896 every Jamaican who paid a small property tax was eligible to vote, although only one per cent of those qualified troubled to register as electors.

Towards the end of the nineteenth century popular resentment against crown colony rule developed, not only in Jamaica, but in most British West Indian territories, and especially in Trinidad to which, as to St Lucia, the United Kingdom had never granted representative government. Yet until 1944 in Jamaica, and even later in the other islands, always excepting Barbados, some form of crown colony rule prevailed. Elected members were not added to the legislatures of Trinidad, Grenada, St Vincent, and St Lucia until 1925, nor to those of British Honduras and four of the five presidencies of the Leeward Islands until 1936.

The political discontents of the last twenty years of the nineteenth century were increased by economic distress. In the decade from 1886 to 1896 the value of sugar exports declined sharply, while wages fell by one-fifth, creating much hardship for working people. The West India Royal Commission of 1897 described the situation of the British Caribbean as 'usually deplorable and sometimes desperate.'[26] In the following year the British Treasury lent Jamaica £100,000 to save the island from bankruptcy. Joseph Chamberlain, then Secretary of State for the Colonies, declared at Westminster that the United Kingdom must be prepared to continue grants to the West Indies if they were not to relapse into anarchy. Some Caribbean islands, especially the smaller ones, lacked resources to pay for their administration. British grants, Chamberlain insisted, should be considered necessary expenses of empire, not doles. 'We cannot allow any part of the territory which we control and over whose finances we have complete authority to fall into anarchy and ruin.'[27]

The virtue of crown colony rule was its amenability to British public opinion, usually more enlightened than that of nineteenth-century Caribbean legislatures. Yet it was necessarily paternal. The wielders of political power were responsible to a distant imperial government, not to the communities in which they served. As most major administrative posts were long reserved for Englishmen, the system gave West Indians no experience of political responsibility and indeed bred distrust of their capacities. It continued the autocratic rule by which the majority of the population had always been governed. When independence was finally achieved in the 1960s, the only type of government which the British Caribbean knew was authoritarian.

Early twentieth-century West Indian politicians consequently tended to look on the state as an instrument of alien rulers and an enemy of the people. Elected members of their legislatures were then everywhere in a minority and unrestrained by any prospect of having to assume responsibility for their proposals. Popular representatives in autocratically governed communities, they tended to form a permanent opposition based not on ideas or principles but simply on criticism of the administration. Under the circumstances this interpretation of their functions was probably inevitable. The results, however, were not confined to crowded hours of glorious intransigence, devoted to chivvying governors and councils. A factious attitude of critical, irresponsible, and permanent opposition to the administration became accepted as the normal atmosphere of political debate. Under independence West Indian statesmen were later tempted to continue the authoritarian rule with which politicians and people alike had long been familiar.

In few places does the dead hand of the past lie as heavily on the present as in the Caribbean. Its history is one of plunder and conquest, coupled with some two hundred and fifty years of slavery. From this unpromising background British West Indians emerged with a polyglot population, diverse cultures, and a determination, after centuries of European control, to shape their own future.

2

Governments, unions, and parties

MODIFICATION OF CROWN COLONY RULE

During the late nineteenth and early twentieth centuries, except in British Guiana and Barbados, some variant of crown colony government prevailed throughout the British West Indies. This system involved rule by governors appointed by the Colonial Office, who might be advised by officials but retained ultimate responsibility for administration. At the end of the 1930s the Moyne commissioners believed that public opinion could prevent arbitrary decisions and that the very unpopularity of the governors' reserve powers provided a safeguard against their frequent or excessive use.[1] Many West Indians were less confident.

Crown colony rule began to be modified when some unofficial members were nominated to the legislative councils. Provision was later made for a number of elective seats, until eventually elected members outnumbered nominated members in both executive and legislative councils. As governors became increasingly obligated to accept advice from elected legislatures, the crown colony system gradually evolved into responsible government. This was finally achieved when members elected on a wide or universal franchise and composing a majority in the executive council became accountable to a wholly elected assembly, with the government formed by the leader able to command a majority in the lower house. This development took place at different times in different parts of the West Indies, the chief common characteristic being the slow and late emergence of full democracy.

In the United Kingdom the Colonial Reformers of the 1830s anticipated, as the Little Englanders of the 1850s and 1860s echoed, Sir George Cornewall Lewis's remark in 1849 that a self-governing dependency was a contradiction in terms. Most British proponents of this view, however, had in mind the white settlement colonies whose Anglo-Saxon peoples seemed to them naturally fitted for eventual self-rule.

As late as 1942 Winston Churchill could still declare: 'We intend to hold what we have. I have not become the King's first minister in order to preside over the liquidation of the British Empire.' Against this statement should be set Clement Attlee's comment on the eve of Burma's independence: 'We want no unwilling peoples within the British Empire. It is for the people of Burma to determine their own future.' By the end of the 1940s it was clear that the United Kingdom wished as many as practicable of the remaining colonies, including the West Indies, to become independent. The old idea that skin colour affected a people's capacity for autonomy died an unlamented death in the Second World War.

Yet while all British parties thereafter agreed that the aim of imperial policy was to bring dependencies to independence, it was still tacitly assumed that many would not achieve this goal for generations. In the meantime leisurely and paternal trusteeship was considered appropriate for colonies so small and poor as to make economic self-sufficiency difficult or impossible. From the standpoint of the United Kingdom, the Caribbean territories, unless federated into a larger and stronger whole, belonged in this category. Few Britons knew or cared much about living conditions in the islands or troubled to ask how their peoples viewed the prospect of protracted dependency.

There were various reasons for what, in retrospect, appears a naive indifference to the wishes of those most closely concerned. Before the Second World War traditional ideas about imperial relationships were little questioned, while public opinion in the West Indies remained at best relatively inarticulate and at worst completely unformed. This was almost inevitable in largely illiterate communities with subsistence standards of living and highly restricted franchises. Significant constitutional advance awaited the advent of adult suffrage, political parties, strong trade unions, and a sizeable middle class.

Unionism is always difficult to develop among unskilled workers. A lively interest in politics is equally difficult to foster in dependencies where all important decisions are made by an imperial government thousands of miles away or by its nominees, while those most affected have little opportunity to direct their own affairs. With the wisdom of hindsight it is easy to see how such conditions bred apathy and obstruction in the British Caribbean and why under 15 per cent of the small number qualified to vote in 1938 in fact did so.

West Indians have been quick to blame the metropolitan power for sins of omission and commission. Yet by establishing liberal political institutions it implanted a tradition of respect for parliamentary democracy, with all that this implies. For centuries, however, these institutions were reserved for the tiny white minority, while trade unions were long proscribed. One reason why economic and social advance came slowly, even in the twentieth century, was that each step forward was halted by a rapid increase in population, once improved health conditions had reduced the death rate. It may not have been to the United Kingdom's credit, yet it was not altogether its fault, that the islands never had enough schools, houses, welfare services, or adequate living standards. In the battle between population pressures and limited natural resources the former were always victorious and still continue to triumph.

For a century after the abolition of slavery there was little political and social progress in the British Caribbean. No West Indian painted a more devastating picture of regional conditions in the 1880s than that drawn by a British civil servant, C.S. Salmon, formerly President of Nevis and Administrator of the Gold Coast. 'Only fifty years ago,' he wrote, 'the people were slaves and treated as cattle. They are uneducated; they are poor; they are heavily taxed. Expensive administrative establishments are kept on foot out of their taxes, while the provision made for educating them is totally inadequate. England had a manifest duty to accomplish in these colonies, and she never even tried to do it. The planters did nothing for education, for religion, or for civilisation. They do nothing now.' Almost all schools except religious foundations were then paid for by the black inhabitants, and half the population was illiterate.

In countries where, as in the West Indies, a major portion of public revenues is raised by levies on imports, especially on imported foods, and where certain exports are also dutiable, taxation bears heavily on the poor. Salmon attacked the system under which large estate owners paid practically no taxes as 'unsound in its incidence, unfair and unjust in its application, and disastrous in its consequences of undernourishment and starvation.'

He was equally caustic about institutions which gave people well fitted for self-rule no voice in how they were governed.[2] Even where an assembly or council had some elected and nominated members, the views of officials usually prevailed. In Trinidad, Tobago, and the Windwards, where the Legislative Councils contained no elective members, the Governors' powers, although often wielded with intelligence and discretion, were absolute. Trinidad's Legislative Council was composed of seven officials and eight members nominated for life by the Governor from among the chief planters and merchants. A proposal in 1890 to add some elective members was dismissed as 'a perilous extreme for this heterogeneous and educationally backward colony.'[3] The only elections then held in that island were for municipal officers in Port-of-Spain and San Fernando, where there were high property qualifications. Similar conditions prevailed in British Honduras. The Leeward Islands' Legislative Council consisted of ten nominated members and ten others indirectly elected by certain insular councils.

The Jamaican Legislative Council was reorganized in 1884 to include six official members and nine elected on a property qualification which enfranchised some 9300 men in a population of about 620,000. Eleven years later the number of elected members was increased to fourteen (one for each parish), as opposed to fifteen who were officals or nominated. Any nine of these elected representatives (who had to pay taxes or meet an income qualification) could veto appropriation or tax bills, while a measure they all opposed could be carried only if the Governor used his reserve powers to declare a question of paramount importance. Under this system clashes between the Governor and the elected members, coupled with efforts to avoid them, occupied an inordinate amount of time. It became increasingly difficult to persuade the ablest men in the island to accept appointments as non-official members because they were expected to vote with the Governor and understandably disliked the role of 'legislative dummies.'

The Jamaican capital of Kingston returned a coloured mayor in 1900. Six years later Robert Love, an able Negro elected to the Jamaican Legislative Council, agitated successfully for dilution of its white membership. By the 1920s black and brown representatives, mostly professional men, formed a majority. Usually, however, they tended to identify themselves with the light-skinned middle and upper classes rather than with the mass of the black population. Suffrage qualifications were lowered in 1909, and ten years later women obtained the right to vote. By the beginning of the 1920s payment of taxes of ten shillings or more a year enfranchised all occupiers of houses in Jamaica.

At the outset of the twentieth century Barbados alone possessed a wholly elected Assembly. Its enactments, however, became effective only when ratified by the largely nominated Legislative Council. Although the island was extremely proud of the constitution it had enjoyed unchanged since the seventeenth century, its twenty-four-member House of Assembly was chosen by a very restricted franchise based on occupational, property, or educational qualifications. A property test was also required for candidates. Barbados' non-elective Legislative Council then had nine members: two officials and seven unofficials nominated by the Governor who presided over the Executive Committee which initiated all government measures and financial bills.

'Although, in theory, the Secretary of State through the Governor is still responsible for the government of Barbados,' E.F.L. Wood observed in 1922, 'it is in fact in the hands of the House of Assembly that political power lies, since, without their consent, the Governor is powerless to carry either votes of money or legislation. Historically, socially, and politically, Barbados is poles asunder from St. Vincent and St. Lucia, which are Crown Colonies where the constitution provides for an official majority responsible to the Secretary of State.'[4] Local government in Barbados was then administered by eleven parish vestries, each with one unofficial nominated member and from ten to sixteen others elected on the same franchise as the Assembly.

The semi-representative constitutions of British Guiana and Jamaica were widely cited as examples of what could and should be established elsewhere in the Caribbean. It did not escape the attention of West Indians that the territories with most provision for self-government were those with the largest white minority nor that for public office inferior whites were usually preferred to more competent men of colour.

Throughout the islands there was little machinery and few efforts made to ascertain public opinion, and no means to ensure that, if elicited, this received consideration. The only method to redress grievances was to petition the Colonial Office: a device almost invariably unsuccessful. The role of the majority of the people was confined to paying taxes and performing heavy labour. Their desire for more self-government sprang from a well-founded conviction that genuine progress was otherwise practically impossible.[5] Tensions between rulers and ruled were heightened by the background of slavery, class stratification based on colour, and conspicuous contrasts between the life of the wealthy few and the poverty-stricken many.

A royal commission on sugar, appointed in 1897 when the industry seemed ready to collapse, considered that the British Caribbean's major need was settlement on the land of as many small peasant proprietors as possible. Greater local production of food would make the colonies more self-sufficient and less dependent on imports. The commissioners criticized the existing concentration on sugar and recommended encouragement of the fruit trade and development of technical and agricultural instruction. 'We have placed the labouring population where it is,' said the *Report*, 'and created for it the conditions, moral and material, under which it exists, and we cannot divest ourselves of responsibility for its future.'[6]

Similar views, expressed a quarter-century earlier by Charles Kingsley, are still voiced today. Few areas have had their problems so minutely analysed by successive officials, committees, and individuals with so few results as the British West Indies. Too often, one witness complained to the 1897 commission, they had been inspected, probed, examined, and reviewed with no effect except to increase mounting piles of voluminous reports.

CONSTITUTIONAL DEVELOPMENTS: 1900-28

By 1900 discontent with crown colony rule was acute, especially in Trinidad. Its Legislative Council, founded in 1831, had no elected members until 1925. The question of constitutional change had been raised as early as 1850. In 1888 a commission was appointed to consider the matter, but no action was taken. Four years later a committee in Port-of-Spain sent a memorandum to the Secretary of State for the Colonies emphasizing the extent of Trinidadians' dissatisfaction with the arbitrary aspects of crown colony government. Three public meetings passed resolutions complaining that the system was 'a great public grievance' in a territory where many people were competent to form intelligent opinions on public affairs. These recommended a legislative council of twenty members, eight nominated and twelve elected on a property qualification, which would have enfranchised from 12,000 to 15,000 of the island's 200,000 inhabitants. Again no action was taken, and six years later the Port-of-Spain city council was suspended for requesting financial assistance from the Trinidad government.[7]

The absence of effective constitutional channels for expression of grievances created deep-seated discontent. During riots in 1903 against the proposed installation of water meters in Port-of-Spain, designed to conserve local water resources, the principal government offices were burned to the ground, sixteen people were shot or bayoneted to death by the police, and some forty others were injured. A British commission of enquiry reported that unnecessary force and brutality had been used and deplored the serious divisions on public affairs between the government and large and influential portions of the community.[8]

A West Indian regiment served with distinction during the First World War which, in Caribbean as in other British colonies, stimulated the movement for greater autonomy. Despite inadequacies in the schools improved education was producing a black and brown intelligentsia of lawyers, doctors, civil servants, and teachers, increasingly dissatisfied with a system which largely confined political power to a few whites. Its members pressed for a larger voice in their government, pointing out that the French West Indies sent representatives to the legislature in Paris and that the United States had established free institutions in Cuba. Yet at the end of the First World War all the British Caribbean islands except Barbados and Jamaica still had wholly nominated legislatures.

Among the most distinguished early leaders of the movement for self-government was T. Albert Marryshow of Grenada. Outstandingly able and strongly critical of crown colony rule, he rallied about him a group of middle-class coloured Grenadians who in 1914 formed a Representative Government Association. The following year he founded the significantly named newspaper, *The West Indian*, which became an effective vehicle for his federalist views. This Association petitioned the Secretary of State for the Colonies to introduce elected representatives in the island's Legislative Council. In 1924, largely through Mr Marryshow's efforts, a council was established with five elected in addition to ten *ex officio* and nominated members.

In most of the smaller islands representative government associations were founded during the first two decades of the century by other middle-class professional men such as Ebenezer Duncan and George McIntosh of St Vincent and Cecil Rawle of Dominica. The latter, like Captain Cipriani of Trinidad and Mr Marryshow, advocated a united West Indies with democratic political institutions. St Kitts-Nevis-Anguilla, where members of the Legislative Council were appointed for life, asked in 1919 for representative government. St Vincent and St Lucia presented similar requests in 1920-1. Other colonies formed associations advocating a wider franchise, constitutional reform, and, in some cases, federation.

As a result of these increasingly vocal movements of protest the Parliamentary Under-Secretary of State for the Colonies, the Honourable E.F.L. Wood (later Lord Halifax), visited British Guiana and most of the islands from December 1921 to February 1922. He reported that he believed the common demand for at least a measure of representative government would eventually prove irresistible. The educated, intelligent minority which supported this would undoubtedly mould majority opinion in the future, especially as elementary school teachers in the West Indies, almost all of whom were black, were actively interested in politics. Indeed in Jamaica and British Guiana some believed that teachers took too much part in political activities. Even where legislative councils had elected members, the system was unsatisfactory because power was divorced from responsibility. In some islands, like Antigua and St Kitts, the most substantial elements in the community (by which Major Wood meant white planters and merchants) opposed representative government, whereas in others, like Jamaica and Grenada, with more peasant proprietors and less pronounced class divisions, they supported it.

Despite the prevalent criticism of isolation and neglect by the imperial authorities Major Wood was impressed by the remarkable attachment of black West Indians to the Crown. African by descent but British in language, customs, and traditions, they wanted to participate in the political institutions they had been taught to admire. Major Wood advised against a mistaken attempt 'to withhold a concession ultimately inevitable until it has been robbed by delay of most of its usefulness and all of its grace.'

His recommendations were nevertheless cautious. He believed neither that there was any significant regional demand for full responsible government nor that this could be prudently conceded in the near future. His principal reasons were the mixture of colours, religions, and races (especially in cosmopolitan Trinidad, which he thought lacked any homogeneous public opinion), the universal absence of a leisured class able to take an active part in political life, the smallness and isolation of many islands, and the tiny proportion of qualified voters.

Yet in Trinidad political advance was urged by the Workingmen's Association, the Legislative Reform Committee (representing the middle classes and small farmers), and the East Indian National Congress. It was opposed by the Chamber of Commerce, the Agricultural Society, and a deputation of East Indians. The latter's objections sprang from fear that substitution of election for nomination might deprive the Indian population of representation in the Legislative Council. Events proved this apprehension unfounded. Although only one East Indian was elected in 1925, after 1928 there were always at least two, and in 1946 four of the nine elected members returned in Trinidad and Tobago were East Indians.

Major Wood's belief that the Leewards were relatively uninterested in constitutional reform reflected the views of local planters rather than the labouring majority. The St Kitts' Representative Government Association, for instance, like the Friendly Society of Antigua, urged increasing the number of elected members.[9] The real, though seldom stated, objection to more self-government was that legislatures elected on a wide franchise would clearly be dominated by the black majority. This was desired neither by Britain nor by the small group of white and brown estate owners and businessmen who at that time formed the colonial ruling élites.

Although since 1889 Tobago had been entitled to return one member to the Legislative Council at Port-of-Spain, Major Wood pointed out that in fact it had never done so. He proposed adding four elected members to the Jamaican Executive Committee. Ultimate control by the Secretary of State should, he thought, be preserved unimpaired by giving governors, in conjunction with official and nominated members, power to carry bills they deemed essential for the good government of their colonies. In most matters, however, if all the elected members were unanimously opposed to a government measure, he believed the dispute should be referred to the Secretary of State for the Colonies.

Throughout the British Caribbean, in Major Wood's opinion, the general public had a completely erroneous idea of the imperial government's financial ability to help these territories. He was apparently surprised by their disappointment at his statement that such assistance, whether through grants or loans, was unlikely. Money was required, he admitted, and could be usefully employed to develop the natural resources of the West Indies, but to his mind should only be sought from private enterprise.

He emphasized the need for a more adequate system of shipping to the United Kingdom and Canada and among the islands, as well as for improvements in telegraphic communications with the outside world. There was then no direct shipping service between Jamaica and British Honduras in the Western Caribbean and the other territories in the East. Letters from Jamaica to Barbados, Trinidad, and British Guiana usually had to be sent via London, New York, or Halifax, with the result that it sometimes took six months to receive a reply. A fortnightly service from Halifax to British Guiana, with steamers calling for a few hours at the Leewards, Windwards, Barbados, and Trinidad, scarcely provided convenient communication among islands which knew little and cared less about each other. 'Sentiment and development,' said Major Wood's *Report*, 'do not flow naturally over the sea from one island to another.'[10]

The Trinidad Workingmen's Association, which had been founded in 1897 but lapsed in 1914, was revived five years later under the leadership of Howard A. Bishop and a group of coloured businessmen. The president was Captain Arthur Andrew Cipriani, a white Trinidadian solicitor and cocoa planter of Corsican descent, whose forebears had settled in the island a century earlier. For eight years mayor of Port-of-Spain, he was the moving spirit in organizing the Trinidadian contingent of the British West Indian Regiment. In this he himself served during the First World War and on his return home devoted his energies to attacking crown colony rule, which he considered a façade for autocracy. To his mind this was merely an alliance between the Colonial Office and local business interests, designed to thwart Trinidadians' reasonable desire for a voice in their own affairs. Under Captain Cipriani's leadership the Workingmen's Association developed into an effective protest group which expanded from its original nucleus in the capital, until by 1928 it had forty-two affiliated branches in various parts of the island and thirteen in Tobago, with thousands of members from both the Negro and East Indian communities.

Trinidad's first general election since Britain acquired the island in 1797 was held in 1925 to return eleven members to the Legislative Council, hitherto wholly composed of nominees and officials. Captain Cipriani was returned at the head of the poll, despite high income and property qualifications for voting, multiplied sixfold for candidates to the Council.[11] A dedicated reformer and for years president of the Caribbean Labour Congress, Captain Cipriani devoted himself to pressing for self-government, legalization of trade unions, better wages, and social and labour legislation.

In those days children from seven years of age during crop customarily worked on sugar estates for as long as twelve hours a day, at a daily rate of fifteen cents. A committee to examine the desirability of restricting hours of labour reported unanimously in favour of an eight-hour day for all except domestic servants and sugar workers during crop. The Trinidad government, however, refused to introduce the necessary legislation on the ground that this would interfere with freedom of contract and impose too great a burden on industry. Captain Cipriani advocated not only an eight-hour working day but old age pensions, minimum wages, compulsory education, increased taxes on the oil industry, and abolition of racial discrimination. He also urged competitive examinations for entry to the civil service and appointment of Trinidadians rather than expatriates. He was one of the earliest supporters of closer association among the British West Indian territories. His constant slogan was 'agitate, educate, confederate.' When all the reforms he espoused were rejected, the Workingmen's Association attacked the government as unwilling either to help the common people or to allow them to help themselves.

Although Captain Cipriani originally failed to secure the legislation he considered necessary, its eventual achievement was largely the result of his efforts. His appeal to the social and political consciousness of Trinidadians, among whom his prestige steadily increased, was eminently effective. 'The people of this Colony,' he told the Legislative Council in 1930, 'have got the education, the ability, the civilisation, and the necessary culture to administer their own affairs ... Crown Colony rule may be well for the jungle and the wilds of Africa, but it has outlived its usefulness in these Colonies.'[12] West Indians, he argued, as free peoples of the British Empire, were as entitled to dominion status as Canadians or Australians.

Trinidad had to wait until 1932 for a Trade Union Ordinance which, unlike the British Trades Dispute Act of 1906, neither safeguarded the right to peaceful picketing nor gave unions immunity against actions in tort. The Workingmen's Association refused to register under the act, although two of its branches, the railway and stevedores' unions, in fact operated as trade unions. A rival body, mainly composed of transport workers, the Trinidad and Tobago Trade Union Centre, was founded in 1929.

In 1932 the Workingmen's Association changed its name to the Trinidad Labour Party, which was affiliated with the British Labour Party and the Socialist International. Captain Cipriani became its leader and a frequent contributor to its organ, *The Socialist*, launched in 1935. As he had dominated the Workingmen's Association, so he dominated the party, but without reliable trade union support it never became very effective. Although by 1938 it claimed a membership of 120,000, or almost one-third of the island's population, it had little real influence after that date.

The almost exclusively Jamaican 'Back to Africa' movement owed its origin to Marcus Garvey (1885-1940), a Jamaican who early in the twentieth century migrated to the United States. There he founded the Universal Negro Improvement Association, based on the slogans of black nationalism and Africa for the Africans. In 1927 his ambition to establish in Africa a black nation to which Negroes from the New World could go proved unsuccessful. After being convicted in the United States of fraud he was deported to Jamaica. Two years later he was elected to the Kingston and St Andrew Corporation Council and founded the People's Political Party.

Jamaica's first party, it advocated self-government, land reform, industrial development, social and labour legislation, and free legal aid for the poor. At that time such aims won no favour with the white and brown members of the community and little more with the black. After an unsuccessful attempt in 1935 to win a seat on the Legislative Council and a period of imprisonment for contempt of court, Mr Garvey left Jamaica for England, where he died five years later. During his lifetime his views were more influential in the United States and Africa than in his native island. Yet he eventually became a legend in Jamaica. In 1964 his remains were brought from England to Kingston and reinterred in Marcus Garvey Memorial Park, where he was enshrined as a national hero.

A physician, Dr Charles Duncan O'Neale, in 1924 founded in Barbados the Democratic League, based on faith in the rights of man. It was supported by *The Herald*, a radical newspaper which had been established five years earlier by Clement Inniss and largely financed by Charles Haynes, a white Barbadian member of a family long distinguished in the island. Among its contributors was Erskine Ward, an outstanding lawyer who a generation later became Speaker of the West Indian Federal House of Representatives. The editor, Clennell Wickham, was an avowed socialist and strong believer in the power of independent journalism. Arguing that Barbados deserved 'free institutions and the full flower of democratic development,' he made the paper a mouthpiece for progressive ideas. As early as 1928 he advocated free trade among the British Caribbean territories and asked: 'Is it too much to hope, or will the West Indian colonies continue to develop each "along its own lines" with the certainty of getting nowhere in the end?'[13]

Wickham tried unsuccessfully to secure the support of an able young coloured barrister, Grantley Adams, who in 1925 returned home from studies at Oxford. During the next two years Mr Adams was a leader writer for the *Barbados Advocate* and subsequently served as editor of the *Agricultural Reporter*. At first more attracted by the ideas of the British Liberal Party than by socialism, Mr Adams later came under the influence of the Fabian Society and British Labour Party. The views of the Democratic League were in fact close to those of contemporary English liberals. The League stood for better food, clothing, education, and housing for the mass of the people, disendowment of the Church of England in Barbados, social insurance, lower qualifications for voting, and a more equitable distribution of wealth. It never succeeded, however, in attracting strong support from the middle and upper classes who then alone had the right to vote and considered such aims too radical.

A proposal to widen the franchise passed the Barbados House of Assembly in 1930 but was defeated by the Legislative Council. When four years later Mr Adams was elected to the Assembly he strongly supported a bill, introduced by C.A. Brathwaite of the Democratic League, to reduce the income qualification for voting from £50 to £30 a year and the freehold qualification from £5 to £3. This speech, he wrote long afterward, was regarded by the island's ruling white oligarchy as a declaration of war. The measure passed the Assembly, only to be rejected by the upper house. Leading members of the white business community clearly resented Mr Adams's stand, and his hitherto flourishing law practice sharply declined.[14] Meanwhile Dr O'Neale, who had recently founded the Barbados Workingmen's Association, was elected to the House of Assembly in 1932. He remained a member until his death four years later.

Major Wood's recommendations, representing minor concessions to West Indian opinion, were accepted by the Colonial Office and implemented in 1923 and 1924. The Montserrat legislature was empowered to elect one of its number to the Legislative Council. The Virgin Islands were given a nominated unofficial member in the Legislative Council, to which an additional official member was also appointed. Dominica obtained a new Legislative Council, composed of the Governor, Administrator, six official members, and six unofficials: two nominated and four elected. Less than 3 per cent of the population, however, was qualified to vote. The St Lucia Council had six official members and six unofficials, half of whom were to be elected and half nominated. The St Vincent Legislative Council included five official and four unofficial members: three elected and one nominated.

Halting political advance in the islands contrasted with constitutional regression in British Guiana. A waterfront worker of Barbadian descent, Hubert Nathaniel Critchlow, who in 1905 led a dockers' strike and subsequently struggled to win recognition for trade unions, in 1919 organized the British Guiana Labour Union, the first such body in the West Indies. Like workingmen's associations in the islands, this mainly represented the interests of unskilled black workers but its principal officers were middle-class business and professional men. Within a few months it had some thirty-six branches and a membership of approximately 13,000. This union managed to secure a ten-hour day and better wages for waterfront workers.

British Guiana's Popular Party was formed in the 1920s by a journalist and former Tobagonian, A.R.F. Webber, who had been influenced by Mr Marryshow of Grenada and Captain Cipriani of Trinidad. In the 1926 election, under the leadership of Mr Webber and Mr Nelson Cannon, this party captured some elective seats in the legislature, to the alarm of white estate owners who feared that its plan for developing the interior might create labour shortages.

A memorial to the Secretary of State for the Colonies from the legislature or Court of Policy resulted in 1926 in an investigatory parliamentary committee on the economy and development of British Guiana. This recommended replacing the Combined Court (the Court of Policy plus six elected financial representatives) by a nominated Legislative Council. Constitutional changes in 1928 did effect this, but substituted for the Combined Court a Legislative Council of fourteen elected members, five nominated unofficial members, eight officials, and two *ex officio* members, presided over by the Governor, who had a casting vote. Thus the elected members could be outvoted and their former control over finance passed to the Governor. Women obtained the right to vote but not to stand as candidates. These changes substituted for the old Dutch system a variant of crown colony government.[15]

Major Wood's *Report* showed little serious effort to attack basic regional problems and less to meet the views of ordinary West Indians. At the time of his visit the political state of the two largest islands was roughly similar to that of England in 1832 at the time of the First Reform Act. In the most politically advanced territory, Jamaica, some 66,000 people, or less than one-twelfth of the population, qualified for the franchise by paying taxes of at least ten shillings a year. Of 400,000 Trinidadians only 25,000 were eligible to vote.[16]

Indirectly, however, the Wood *Report* was responsible for the passage in 1929 of the first Colonial Development Act. This empowered the British Treasury to make grants or loans up to a total of one million pounds a year to any dependency for capital expenditures likely to benefit British industry. Despite its emphasis on aiding the United Kingdom rather than the colonies, the measure marked a milestone in imperial policy. It helped to accelerate West Indianization of the civil service and established a precedent for the subsequent series of Colonial Development and Welfare Acts whereby successive British parliaments voted large sums to improve living conditions in the dependencies. Although West Indians frequently pointed out that these grants were never large enough to meet urgent needs, they nevertheless inaugurated a significant new departure in colonial policy. After the outbreak of the Second World War the United Kingdom's financial position was consistently precarious, yet all British parties acknowledged a responsibility to reverse ancient roles by subsidizing colonies from which they had once profited.

THE DEPRESSION AND ITS RESULTS

The modern history of the British Caribbean dates from the depression of the 1930s, when overproduction and low prices threatened with virtual extinction the sugar industry, which employed some 176,000 of the two million West Indians. The price of sugar dropped from £23.10.0 a ton in 1923 to £5.0.0 in 1934.

A British royal commission chaired by Lord Olivier, sometime Governor of Jamaica, estimated in 1930 that, if sugar production were abandoned, the working population affected would be 100 per cent in St Kitts and Antigua, 66 per cent in Barbados, 50 per cent in British Guiana, 33 per cent in Trinidad, 25 per cent in St Lucia, and 10 per cent in Jamaica. Its major recommendations were encouragement of alternative crops such as rice and fruit, settlement on the land of small peasant proprietors, and improved housing for labourers on sugar estates.[17]

By 1933 prices for the islands' principal exports had been almost halved, wages reduced, taxes raised, and unemployment increased. When work was available, male agricultural labourers earned from one shilling and threepence a day in the small islands to two shillings in Jamaica. Women were paid even less. Two-thirds of the population of Barbados and many in other territories were living in houses with one or two rooms. Old age pensions, minimum wage legislation, and workmen's compensation schemes were in their infancy and everywhere inadequate. Most employers were strongly opposed to trade unions, no collective bargaining machinery existed, and only a handful of the population was entitled to vote. Industrial and political means to redress grievances were equally lacking.[18]

'The common man, alive to these conditions,' commented a distinguished Jamaican a decade later, 'would no longer endure them and was prepared ... to raise hell in his own way to call attention to his wrong.'[19] Ordinary people were badly paid or out of work, badly housed, badly fed, and often in poor health. Intolerable social and economic circumstances created bitter resentment which in each territory eventually erupted into strikes and violence too widespread to be ignored. They also gave rise to effective labour movements from which, in turn, sprang political parties whose pressure for self-government was ultimately successful.

The first outbreak occurred in May 1935 among the unemployed sugar workers of St Kitts, where most land was occupied by estates owned by absentee white proprietors. In the same year there were riots and a sit-down strike by Trinidadian oil workers, succeeded by a hunger strike. Jamaican wharf labourers and St Lucians engaged in coaling ships also struck, and there were protests against increased customs duties in St Vincent, whose Workingmen's Association, founded in 1933, pressed for constitutional and land reform.

Another series of strikes by sugar workers for higher wages occurred in 1935 in British Guiana, where a commission of enquiry emphasized the need for machinery to discuss grievances. Two years later, during other strikes, the Manpower Citizens' Association was formed. Originally an Indian sugar workers' union, it subsequently included African bauxite workers before the establishment of the British Guiana Mine Workers' Union. Within two years it had secured 10,000 members, launched the *Guiana Review*, then the territory's only labour paper, and was advocating constitutional reform and labour legislation.

In addition to two large general unions, the British Guiana Labour Union and the British Guiana Workers' League, there were by 1938 a number of smaller unions among postmen, transport workers, and government employees. Most were represented in a co-ordinating body, the British Guiana Trade Union Assembly, as well as in a wider organization, the British Guiana and West Indian Trade Union Congress, founded in 1926 by regional labour leaders.[20] The latter body, at a meeting in Georgetown in November 1938, advocated federation, a legislature elected by universal suffrage, state ownership of public utilities and the sugar industry, free and compulsory education, and social and labour legislation.

The British Guiana Department of Labour, established in the same year, collected statistics on wages, prices, living costs, and working conditions. It also provided conciliation officers for disputes where negotiations between employers and employees had been unsuccessful. Dangerous trades were regulated by law in 1938, as was the employment of children and young people. A workmen's compensation scheme was already in effect. Wages of unskilled male labourers then ranged from two to three shillings a day, while those of female employees averaged one shilling and eightpence. Domestic servants earned, in addition to meals, between one and a half and three pounds a month.[21]

During riots at Barbados in 1937 fourteen people were killed and forty-seven wounded. The immediate cause was the arrest as an agitator of Clement Payne, an adherent of the Trinidadian working-class leader Uriah Butler. Although successfully defended by Grantley Adams in the Court of Appeal, Mr Payne was finally deported, while several other labour leaders were sentenced on charges of sedition. Mr Adams insisted that the real reasons for the uprising were economic: his phrase was 'stark poverty.'

A British commission appointed to enquire into these disturbances stressed four major problems: overpopulation, bad housing, unemployment, and inadequate earnings. It also considered the island singularly backward in labour organization and found 'no justification, short of bankruptcy of trade and industry,' for the prevalent low wages (averaging $1.78 a week) which made decent living conditions impossible. Many businesses, the commissioners pointed out, could afford to pay high dividends and comfortable salaries to their senior employees. Until the distribution of earnings between masters and men was fundamentally changed, they believed the majority of workers would inevitably continue to feel hatred and bitterness.[22] Like the Moyne Royal Commission after them, they advised the development of trade unions and the creation of departments of labour.

In 1938 Grantley Adams became vice-president and in 1939 president of the Barbados Progressive League, established in the previous year by Hope Stevens to press for social legislation and a wider franchise. The League later changed its name to the Barbados Labour Party, whose organ was *The Beacon*, founded in 1946. Hugh Springer, a brilliant young Barbadian recently returned from studies at Oxford, served from 1941 to 1947 as general secretary of the Progressive League and in 1941 helped to found the supporting Barbados Workers' Union. This organization, which owed much to the advice of the English trade unionist Sir Walter Citrine, developed slowly because of widespread fears of employers' disapproval, but by 1946 boasted almost 11,000 members.[23] Grantley Adams believed that the decline of the Trinidad Labour Party was caused by its lack of a trade union base. He was determined to avoid this in Barbados by establishing close co-operation between the party and the union.[24] In 1942 Mr Adams was appointed by the Governor to the island's Executive Committee.

The agricultural and waterfront employees, who formed the bulk of early adherents to the Barbados Workers' Union, were gradually joined by men and women in diverse occupations. It emphasized trade union education and eventually developed into one of the region's strongest and most effective labour movements. The alliance between it and the Barbados Labour Party, described by a local journalist as more a twinship than an affinity,[25] led to the establishment of a Department of Labour, social and industrial legislation, and Whitley Councils in the civil service. Three more unions were registered in 1945: the Barbados Overseers Association, the Congress Trade Union, and the Barbados Clerks Union. The same year saw the establishment of two employers' organizations: the Sugar Producers' Association and the Shipping and Mercantile Association.

During 1937 further labour stoppages occurred in British Guiana, Jamaica, and St Lucia. Two years later a sugar workers' strike in the latter territory resulted in the formation of the island's first trade union, supported by both agricultural and urban workers. A general strike in Trinidad originated among the predominantly Negro oil workers, headed by a Grenadian champion of 'the barefoot man,' Tubal Uriah Buzz Butler, whose views were an odd mixture of the Bible and Marxism.[26] Butler had served in the West India Regiment during the war and had originally been a devoted follower of Captain Cipriani. Although each attacked the colonial régime, both were staunch supporters of the British connection.

During 1935 Mr Butler had led the unemployed in a hunger march and the following year, after being expelled from the Trinidad Labour Party for extremism, he founded the British Empire Workers' and Citizens' Home Rule Party. When in June 1937 he threatened to call a sit-down strike in the oil fields, the police tried to arrest him. The disturbances spread to other parts of the island and soon involved East Indian sugar workers. The major issues were a demand for higher wages and widespread resentment against a political system which enfranchised less than 7 per cent of the population. Before order was restored fourteen people were killed, fifty-nine wounded, and hundreds arrested.

Mr Butler, whose star rose as Captain Cipriani's declined, was hailed as a hero by the ordinary people, although he himself admitted that he neither represented nor controlled the majority of the oil workers. He was, however, the first effective Negro leader to emerge in Trinidad.

When the Second World War broke out in 1939 he was interned, without trial by jury or specific charges levelled against him, and was succeeded as party leader by an East Indian lawyer, Adrian Rienzi. The latter had originally belonged to the Trinidad Labour Party but left in 1936 to found the Trinidad Citizens League. By that time Captain Cipriani had come to consider Mr Rienzi quasi-Marxist, while Mr Butler and Mr Rienzi had become impatient with Captain Cipriani's belief in constitutional gradualism.

West Indian political leaders commonly argued that white ruling groups in the islands were mainly interested in extracting profits from neglected and poverty-stricken people. There were, however, exceptions. During the Trinidadian Legislative Council's debate on 9 July 1937 on local riots the Acting Colonial Secretary stated: 'In the past we have had to salve our consciences with humbug and ... labour with platitudes. Those days have gone by; we can no longer say to labour we recognize your hardships but we cannot afford to remedy them ... A decent wage for labour and decent conditions should be a first charge on industry ... It is far more in the interests of this colony that the profits of oil should be expended on our own people than on shareholders in other countries.' The speaker might have been Captain Cipriani instead of a senior British civil servant.

A commission appointed by the United Kingdom to enquire into the troubles of 1937-8 found many Trinidadian estate owners largely indifferent to the welfare of their employees. There was then no collective bargaining machinery for discussion of grievances, although working-class opinion, fostered by the spread of education, was becoming articulate. The purchasing power of wages had declined as a result of inflation, and although an enabling act to permit establishment of a minimum wage board had been passed in 1935 and a Wages Advisory Board set up, this body had made no recommendations and taken no action.

Under such circumstances many workers considered strikes the only means to secure higher wages and redress grievances. The commission recommended improvements in health, housing, education, and workmen's compensation, encouragement of authorized trade unions, establishment of a labour department and an industrial court, and appointment of conciliation officers.[27] It did not, however, accept the contention of the Trinidad Labour Party and other local groups that desire for more self-government was an important cause of unrest, but attributed this to bad living and working conditions.

A direct result of the disturbances of 1937 was acceleration of the labour movement. The Clerks' Union had been founded in 1933 by the Trinidad Labour Party, the Amalgamated Building and Woodworkers' Union in 1936, and the Printers' Industrial Union shortly afterward. The Oilworkers Trade Union was formed in 1937, as was the All-Trinidad Sugar Estates and Factory Workers' Union, which early the next year called an unsuccessful strike. The Negro Welfare and Cultural Association, a radical, working-class body long active in Port-of-Spain, organized the Seamen and Waterfront Workers' Union and the Public Works Workers' Union. The Shipwrights' Union, like that of clerical employees, originated as a branch of the Labour Party. The Trinidad and Tobago Union of Shop Assistants and Clerks was formed as a rival to the Clerks' Union. Two large general unions were founded by leaders of the oil workers' and sugar labourers' unions: the Transport and General Workers' Union and the Federated Workers' Union, most of whose members were railway and construction men. By the beginning of 1939 three labour papers were published in Trinidad: *The People, The Socialist* sponsored by the Labour Party, and *The Pilot*, the organ of the Seamen and Waterfront Workers' Union.[28] This proliferation of industrial organizations weakened the Trinidad Labour Party as most people, particularly in the southern districts, tended to concentrate their support behind the unions.

During a period of industrial unrest after the First World War labour unions were formed in Jamaica among longshoremen, cigar workers, and industrial employees. Legalized in 1919, a year marked like its predecessor by strikes and riots, registered unions were freed from liability to prosecution as conspiracies in restraint of trade. They remained subject, however, to actions for civil damages and even peaceful picketing was prohibited. At the request of the Jamaican government this provision was expressly omitted from the Trade Union Act of 1919. As the Moyne *Report* noted in the late 1930s, British Guiana was then the only Caribbean colony where, as in the United Kingdom, unions were protected against actions for damages owing to strikes. The Moyne commissioners saw little purpose in conceding the right to strike, while at the same time removing all possibility of its effective use.[29]

The Jamaican Longshoremen's Union, founded in 1918 by A. Bain Alves, four years later became the first labour body in the island to register under the new dispensation. In 1935 A.G.S. Coombs formed the Jamaica Workers' and Tradesmen's Union which for the next three years remained the country's principal labour organization. Its energetic treasurer was a money-lender destined for fame, Alexander Bustamante (né Clarke), a picturesque man of the people and an orator with a striking presence, warm heart, and unfailing gift for the common touch.

In 1937, when agricultural incomes averaged under twenty-five shillings a week, most Jamaicans were employed for only six months out of twelve. Unrest in the island led to the establishment by middle-class radicals of the National Reform Association. Led by Kenneth Hill, a journalist, it advocated legalization of trade unions, adult suffrage, and wider self-government. The Federation of Citizens' Associations, formed about the same time, pressed for abler parochial councillors to improve the calibre of local government. It promptly gained control of the Kingston and St Andrew municipal council. Jamaicans in New York City, led by W. Adolphe Roberts and W.A. Domingo, in 1936 founded the Jamaica Progressive League. It emphasized cultural nationalism, a creed expounded by *Public Opinion*, a weekly journal established a year later by O.T. Fairclough, a bank official, and later edited by the teacher and nationalist H.P. Jacobs.

During 1937 there were strikes and demonstrations for a public works programme, unemployment relief, and higher wages on Jamaican sugar estates. Forty-six people were killed, over four hundred injured, and several thousands arrested and prosecuted. Early in 1938 a series of mass meetings was organized in various parts of the island by Messrs Bustamante and William Grant. The latter was an adherent of Marcus Garvey's black nationalism movement.

Of the island's twelve unions, mostly small craft organizations, the most important were the Jamaica Workers' and Tradesmen's Union formed in 1936 and mainly supported by waterfront and agricultural labourers, and the Jamaica United Clerks' Association, which represented many Kingston shop assistants. By 1939 the four largest Jamaican unions had 8,500 members, or some 3 per cent of the island's wage earners. Five years later there were twenty-five unions with 46,000 members, or almost 16 per cent of the gainfully employed.[30]

Between January and May 1938 there were further strikes by sugar workers, wharf labourers, road construction gangs, and street cleaners. In upheavals all over the island rioters stopped bus services, broke street lamps, set Chinese grocery shops on fire, stoned the police, and generally brought business to a standstill. The Governor declared a state of emergency, and before order was restored eight people were killed, almost two hundred injured, and more than seven hundred arrested.

Mr Bustamante announced that he was prepared to fight, had 100,000 people behind him, and 'if there is going to be a master in Jamaica then I am going to be that master.'[31] His imprisonment on a charge of sedition and incitement promptly established his reputation as a hero. The other outstanding leader who came to the fore was Bustamante's cousin, Norman Washington Manley, KC, a Rhodes scholar and leading barrister. 'I give up my law practice,' he declared, 'to take into my hands the case of the people of Jamaica before the bar of history, against poverty and need – the case of my country for a better life and freedom in our land.'

Although for the next year the cousins co-operated, they could scarcely have been more dissimilar. A cultivated, aloof, professional man of conspicuous integrity, Mr Manley lacked his cousin's warm humanity and was obviously most at ease with the middle classes. He soon developed into an expert parliamentarian. Mr Bustamante, who had only an elementary school education, according to his own picturesque account had previously led an adventurous life in Cuba and Spain, as well as in North, South, and Central America. A flamboyant orator, he liked to explain with more gusto than accuracy that he had been 'raised in the gutter.' Years later Sir Grantley Adams neatly characterized the cousins: "Manley is a statesman who will never be a politician. Bustamante is a politician who will never be a statesman.'[32] For three decades the two men dominated the public life of Jamaica.

Mr Manley had distinguished himself in 1937 by helping to persuade banana firms to establish a welfare fund, supported by a royalty of one penny on each stem of bananas shipped from the island. This provided funds for Jamaica Welfare, an organization which fostered cultural and community development, especially in rural districts. In the following year Mr Manley managed to secure the release of Mr Bustamante and Mr Grant and to win the confidence of the working people.

As the island then had no machinery for collective bargaining, the appointment by the Governor in May 1938 of a Board of Conciliation represented a major advance. Its members, men of liberal views and high standing in the community, discussed the strikers' grievances with an unofficial trades union committee whose principal spokesmen were Messrs Bustamante, Manley, and Noel Nethersole, also a lawyer and former Rhodes scholar. The board had managed to settle the dock strike and other outstanding disputes in Kingston when renewed violence led to a commission of enquiry into the disturbances. Believing the chief causes to be poverty and unemployment, it recommended an enlarged police force and a body of special constables to deal with future emergencies.

Its *Report* paid generous tribute to Mr Manley as the man most responsible for re-establishing confidence and halting further disorders. 'Both sides,' in the opinion of its members, 'were gainers by his intervention. Employers had someone with whom to negotiate, who understood conditions in the island and who knew what demands could reasonably be made and what could not. On the other hand, the labourers had at their disposal and working wholeheartedly on their behalf one of the best brains in the country and one of the most disinterested ... We think that his services to the community as a whole were invaluable.'[33]

Prompt enactment of social legislation in Jamaica was constructive. In 1937 the Shop Assistants Act limited hours of work, and in the same year minimum wage and workmen's compensation measures were passed. The Trade Union Act of 1919 was amended to permit peaceful picketing, prohibit civil actions against unions for losses suffered through strikes, and abolish their liability for breach of contract during strikes. A slum clearance and housing law was placed on the statute books in 1939, as was a Trade Disputes (Arbitration and Enquiry) Act requiring mediation, conciliation, and arbitration of industrial disputes.

These were followed in 1940 by a Factories Act which enforced inspection. The Children and Young Persons Act of 1941 limited hours of work and restricted employment of children and youths in dangerous occupations. Also enacted in that year were the Dock Workers (Protection against Accidents) Act and the Employment of Women Act, specifying hours and conditions of work for female employees. In 1942 a Labour Advisory Board, with representatives of the government, employers, and employees, was established to discuss proposed labour legislation.

In May 1938 the National Reform Association adopted Kenneth Hill's proposal that dockers form a trade union under the leadership of Mr Bustamante, who was then in jail. On his release he became life president, with wide powers over the organization, finance, and policy of the Bustamante Industrial Trade Union, which within half a year numbered over 6,000 members.[34] This was a general union of skilled and unskilled workers in varied occupations such as agriculture, transport, commerce, docking, and shipping. From its inception it attracted many sugar and banana estate labourers who were among the most poorly paid employees in the island. The general secretary, Hugh Buchanan, and the solicitor, Ross Livingstone, joint editors of *Jamaica Labour*, were charged in July 1938 with seditious libel and sentenced to six months in jail for publishing articles alleging that the government was determined to kill all workingmen or women who raised their voices in defence of labour. This apparently enhanced their reputation and that of the union. By August of that year friends and foes alike recognized Mr Bustamante as *the* labour leader of Jamaica.

When a local journalist charged him with authoritarianism and ambition for political power, he replied frankly in an article published in the *Daily Gleaner*: 'Yes, I want power, sufficient power to be able to defend those weaker than I am; those less fortunate, and that's what I have today – Power ... It has been stated that I want to be a dictator. Yes, I do want to dictate the policy of the unions, in the interests of the people I represent, and the only ones who are giving results today are the dictators ... The voice of labour must be heard and it shall be heard through me.'[35]

In September 1938, at a meeting in Kingston attended by Sir Stafford Cripps, Mr Manley founded the People's National Party and announced his support for West Indian federation, a goal already widely accepted in the Eastern Caribbean.

The first effective Jamaican movement for self-government, the People's National Party also advocated adult suffrage, social and economic reform, strong trade unions, land settlement, and, as an ultimate aim, dominion status. The new party absorbed two older bodies, the National Reform Association and the Federation of Citizens' Associations. Two years later it formally espoused moderate socialism like that of the British Labour Party.

An unsuccessful general strike called by Mr Bustamante in January 1939 resulted in the formation of a Jamaican Department of Labour. He joined the People's National Party early in the year, but before its close withdrew, taking with him the Bustamante Industrial Trade Union which included most of the island's organized workers. Its remaining labour bodies retained their affiliation with the party and the following year, under Mr Manley's aegis, formed the Trades Union Advisory Council. A decade later this body changed its name to the Trade Union Congress.

In September 1940 Mr Bustamante made an inflammatory speech, threatening to call dock workers out on strike. As a consequence he and several other trade union and political leaders were imprisoned for months without trial. This proved a distinct asset to his meteoric career. West Indians are second to none in their enthusiasm for a martyr, a role for which Mr Bustamante displayed remarkable innate ability. Sir Alexander Grantham, Governor of Jamaica from 1938 to 1941, conceived an affection for him, despite their frequent opposition, and dissented from the view that he was only a rabble-rouser. 'He could harangue and sway a crowd like no one else in the island,' wrote the Governor, 'but this was only the outward expression of his love for humanity, especially for the humble workers. He inspired great loyalty amongst his followers and they did not in the least mind his driving around in a large motor-car and indulging his taste for champagne.'[36]

During Mr Bustamante's imprisonment his union, whose membership and funds had been drastically declining, was nursed back to health by Messrs Manley and Nethersole. In 1941 they successfully negotiated with the Sugar Manufacturers' Association the first island-wide agreement for higher wages linked to increases in the cost of living. When after seventeen months' internment Mr Bustamante emerged from jail in February 1942, Mr Manley was able to hand back to him a union whose membership had more than doubled. The day after his release, however, Mr Bustamante broke with his cousin in a much publicized split which proved the beginning of a permanent estrangement. At first Mr Bustamante tended to favour the conservative Jamaica Democratic Party, formed in 1943 by Robert (later Sir Robert) Kirkwood to represent the interests of white estate owners and businessmen. Shortly after the election of 1944, in which it won no seats, the Democratic Party disintegrated. Later in

1943 Mr Bustamante founded the Jamaica Labour Party as the political arm of the Bustamante Industrial Trade Union, in opposition to Mr Manley's predominantly middle-class, although nominally socialist, People's National Party, which thus found itself without union support.

Although the shrewdly named Jamaica Labour Party was in fact more conservative than its rival and more successful in winning support from business interests, it soon attracted the mass of unskilled workers. Despite relying on support from private enterprise, the party pressed for wage increases. Its leader's distaste for radical ideas ranged from attacks on socialism to condemnation of birth control. Less highly organized than the People's National Party, it was mainly united by the personal appeal of Mr Bustamante.

The labour label of most West Indian parties, regardless of their views, has been described as 'one of their more endearing oddities.'[37] The explanation is simple. As all the islands have an overwhelming preponderance of unskilled workers, a party which does not profess to represent their interests has no chance of success. In the British Caribbean, as in Australia and New Zealand, to call a party 'conservative' would always have meant political suicide, although many have in practice been moderately conservative. Events were to show that if the Jamaica Labour Party dared not advocate conservatism, the People's National Party dared not practise socialism. The radicalism of the latter long proved as moderate as the Toryism of the former.

Both were dominated by leaders whose power was more important than the formal party structures. The 1938 constitution of the People's National Party provided for large numbers of small groups in various parts of the island. Although individuals were allowed to join and there were some affiliated societies, most supporters were members of local groups. Centres for political indoctrination and electoral support, these helped to lend a semblance of democratic decentralization and to send delegates to annual constituency conferences which selected candidates for the island legislature.

The party holds an annual conference, usually in September, attended by some one thousand delegates. Here the platform is expounded by senior members and a major address is delivered by the leader. Delegates elect the president and four vice-presidents of the party, in addition to twenty-five members of the National Executive Council. Other members of the Council are party officers, members of the parliamentary party, two representatives from each constituency with at least twenty groups, and one from each with less than twenty. The Council, which sometimes numbers more than one hundred, meets monthly and serves to keep the party leaders in touch with local opinion, while the major policy-making body is the Executive Committee.

The emergence of Mr Bustamante and Mr Manley as rival political leaders had three major consequences: the development of the first firmly rooted two-party system in the British Caribbean, a connection so close as to be almost a fusion between unions and parties, and a tradition of charismatic leadership. The two wings of the Jamaican labour movement became and have since remained affiliated with the two major parties.

THE ORDE BROWNE *REPORT*

The appalling succession of strikes, riots, and labour revolts in the 1930s, euphemistically described as 'disturbances,' were in most territories marked by bloodshed and mob violence. When in 1938 West Indian affairs were debated at Westminster, a Labour member, Arthur Creech-Jones (later Secretary of State for the Colonies) contended that the adult suffrage enjoyed in the French islands ought to be extended to the British Caribbean, where only one in nineteen Jamaicans and one in fifteen Trinidadians then had the right to vote.[38] The United Kingdom, he wrote later, bore 'a grave responsibility for a colonial policy based on cheap labour and cheap raw materials ... the hopeless squalor of today is ... the measure of ... [its] shortcomings and of our economic neglect.'[39]

In the House of Lords Lord Olivier, a former Governor of Jamaica, roundly declared on 23 February 1938 that the British public did not pay enough for its sugar to enable the West Indian industry to provide decent wages. The Secretary of State for the Colonies, Malcolm MacDonald, described prevalent Caribbean discontents as a protest against economic distress and its consequences: uncertain employment, low wages, and bad housing.

As a result of widespread criticism both within and without the United Kingdom Major C. St J. Orde Browne, labour adviser to the Secretary of State for the Colonies, was asked to examine labour conditions in the West Indies, which he visited from September 1938 to April 1939. His *Report* noted that since the end of the First World War various diseases had afflicted the islands' major crops: sugar, bananas, cocoa, limes, coffee, citrus, coconuts, and pimento. When the Panama Canal was completed, many West Indian labourers returned home to increase the numbers of unemployed in the British Caribbean, where rising birth rates accentuated prevalent shortages of work.

Conditions were already critical before the depression of the 1930s. At a time when survival of the sugar and banana industries demanded the greatest possible efficiency, mechanization was deliberately withheld to provide more employment. 'The existing situation,' Major Orde Browne observed in words often re-echoed, 'may be described as an attempt to make the various industries carry a population appreciably larger than the economic position warrants. A general readjustment is clearly essential.'[40]

Underemployment was as serious as unemployment. Like many other analysts of West Indian problems, Major Orde Browne thought the most promising remedy was encouragement of independent peasant proprietors to make less necessary large-scale imports of food which could be locally produced. This prescription, although often recommended as a cure for a major West Indian problem, has not been universally approved. The settlement of more small farmers on little plots which they own, while desirable socially, does not necessarily increase productivity and may cause it to decline.

Despite diverse views on this matter there could be no disagreement with Major Orde Browne's observation that proteins, fats, and vitamins were conspicuously lacking in the diet of most West Indians, with the result that, while few actually went hungry, malnutrition was widespread. He found housing deplorable, overcrowding general, sanitation frequently absent, tuberculosis, malaria, and venereal diseases prevalent, and cleanliness, despite creditable attempts, almost impossible to achieve. Wages, while undeniably low, might have sufficed for a reasonable standard of comfort were not so many people only intermittently employed. Most families, labouring under a load of debt completely disproportionate to their resources, lived in a constant state of insecurity, although not of actual want.

'A social and economic study of the West Indies,' it was aptly said, 'is necessarily a study of poverty.'[41] Manual and agricultural labour were generally disdained, yet few young people secured enough education to equip them for other occupations. As Major Orde Browne emphasized, all the British Caribbean territories needed responsible trade unions, departments of labour with facilities for compiling statistics on employment, conciliation boards, workmen's compensation schemes, labour legislation, and collective bargaining arrangements. He also stressed the need for cheap or free medical care and facilities for technical training.[42] As a result of his *Report* the Colonial Office thereafter actively encouraged labour legislation throughout the area. His illuminating but depressing analysis convinced the United Kingdom of the necessity for a more elaborate enquiry into the causes of West Indian discontents.

THE MOYNE *REPORT*

A royal commission chaired by Lord Moyne was consequently appointed to investigate social and economic conditions in the British Caribbean and make appropriate recommendations. Between November 1938 and March 1939 the commissioners visited all the British and certain American, French, and Dutch West Indian territories. Most hearings, often held before large and sometimes demonstrative audiences, attracted wide publicity which stimulated thought and discussion on regional issues. The commissioners considered the disturbances of the 1930s as symptoms whose principal causes were low earnings and irregular employment. In this view the Secretary of State for the Colonies concurred.

The Moyne *Report* viewed the region's problems as essentially agrarian. Agriculture, industry, and public finances had all suffered severely from the depression of the 1930s. World market prices for the West Indies' principal exports had sharply declined. Accepted colonial policy then was that each administrative unit, regardless of size, should be financially independent and receive assistance from the imperial exchequer only when local resources proved inadequate to meet absolute necessities. This system resulted in very low standards of living at a time when increased education, improved communications, and the ubiquitous presence of prosperous tourists and white members of the business community created a demand for better conditions. Yet the combination of a rapidly rising birth rate, a falling death rate, and worldwide economic depression threatened the maintenance of even existing low standards of living.

'Serious discontent,' the commissioners noted, 'was often widespread in West Indian colonies during the nineteenth century ... But the discontent that underlies the disturbances of recent years is a phenomenon of a different character, representing no longer a mere blind protest against a worsening of conditions, but a positive demand for the creation of new conditions that will render possible a better and less restricted life. It is the co-existence of this new demand for better conditions with the unfavourable economic trend that is the crux of the West Indian problem of the present day.'[43]

The commission believed that traditional exports and new industries could not provide sufficient employment for rapidly increasing populations without a new agricultural policy, which abandoned the time-honoured reliance on production for export (long encouraged by the United Kingdom) and encouraged increased production of food for domestic consumption. It recognized, however, that such a change could not come quickly. The introduction of mixed farming would amount almost to an agricultural revolution. In the meantime many urgent needs of the British Caribbean peoples demanded large expenditures which not even the wealthiest colonies could hope to undertake from their own resources.

Hence the Moyne *Report*'s first recommendation was a West Indian welfare fund, financed by an imperial grant of one million pounds a year for a twenty-year period. This would provide for labour departments, settlement on the land of small farmers, welfare facilities, and improved education, health, and housing in the various territories. It should be administered by a comptroller responsible to the Secretary of State for the Colonies and with headquarters in the Caribbean, who would co-operate with, but be independent of, the local

West Indian governments. He and his staff should conduct research, propose schemes for development and social reform, consider projects submitted by the colonial governments, and supervise the administration of grants.

Like Major Orde Browne, the commissioners considered modern labour legislation essential. While agricultural employers had effective organizations, their workers normally had few or none. In the previous decade successive secretaries of state had repeatedly urged British Caribbean governments to encourage trade unions. The Moyne commissioners, however, found no real effort, until very recently, to assist such developments. Hence collective bargaining was impossible, wages were low, and labourers forced to accept whatever rates of pay were offered. Inadequate earnings and irregular employment were the major causes, the commissioners believed, of the disturbances of the past few years.

The *Report* recommended that the comptroller's staff should include a labour adviser, in addition to experts on education, medicine, social welfare, and town planning. Unions should be protected against actions for damages resulting from strikes, peaceful picketing legalized, local wage boards and a West Indian industrial court established, and labour departments set up in each colony. It also advocated Whitley Councils, on the British model, for civil servants and teachers, and factory legislation made effective by provisions for inspection. Employment of children under fourteen outside their homes, whether in agriculture or industry, should be prohibited.

The plight of the unemployed, accentuated by the seasonal nature of most work on the land, was 'serious to the point of desperation.' Poor relief was usually confined to the old and infirm, while the majority of territories gave no public assistance to able-bodied men out of work. The commissioners urged consideration of unemployment insurance for those regularly employed and workmen's compensation schemes, based on the Ontario Act, for agricultural as well as other workers. While approving attempts to develop commercially sound industries, they saw little prospect of industrial development on a scale sufficient to minimize unemployment. The Leewards and Windwards had practically no industry apart from agriculture.

This somewhat pessimistic assessment of industrial potential, stemming from the depression of the 1930s as well as from the lack of natural resources and accessible markets, led to an emphasis, later partially modified, on welfare rather than economic development. The commissioners believed that West Indian standards of living must largely depend on more intelligent employment of resources, more intensive use of land, and much expanded agricultural research. They recommended encouragement of mixed farming, fishing surveys, improvement of water supplies, and assistance with drainage and road-building programmes.

Facilities for communication, they pointed out, were better between the West Indies and the outside world than within the British Caribbean. This hampered inter-island trade and other relationships which ought to be expanded if more political and administrative co-operation were to be achieved. They proposed that, when the war ended, the United Kingdom should provide two vessels to ply between the smaller islands, and that wireless, telephone, and local broadcasting services should be introduced as soon as possible throughout the area. Regular air service in the Eastern Caribbean was also urgent.

The commissioners did not approve immediate self-government based on universal suffrage (although they unanimously agreed that this should be the ultimate goal), because this would make impossible the financial control required for substantial monetary aid from the United Kingdom. More participation in government by West Indians, however, they considered necessary for significant social advance. Hence they advocated a wider franchise, lower qualifications for candidates, appointment of only three *ex officio* members to local legislatures, and consideration of a system of advisory committees to give elected representatives insight into the practical details of government. Only one executive council in the whole British Caribbean then contained a representative of labour. The Moyne commissioners recommended broadening their bases to give a voice to all important sections of the community.

They thought the chief weakness of the crown colony system was less its apparent autocracy than the fact that unofficial members of the legislatures, debarred from administrative control, tended to be consistently hostile towards governments and officials, whom they considered dominated by representatives of vested interests. This attitude, supported by opposition from a critical press, made able British civil servants reluctant to accept appointments in the West Indies, where they were often targets for personal attacks, properly directed against government policies, not those who implemented them. An allied problem was that racial discrimination, although everywhere deprecated and nowhere sanctioned by law, appeared to be increasing. Where employers and employees were of different colours, economic and racial issues were easily confused. This posed a serious obstacle to the harmonious political development necessary for wider autonomy. The commissioners recommended that local governments should make much more effort to explain the reasons for their decisions and to prevent colour prejudice. They also urged unification of public services and common entrance qualifications throughout the area, although this would involve overcoming considerable diversities in salaries and conditions of work. Between equally suitable candidates, they thought it indisputable that preference should be given to West Indians.[44]

Lord Moyne became Secretary of State for the Colonies in 1941. The Moyne *Report*, the most comprehensive survey of the West Indies ever undertaken, remains the classic source of information on the British Caribbean at the end of the 1930s. Its strong emphasis coloured subsequent thinking, both of West Indians and the Colonial Office.

AFTERMATH OF THE MOYNE *REPORT*

A landmark in the history of the West Indies, the Moyne *Report* heralded a new era in imperial policy, although the Jamaican People's National Party dismissed it as a futile effort to substitute social services for significant political and economic reform. It nevertheless destroyed any excuse for ignorance of conditions in the British Caribbean. The strikes and riots of the 1930s stemmed partly from economic recession, which reduced already low standards of living, and partly from a growing desire for more self-government. Such pressures, coupled with dawning awareness of regional interdependence, were not peculiar to the West Indies.

In many countries depression created demands for unemployment and health insurance. During the Second World War the British National (but predominantly Conservative) administration commissioned a Liberal, Sir William Beveridge, to produce a report on social insurance and allied services, later implemented by the Labour Government. Throughout the western world the advent of the welfare state permanently altered concepts about the proper relationship between the citizen and the state.

These developments had a marked effect on British colonial policy, although imperial authorities still considered economic viability among the acid tests of a dependency's readiness for autonomy. Mr Manley argued in 1951 that this view was unreasonable because few nations were completely self-sufficient. He attacked it as 'a colonial idea, carefully given to us by our colonial masters, and to be totally repudiated by us.'[45] His contention ignored both the distinction between viability and complete self-sufficiency and the implications of expecting one country to pay for but exert no control over the policies of another. Had their roles been reversed, West Indians might have had more sympathy for the United Kingdom's attitude.

While the full text of the *Report* was not released until 1945, its recommendations were published in February 1940 at one of the darkest periods of the war.[46] This abbreviated version made Englishmen aware of West Indian problems, roused their consciences, and led directly to the Colonial Development and Welfare acts of the 1940s and 1950s. Although calling for very large expenditures at a time when the United Kingdom's own survival was threatened and its standard of living drastically reduced, the proposals were promptly accepted by the British government.

On the day of their publication the Secretary of State for the Colonies, Lord Lloyd, presented to the British parliament a statement of policy on colonial development and welfare. To implement the Moyne Commission's recommendations, the government established a central organization, presided over by a comptroller with a technical staff. As advisers consulting with West Indian administrations without any derogation from the powers of local legislatures, the comptroller and his assistants drew up plans for development and welfare throughout the British Caribbean. Their implementation proved in practice to require considerable tact, as territorial governments understandably feared that imperial grants might involve financial controls.

The British government recognized the inability of many colonies to finance from their own resources urgently needed research, expanded administrative and technical staffs, and adequate standards of health and welfare. The primary aim of its colonial policy was 'to protect and advance the interests of the inhabitants of the Colonies.'[47] The Colonial Development Fund, established in 1929, was promptly enlarged and its scope expanded to include a variety of welfare and educational projects.

This policy represented a marked departure from the original object of promoting commerce with or industry in the United Kingdom. Under the new scheme primary emphasis was placed on improving the economic position of the colonies. Funds were made available for both capital and recurrent expenditures on such services as health, housing, education, and agriculture. Colonial governments were invited to prepare long-term development programmes, so that they might be actively associated with the Colonial Secretary in the initiation and execution of policies for their own well-being.

The Colonial Development and Welfare Act of 1940 (which superseded that of 1929) was carefully debated and approved with little criticism at Westminster in May 1940, when the British army was retreating to Dunkirk and the United Kingdom's own existence was at stake. This measure appropriated £50 million annually, over a ten-year period, for social and economic development throughout the colonial empire, with an additional £500,000 a year devoted to research and the remission of loans made under the act of 1929. Of this sum approximately one-fifth was allocated to the British Caribbean under the administration of the Comptroller for Development and Welfare in the West Indies.

The act broke new ground by establishing the duty of British taxpayers to contribute towards the development of the colonial peoples for whose good government they were responsible.[48] As early as 1930 the Labour administration of Ramsay MacDonald had urged British colonial governments to enact trade union legislation. Because most were unenthusiastic and in financial difficulties as a result of the depression, little had been accomplished.

The requirement of a certain minimum of labour legislation and encouragement for trade unions, as a condition for eligibility under the Colonial Development and Welfare Act of 1940, was intended to persuade colonial governments to enact such measures. The Bahamas significantly preferred to forego grants rather than to legalize trade unions. In the West Indian territories Frank Norman, an experienced British civil servant appointed as labour adviser to the Comptroller of the Colonial Development and Welfare Organisation, supported labour legislation where this was inadequate and helped local governments to secure personnel competent to deal with industrial matters.[49]

A labour officer was appointed in 1938 in Trinidad at that island's request, and similar public servants were subsequently seconded to other West Indian territories. By 1941 every British Caribbean colony had full-time officials to supervise working conditions. Four years earlier there had been none. From 1942 on these officers were often experienced British trade unionists. In many islands labour advisory boards or Whitley Councils composed of representatives of both employers and employees were established to resolve industrial disputes. These developments fostered the growth of the trade union movement, especially in British Guiana, Jamaica, and Trinidad, while labour organizations were also assisted by advice and aid from the British Trades Union Congress.

Largely because of the recommendations of the Moyne Commission, by the end of the Second World War West Indian unions were well established. Unlike their predecessors founded after the First World War, these labour bodies were in the vanguard of the crusade for autonomy, linked in some territories with anti-white racialism. Most of these movements of social and political protest organized workers in a wide variety of occupations into large, blanket unions, often led by emotional and charismatic leaders.

The Colonial Development and Welfare Act of 1945, more flexible than its predecessor, between 1946 and 1956 increased the funds available to £140 million: a heavy burden for British taxpayers crippled by six disastrous years of war. Of this sum £15.5 million were set aside for the British Caribbean. Later Colonial Development and Welfare Acts provided even larger although always inadequate appropriations. Grants and loans available under these measures from 1940 to 1953 totalled almost £28 million, or more than twice what the Moyne Commission recommended. These figures do not include financial assistance for administration, aid in catastrophes such as fires, hurricanes, and earthquakes, or allocations for *ad hoc* projects like surveys, research studies, and higher education.

The Development and Welfare Organisation promptly set up headquarters in Barbados and began by establishing *rapport* with the various West Indian governments and examining Caribbean problems to determine priorities. While accurate surveys and statistical information were prerequisites for objective study of social conditions, it was not difficult to see what should be done.

Highest priority was accorded development projects designed to make amenities in country districts more comparable to those in larger centres and hence to help check the drift, as marked in the Caribbean as elsewhere, from rural to urban areas. The financial aid required for housing alone was far greater than had originally been contemplated.[50]

Most territories needed better roads, streets, and bridges. Often even more urgent were modern water supplies and sanitation facilities. Islands like Antigua, Anguilla, the British Virgins, the Turks, Caicos, and Caymans, without springs or streams and often with brackish and inadequate wells, depended on catching rainwater from roofs. During periods of drought water shortages were frequently serious. In all these territories the Colonial Development and Welfare Organisation approved projects for catchment basins and storage reservoirs.

Launched under considerable difficulties during the war, many early schemes were designed to improve public health by providing treatment and control of chronic illness resulting from such preventable but endemic maladies as yaws, malaria, tuberculosis, and venereal disease. Other projects included training medical personnel, developing school, maternity, and infant welfare services, establishing health centres, and improving hospitals. As social legislation was everywhere rudimentary, education and welfare officers were appointed in most of the islands.

The Development and Welfare Organisation also inaugurated topographical surveys of colonies which lacked accurate maps and gave grants for training West Indian surveyors in Canada. Specialists were imported to assist in setting up vital statistics departments, and architects to make housing studies and plan hospitals, schools, and health centres. All these consultants aided in training local staff.[51] Wherever possible, emphasis was placed on helping people to help themselves. Needs were so great that almost infinite sums could have been usefully expended.

By the end of the Second World War giant strides were still required to raise social services and living conditions in the British Caribbean to an adequate standard. Education, health, and housing, in particular, remained conspicuously deficient, while modest wage increases were largely cancelled by rising costs. In 1943, for instance, the annual wages of agricultural workers in Barbados averaged from £20 to £25.[52] Pressures for social and economic advance, paralleled by an equal demand for responsible government, emphasized the importance of greater productivity to make the territories more financially viable. Yet in the seven years since the Moyne commissioners had visited the West Indies productivity had increased very little.[53]

In the spring of 1948 the British Parliament passed the Overseas Resources Development Act which created two public bodies: the Overseas Food Corporation with assets of £50 million, and the Colonial Development Corporation, with assets of £110 million. The former was to further the production and marketing of foodstuffs. The latter was to survey regional needs and develop local resources through projects too costly for unaided public or private action. Despite the fact that these undertakings designed to increase production were supposed to be commercially sound, the Colonial Development and Welfare Organisation in fact incurred serious losses. Its activities ranged from developing timber resources in British Guiana, to operating the salt industry in the Turks and Caicos, and rebuilding St Lucia's capital, Castries, after a disastrous fire.

Although the disinterested and expert advice of the Colonial Development and Welfare Organisation was undoubtedly valuable, its projects had drawbacks. Most were small, pilot, *ad hoc* schemes which scarcely touched the fringe of British Caribbean problems. Least attention was given to the urgent need for planned economic development. A major reason for this was that responsibility for suggesting proposals lay with the various West Indian governments, while officials of the Development and Welfare Organisation in Barbados were restricted to giving advice and making recommendations to the Secretary of State for the Colonies. Local governments were hampered by wartime shortages of material and skilled personnel, especially by the scarcity of West Indians qualified as technicians, engineers, architects, economists, and agricultural advisers. Moreover, it was difficult for insular administrations accurately to forecast the sums available for development after meeting their normal expenses. No one authority was empowered to examine and recommend a unified attack on the problems of the British Caribbean as a whole.

A broad regional approach, although clearly desirable, was hard to achieve. The most populous and prosperous territories resented any suggestion that the needs of their poorer neighbours should be accorded precedence. The West Indies' steady pressure for increased autonomy was meeting with growing success. The more self-government they obtained, the more jealous of each other they became, the more eager to guard their own interests, and the less willing to receive British suggestions about possible solutions to their difficulties.

By the middle of the twentieth century it was clearly impossible for the United Kingdom effectively to attack Caribbean problems without the active co-operation of West Indians. If their society was to be refashioned it must be on lines of their own choosing. They suspected white officials, even when well-meaning, of condescension, and complained that these were unlikely to remain in the region long enough to understand the islands and their people.

If such views did less than justice to certain outstanding British colonial civil servants, such as two Governors of Jamaica, Lord Olivier and Sir Hugh Foot, they yet reflected an attitude widespread among West Indians eager to administer and develop their lands as they wished. Fulfilment of this understandable desire was complicated by the fact that a large part of the funds required for raising Caribbean living standards had to be provided by Britain.

THE CARIBBEAN COMMISSION

Some efforts were made to achieve international co-operation. By the lend-lease agreement of 1941 the United Kingdom obtained fifty American destroyers in exchange for ninety-nine year leases of land for naval and air bases in the Bahamas, Jamaica, British Guiana, Trinidad, St Lucia, and Antigua. Trinidad, in particular, bitterly resented this arrangement, although work on the American bases provided welcome employment. In St Lucia, however, the agreement resulted in neglect of peasant agriculture and shortages of labour on sugar and banana estates.

As the plan meant that Americans would be living and exercising considerable authority in British territories, some machinery for co-operation was obviously desirable. The United Kingdom's stirrings of conscience about its Caribbean dependencies, quickened by knowledge of the deplorable conditions revealed in the Moyne *Report*, were, moreover, paralleled in the United States by an awakening sense of responsibility for Puerto Rico and the American Virgin Islands.[54]

The Anglo-American Caribbean Commission was established in 1942 as a practical experiment in economic and social co-operation between the United States and Britain. Its co-chairmen were Charles Taussig, an American businessman who, as president of the American Molasses Company, had long been familiar with the area, and Sir Frank Stockdale, British Comptroller for Development and Welfare in the West Indies. The latter's appointment indicated the close relationship which the United Kingdom wished to maintain between the Caribbean Commission and the Development and Welfare Organisation. On Sir Frank's retirement as comptroller his successor, Sir John Macpherson, replaced him as British co-chairman of the commission. The headquarters of the American section were in Washington and of the British section in Barbados. These operated as separate entities responsible, not to any common authority, but to their own governments. At the outset the commission had six members, half appointed by the United States and half by the United Kingdom.

During its first three years the commission served mainly as a co-ordinating supply agency for British and American Caribbean territories. This was vitally important in wartime, when disruption of transatlantic shipping and enemy submarine activity in the area made the West Indies so short of food that on occasion their peoples went hungry. Establishment of a schooner pool and encouragement of more local production of food, including fish, early illustrated what could be accomplished by mutual co-operation and substitution of regional for local attacks on common Caribbean problems. During the war the commission arranged for temporary employment in the United States of agricultural and industrial workers from the Bahamas, Jamaica, British Honduras, and Barbados. It also formulated a programme for intercolonial co-operation on forestry, fisheries, agriculture, and nutrition.

In 1943 the commission formed an advisory body, the Caribbean Research Council, to survey needs, co-ordinate scientific and industrial work in the area, recommend research projects, and facilitate the exchange of information. The next year the commission established a regional consultative organization, the West Indian Conference, with two delegates from each of fifteen Caribbean territories. A weakness during its early years was that, while the United States usually nominated Puerto Ricans and Virgin Islanders as delegates, the United Kingdom almost always appointed English colonial officials to represent the British West Indies.

The conference, like the parent commission, was an advisory and consultative, not an executive, body. Its first biennial session met in Barbados in March 1944, the second in St Thomas two years later, the third in Guadeloupe in 1948, and the fourth in Curaçao in 1950. These were the first international discussions at which West Indian colonies were directly represented. Although the majority of the twenty-nine delegates to the St Thomas conference were white, fourteen were elected members of island legislatures. These meetings considered such matters as improvements in nutrition, expansion of fisheries, industrial development, and public health measures. Their proposals were subsequently studied by the commission which, if it approved, recommended appropriate action by the metropolitan governments concerned.

When in 1945 France and the Netherlands were invited to join the commission, as their West Indian holdings gave them an obvious interest in the area, its name was changed to the Caribbean Commission. The following year it acquired headquarters in Port-of-Spain, where an international secretariat was established at Kent House to encourage co-operation between the metropolitan powers and their West Indian territories and to further scientific, economic, and technological development in the region.[55] It was agreed that the commission should include Caribbean representatives. Of the four members of the British section two were West Indians: Garnet (later Sir Garnet) Gordon of St Lucia and Norman Manley of Jamaica.

The commission and its auxiliary bodies met frequently, published research studies on wide-ranging problems of labour, education, health, welfare, and housing, established a Caribbean Medical Centre in Trinidad for the control of venereal disease, developed uniform quarantine procedures throughout the British West Indies, and encouraged tourism and diversified farming. The commission accustomed the four metropolitan powers and West Indians to co-operation and demonstrated the value, stressed a decade earlier by the Moyne *Report*, of a comprehensive regional approach to similar problems. Among the ablest members of the commission's staff until his departure in 1955 was Dr Eric Williams of Trinidad, who subsequently formed his country's first successful political party and led it to victory.

Despite the commission's broad programme, its high costs and lack of concrete accomplishments were increasingly criticized, especially by the United Kingdom. It was also attacked for alleged impracticality and diffusion of activities. Never more than advisory, it was specifically debarred from considering the political issues closely related to social and economic problems. It conducted research, sponsored conferences, provided technical assistance, and made recommendations, but had no authority to implement its proposals. The metropolitan powers alone were responsible for policy and action. This produced frustration and delay and lent colour to the charge that the commission was an expensive and not conspicuously useful luxury.

It was succeeded in 1961 by the Caribbean Organization which had broadly similar aims. This new body illustrated the West Indies' constitutional progress since 1942. The United States, the United Kingdom, and the Netherlands were observers, not members. France, however, continued as a member to represent French Guiana, Martinique, and Guadeloupe, which were departments of France. The other members were the West Indies Federation, British Guiana, the Netherlands Antilles, Surinam, Puerto Rico, and the British and American Virgin Islands. To the governing body, the Caribbean Council, each member territory sent one delegate. The Caribbean Organization, like its predecessor, was mainly advisory and consultative, designed to foster co-operation and understanding and, in the words of Governor Munoz Marin of Puerto Rico, to serve as a clearing-house for ideas. Its principal activities were promoting tourism, sponsoring trade missions and conferences, and providing information on business opportunities in the area.

When in 1962 the Federation of the West Indies collapsed, its constituent units automatically ceased to belong to the organization, but were invited to join as individual members. Jamaica and Trinidad and Tobago, on becoming independent, declined to do so. The remaining eight members of the defunct Federation indicated their willingness to join, but France objected, unless she was given ten votes on the council where hitherto each member had had one. The British West Indian colonies were then invited to participate as special observers. The organization's fate was sealed in November 1964 when Puerto Rico, to which its headquarters had been transferred, withdrew. Surinam and British Guiana did likewise. Under these unpropitious circumstances it was agreed in 1965 to disband the Caribbean Organization. Its demise was but one of many indications that co-operation among West Indian territories, however sensible in theory, was singularly difficult to achieve.

3

Politics and labour

To the British Caribbean the Second World War brought more rapid political than social and economic advance. In the latter field, as an International Labour Office study noted, the decade from 1940 to 1950 was one of 'promise rather than fulfilment, of study and planning even more than of effective action.'[1] When war broke out in 1939 the franchise was severely restricted throughout the area. In St Lucia only 2.2 per cent of the population were entitled to vote, in British Guiana 2.9 per cent, in Barbados 3.4 per cent, in Jamaica 5.5 per cent, and in Trinidad 6.5 per cent.[2]

A despatch of 7 March 1941 from the new Secretary of State for the Colonies, Lord Moyne, to the Governor of Jamaica, Sir Arthur Richards, proposed constitutional reform and explained that the United Kingdom was willing to introduce universal suffrage in that island immediately. He recommended reducing the official and almost doubling the elective members of the Legislative Council and also urged modernization of local government and compilation of reliable population statistics.

The Jamaican constitution of 1944 largely implemented reforms advocated by a select committee of the Legislative Council. These called for a wide measure of internal autonomy and a quasi-ministerial system. Full responsible government, urged by the People's National Party and supported by the Governor, was rejected by the Legislative Council. The scheme finally adopted was a compromise between radical and conservative views. Its salient characteristics were a thirty-two-member House of Representatives elected by universal adult suffrage; an appointed upper house or Legislative Council (with a one-year suspensory veto) composed of three officials – the Colonial Secretary, the Attorney General, and the Financial Secretary; and a minimum of ten unofficial nominated members. Property qualifications for members of the House of Representatives were removed and anyone entitled to vote became eligible for election to the lower house.

The principal policy-making body, the Executive Council, was chaired by the Governor and composed of ten members, of whom half were drawn from the wholly elected lower house. As all measures had to be approved by a majority of this council before being discussed in the legislature, initiation of public policy was transferred from officials to unofficials. Since, however, elected members were not in a majority and lacked full ministerial responsibility, they did not exercise effective control. The Jamaican Privy Council, with sharply curtailed powers, included the Colonial Secretary, the officer commanding troops, the Attorney General, the Financial Secretary, and two nominated unofficials. It advised the Governor on the exercise of the royal prerogative and discipline of the civil service.

Control of expenditures was vested in the House of Representatives. The five elected members of the Executive Council, who chaired the five principal committees in the lower house, had most of the functions, but not the titles, of cabinet ministers. The Governor retained reserve and veto powers and the right, if supported by the Executive Council or Secretary of State for the Colonies, to assent to measures not passed by the legislature.

The People's National Party bitterly resented the Governor's statement that 'the majority of Jamaicans do not want self-government.'[3] Yet eighteen years later the far from conservative West Indian Economist supported this view, because before 1944 most of those qualified to vote in fact did not trouble to register. It concluded that they did not desire adult suffrage then and even in 1960 had no interest in self-government. Many Jamaicans, it contended, resented political activity as an interference in their daily routine. Because the parties emphasized class interests rather than political programmes, educated people often declined to participate in what they considered the lower-class activity of voting. 'Three-quarters of a century of growing democracy,' the journal observed caustically, 'have found the people of Jamaica, at each stage, indifferent to the changes brought about by a minority: unwilling to welcome them, yet little disposed to voice opposition.' As late as 1969 The Gleaner's political reporter maintained that, since almost one-third of the Jamaican electorate were 'conscientious non-voters,' they were naturally unwilling to be photographed and fingerprinted for the voting register.[4]

In the Jamaican general election of December 1944, the first in any British West Indian territory held under universal suffrage for a wholly elected House of Representatives, about 58 per cent of those eligible voted. An electorate of some 663,000 (in contrast with 73,230 in 1943) cast 365,090 ballots.[5] Most voters, having little or no familiarity with political parties, clearly found personalities more appealing than policies.

The People's National Party, mainly supported by the educated middle class in the towns, campaigned on a platform of self-government, public ownership, and socialism. The Jamaica Labour Party, with its strength in the countryside and the more conservative sections of the business community, preferred an emotional appeal to that of the unity of labour. Its leader, Alexander Bustamante, frankly explained that he himself chose each candidate and determined all party policies. Local legend credited him with saying that if he put up a dog in a Jamaica Labour Party constituency, he could guarantee its election. He attacked members of the People's National Party as communists and atheists and the self-government they advocated as simply substitution of a brown man for a white on the backs of black men.

To this appeal the largely illiterate and overwhelmingly working-class electorate responded by returning twenty-three Jamaica Labour Party candidates, five Independents, and four members of the People's National Party. The relatively sophisticated capital of Kingston returned the Jamaica Labour Party in five out of six constituencies. Norman Manley, Noel Nethersole, and Kenneth Hill, leading members of the People's National Party, all lost their seats. Only one white candidate was elected: a significant illustration of the relatively minor political role which members of the former ruling group were destined to play in the future. The Jamaica Democratic Party, founded immediately before the election and led by Abe Issa of Syrian descent, one of the island's leading businessmen, failed to capture a single seat and was dissolved shortly afterward.

The popular vote was much more evenly divided than were seats in the legislature. The Jamaica Labour Party won 41.4 per cent, Independents 30 per cent, the People's National Party 23.5 per cent, the Jamaica Democratic Party 4.1 per cent, and others 1 per cent. Among the minor parties which jointly polled less than 3500 votes and expired promptly after the election were the Federation of Citizens' Association, the Jamaica Liberal Party, J.A.G. Smith's Party, the United Rent Payers Party, and the Jamaican Radical Workers Union.[6]

The opening of the new legislature on 9 January 1945 was attended by the Secretary of State for the Colonies, Colonel Oliver Stanley. The policy of the United Kingdom, he said, was to help the British Caribbean peoples advance towards self-government and improved standards of living. Ultimately, however, the future of the West Indies was in their own hands, dependent on their skill, energy, enthusiasm, and hard work. 'We believe,' he told the American Foreign Policy Association in New York, 'that all Colonial Powers in any given region and other countries who have a particular interest in the region, should meet together in order to discuss their common problems, and to help each other to find their common solutions.'[7]

A quarter-century later, noting that Mr Bustamante obtained power with no specific platform and no strong desire for political office, the Jamaican *Gleaner* attributed his success to his having given the masses a cause for which to struggle. Even his lack of a coherent programme may have been advantageous in a community where parties and political ideas were both unfamiliar. His capacity to understand and identify himself with ordinary people was perhaps his most conspicuous asset. When he became the island's first elected Chief Minister but showed no intention of resigning as leader of the Bustamante Industrial Trade Union, the press criticized his combining the roles of union leader and head of the government. He retorted indignantly that no one in Jamaica was wise enough to say how his party and union should be run.[8] His electoral success was clearly based on the supporting union, which claimed as members some 80 per cent of Jamaican trade unionists. In 1945 19 per cent of Jamaican wage earners, of whom more than half were agricultural labourers, belonged to trade unions. Of their 58,156 members, 46,538 belonged to the Bustamante Industrial Trade Union. No other labour organization in the island then boasted as many as 2,500 members.[9]

Mr Manley saw the writing on the wall and in 1945 linked the Jamaican working-class movement with that of the Eastern Caribbean by affiliating his People's National Party with the Caribbean Labour Congress. Four years later he converted his island's Trade Union Council from a federation of fourteen small unions into one general trade union which supported his party. By 1950 16 per cent of the organized workers in Jamaica had joined the council.

The value of union support was demonstrated in the general election of 1949 when 65.2 per cent of the electorate cast their ballots and the People's National Party won 43.5 per cent of the total vote, in contrast with 42.7 per cent for the Jamaica Labour Party. The latter retained office, however, although with a much reduced majority. It captured seventeen seats, as opposed to thirteen for the People's National Party and two Independents. Two minor groups, the Agricultural Industrial Party and the United Party of Jamaica, with only one per cent of the vote between them, failed to return any members.

The strength of the People's National Party was concentrated in the urban area of Kingston and St Andrew, five of whose six seats were taken by its candidates. These included such party stalwarts as Norman Manley, Florizel Glasspole, Kenneth Hill, Wills Isaacs, and Noel Nethersole. All except Manley held office in one or more trade unions: Glasspole and Nethersole in six and Hill in four. The campaign hinged on a demand for full and immediate responsible government put forward by the People's National Party.

The Jamaica Labour Party again attacked its rival as a group of irresponsible radicals whose views verged on communism.[10] Bustamante and his followers, whose major support was in the rural areas, then showed little real interest in self-government and none in adult education. Mr Bustamante was the moving spirit and virtual dictator in both his party and his union. The latter was 'a remarkable example,' observed a local journalist, 'of a union which wanted to steer clear of politics and yet became a political instrument.'[11]

POLITICAL AND LABOUR ADVANCES
IN TRINIDAD AND TOBAGO: 1938-50

Meanwhile the Trinidadian labour movement made steady progress. From 1937 to 1957 the number of unions increased from five to sixty-seven and in the latter year labour organizations boasted more than 50,000 members. The Seamen and Waterfront Workers' Trade Union in 1938 concluded an agreement with the Shipping Association covering wages and working conditions for stevedores, lightermen, and boatmen. An arbitration tribunal formed during the same year to settle a dispute in the oil industry was the first such body in the British Caribbean. In 1945 the All-Trinidad Sugar Estates and Factory Workers' Trade Union successfully negotiated with the Sugar Manufacturers' Association establishment of a Joint Consultative Committee to discuss problems affecting field and factory labourers. The oil workers were already strongly organized and had secured several collective agreements providing for a conciliation board, wage increases, and holidays with pay. By 1942 the Trinidad oilworkers' trade union was said to include 8000 of the industry's 9000 employees.[12]

The number of elective members in Trinidad's Legislative Council was increased in 1941 from seven to nine, while official members were reduced from twelve to three, which produced a majority of unofficials. The first elected member of the legislature was appointed to the advisory Executive Council in 1931. Ten years later a second elected member was added to this body, with which the Governor was required to consult.

Captain Cipriani found his position as an elected member difficult since he often disagreed with the Council's decisions, and consequently resigned in 1943. The appointment in that year of the trade unionist elected member of the legislature, Adrian Rienzi, to the Executive Council gave elected members a majority of one over unofficials. Throughout the British Caribbean politically minded West Indians hailed each increase in the number of elected members and each decrease in officials as a significant advance towards self-government.

On the recommendation of a franchise committee of the Trinidadian Legislative Council universal adult suffrage based on a simple literacy test was introduced in 1946. Income qualifications for candidates were lowered to BWI $960 a year or ownership of real estate valued at $5000 or more. At the time of the general election in 1946 there were 259,512 voters, in contrast with 25,822 in 1933.

In this contest over half of the 45 per cent of the population who had registered as voters cast their ballots, but no party secured a clear majority. Three seats were won by the United Front, a radical coalition composed of the West Indian National Party and the East Indian National Council, supported by the Federated Workers Trade Union.

The West Indian National Party, which included both blacks and East Indians, had recently been founded by two black physicians, Dr Patrick Solomon of Trinidad and Dr David Pitt of Grenada, who was a socialist member of the San Fernando borough council. This party advocated socialism, responsible government, free education and medical care, nationalization of oil and asphalt, land redistribution, government control of public utilities, and production of sugar by co-operatives instead of private estates. Neither the business community nor the majority of trade unions evinced much sympathy with such a programme. As the leading members were pronounced individualists of diverse views, the party never became very effective. Similar difficulties dogged its successor, the Caribbean Socialist Party, founded in 1947 by Dr Solomon, who had been elected the previous year as a United Front candidate.

Uriah Butler's British Empire Workers' and Citizens' Home Rule Party in 1946 also won three seats, of which two were held by East Indians. It was supported by the British Empire Workers', Peasants', and Ratepayers' Union, strongly criticized by a British labour adviser as a political organization designed to promote Butler's messianic career. 'Although Mr Butler himself has become more moderate in his public utterances,' wrote F.W. Dailey, 'and is at pains to denounce Communism, ... the irresponsible and violent type of worker seems to be attracted and fostered by his Union ... and a very unsatisfactory state of affairs as regards the Union funds has once more been revealed by the auditors of the books.'[13]

Mr Butler himself was defeated by a United Front candidate, Albert Gomes, a labour leader and former socialist of Portuguese descent, who from 1942 to 1944 had been president of the Federated Workers Trade Union. Originally a member of the West Indian National Party, in 1947 he established a rival body, the Party of Political Progress Groups. He was one of three elected members of the former legislature to retain his seat in 1946.

None of these parties endured long or had a clearly formulated policy, save a common concern for constitutional and social reform. Yet despite continued ethnic tension in Trinidad their interracial character was important, as it accustomed blacks and East Indians (who in 1946 won four of the nine elective seats) to working together for political ends. Only in the early 1950s did the island's first purely racial political organization come into existence: the People's Democratic Party, founded by an East Indian, Bhadase Maraj. Until his death in

1971 he remained a leading public figure. The communist-oriented West Indian Independence Party, established in 1952, was supported by the Oilworkers' Union under John Rojas and the Federated Workers' Union under Quintin O'Connor.

The major bond among elected members was dislike of the colonial government. Enthusiasm for opposition, a characteristic of partially elected legislatures throughout the West Indies, remained a marked feature of politics in Trinidad, which early established a reputation for obstruction and party splits. Its people, Albert Gomes complained in 1946, had 'not yet begun to think politically.'[14]

Trinidadians continued to be dissatisfied because their legislature, unlike those of Barbados and Jamaica, was not wholly elected. At the instance of the elected members a committee of the Legislative Council was appointed in 1947 to consider further constitutional reforms. Most of its recommendations were embodied in the revised constitution of 1950 which introduced a ministerial system and the colony's first predominantly representative legislature.

Two minority reports were appended to this committee's proposals. One by Rangit Kumar, president of the East Indian National Congress, clearly showed his compatriots' fear of a responsible government almost certain to be dominated by the black majority. He urged retention of crown colony rule as the only system guaranteed to safeguard the position of ethnic minorities, including British businessmen with substantial interests in the colony. The other report, by Dr Patrick Solomon, advocated a wholly elective bicameral legislature and full responsible government in domestic affairs. 'There can be no transition by easy stages,' it contended, 'from the present position where the Executive is regarded with intense suspicion and antagonism to that in which it clearly becomes a people's government. Our people are willing, even eager, to accept responsibility, but it must be given to them now, before they learn to believe that it can be purchased only at the price of violence.'[15]

The constitution of 1950 provided single-chamber government by a Legis-lative Council with three *ex officio*, five nominated, and eighteen elected members, in addition to a Speaker, with a casting vote only, appointed by the Governor from outside the Council. The Governor lost his seat in the House, where his place as president was assumed by the Speaker. The Executive Council ceased to be advisory and became the principal policy-making body. It was composed of five members chosen by the Legislative Council from its elected component, one nominated, and three *ex officio* members, in addition to the Governor who as chairman had a casting vote. This gave elected members a majority of one. The Governor's reserve powers were to be exercised with the consent of the Executive Council, or, failing such consent, with the approval of the Secretary of State for the Colonies. He promptly appointed the elected members of the Executive Council, thereafter styled ministers, to take charge of certain departments.

These changes did not go far enough to satisfy some Trinidadians who wanted more than half the members of the Executive Council to be elected and nominated members to be eliminated. Nevertheless they inaugurated a larger measure of responsible government than Jamaica then enjoyed and represented a distinct liberalization of the constitution.

The chaotic state of Trinidadian politics was demonstrated at the general election of 1950 when 18 elective Legislative Council seats were contested by 141 candidates, of whom 91 stood as Independents and the remainder as representatives of five different parties. Butler's British Empire Workers' and Citizens' Home Rule Party, supported by black oil workers and East Indian sugar workers, won six seats; the new and conservative Party of Political Progress Groups, the Trinidad Labour Party, and the Caribbean Socialist Party each secured two; while Independents captured six.

Although Mr Butler's party returned most members, the Legislative Council elected none of them to the Executive Council, but instead chose one representative of the Political Progress Groups, one Caribbean Socialist, and three Independents. Thus there was no ruling party and no official opposition.

POLITICAL ADVANCE IN BARBADOS: 1943-54

Development of unions was a major recommendation of the Moyne Commission, among whose members was Sir Walter Citrine, general secretary of the British Trades Union Congress. His encouragement and interest helped to foster labour movements in Antigua, St Kitts, and Barbados and led to a practical concern with colonial trade unionism by the British Trades Union Congress. In 1954 alone the Congress allotted £6000 to the West Indies, to assist such projects as union buildings in Trinidad and Barbados and labour organization in Jamaica and British Guiana. It also provided scholarships to enable West Indians to study union techniques in the United Kingdom.

During the 1940s and 1950s Barbados made steady social and political progress. Succession duties were introduced in 1941 and income taxes increased in the following year. The suffrage was widened in 1943 as a result of recommendations by the Moyne *Report* and efforts by the Governor, Sir Grattan Bushe, and Grantley Adams and his supporters. This reform, which passed the predominantly white Assembly by only one vote, reduced the income qualification from £50 to £20 per annum, thus enfranchising most urban workers and many agricultural labourers. It also gave women the right to vote and stand for election to the lower house. Although the measure increased the electorate from 7,600 to over 20,000, income requirements continued to exclude most rural workers on sugar estates. By 1949 the average annual income in Barbados was £27, in contrast with about £15 in St Vincent and £100 in the United Kingdom.

The general election of 1944 returned a majority of blacks to the Assembly. The avowedly socialist Barbados Labour Party won eight seats. Hugh Springer was appointed to the policy-making Executive Committee, to which for two years Grantley Adams had belonged. He became Chief Minister in a coalition government composed of the Barbados Labour Party and another socialist group, the West Indian National Congress Party, founded in 1944 and led by W.A. Crawford. The opposition was formed by the conservative Electors' Association, established in 1941 and composed mainly of white merchants and planters. Most members of the Congress Party and Progressive League were soon absorbed into the Barbados Labour Party, which at the general election of 1946 won nine seats. In the first Barbadian government dominated by men of colour Mr Adams headed both the Barbados Labour Party and the Barbados Workers' Union. Two years later his party won twelve seats, the Electors' Association nine, and the Congress Party three.

In 1946 Sir Grattan Bushe, the Governor, introduced a semi-ministerial system by stating that he intended in future to ask the person he considered best able to command a majority in the Assembly to join the Executive Committee and to propose fellow members of that house for appointment to it. He inaugurated this régime by asking Mr Adams to join the Executive Committee and nominate its other elected members. This arrangement made the Barbados constitution the most advanced in the British West Indies.

Yet while this was an important step towards full responsible government, it presented difficulties, as ministers lacked authority to control their departments. Although executive power was distributed among the Governor, the Executive Council, and the Executive Committee, the latter became the chief instrument of policy. The equivalent of the Executive Council in other islands, it initiated all government measures, introduced money bills, and prepared estimates. The Barbados Executive Council resembled the Jamaican Privy Council, which under the 1944 constitution advised the Governor on the exercise of the royal prerogative, as the Governor of Barbados never held the reserve powers possessed by most colonial governors.

Universal suffrage, introduced in 1951 when income and property qualifications were abolished, tripled the number of registered voters, while payment of legislators widened the basis of representation. At the general election of 1951 the Barbados Labour Party, standing for responsible government, was again victorious. Early in 1954 the island obtained a full ministerial system, with Mr

Adams translated from Chief Minister to Premier. Concerned to maintain constitutional propriety, he promptly resigned as president of the Barbados Workers' Union, a post in which he was succeeded by the experienced trade unionist Frank Walcott.

Barbados still, however, lacked complete cabinet government, as three senior officials and a member of the nominated Legislative Council continued to be members of the Executive Committee, over whose deliberations the Governor presided. Foreign affairs and control over the police and civil service remained the responsibility of officials appointed by the United Kingdom.

The fifteen-member upper house, which since 1947 had only a one-year suspensory veto, was appointed by the Governor for a five-year term, with the Chief Secretary (previously called Colonial Secretary) as its spokesman until 1959. Relations between the Assembly and Legislative Council were frequently strained, especially as most members of the former were brown or black, and most of the latter white.[16]

Major credit for these constitutional advances and for such reforms as adult suffrage, workmen's compensation, and a peasant loan programme belongs to Mr Adams. A skilled and ardent politician and parliamentarian, he was also a man of courage, dedication, and integrity. In 1948 he was appointed to the United Kingdom delegation at the first meeting of the United Nations in Paris. There he ably defended British colonialism against attacks by the USSR. 'Give me,' he said, 'the British way of life.' In the following year he served as vice-president at the inaugural conference of Free Trade Unions of the World, later known as the International Confederation of Free Trade Unions.

POLITICAL ADVANCE IN THE LEEWARDS: 1931-53

In the Leewards and Windwards constitutional reform came slowly. The former, as settlement colonies, had from the beginning of British rule been governed under the old representative system, with legislative council members elected under a highly restricted franchise. Like the other British West Indies, they reverted in the latter part of the nineteenth century to crown colony government, under which elective seats were first reduced and later abolished.

From 1871 to 1956 the Leewards were united in a federation described in the following chapter. Their constitutions were reformed in 1931 to provide the same number of elected as of nominated official and unofficial members. The property or income and literacy qualifications required for voters were from four to five times higher for candidates.

In response to local pressures the Secretary of State for the Colonies agreed in 1949 to the appointment of a committee on constitutional reform, composed of elected and nominated members of Legislative Councils in all the Leeward Islands except St Kitts, where elected members declined to serve. This committee recommended an adult franchise subject to a simple literacy test, abolition of property qualifications for candidates, an increase in the number of elected members in the Legislative Councils, and trial of the committee system of government.

New constitutions embodying these proposals were introduced between 1951 and 1953. These provided adult suffrage without the literacy test retained in the Windwards and Trinidad and Tobago. The Legislative Councils were composed of the Administrator as President, with a casting vote only, the Financial Secretary and Attorney-General *ex officio*, three unofficial members (of whom one belonged to the Executive Council) nominated by the Governor in Antigua and St Kitts, and two in Montserrat and the Virgin Islands. Eight additional members in Antigua and St Kitts-Nevis-Anguilla, six in the British Virgins, and four in Montserrat were elected by universal suffrage. The elected representatives chose three of their own number as members of the Executive Council and elected a Deputy President to preside, in the Administrator's absence, over meetings of the Legislative Council. The latter, however, by a two-thirds majority vote, could remove elected members of the Executive Council. The Governors, although normally required to consult with the Executive Councils, were empowered to act contrary to their advice.

In the course of 1951 and 1952 unofficial members of the Leeward Islands presidential legislatures were empowered to return some of their elected members to the General Legislative Council, where they formed a majority. Unofficial members of the General Council nominated certain elected members to the federal Executive Council. Candidates in the Leewards and Windwards did not have to meet a property qualification but forfeited a deposit of £120 if they did not secure a substantial fraction of votes cast. A committee system was introduced by appointing elected members of the Executive Councils as chairmen of small advisory committees to deal with certain departmental subjects.

In 1950 the General Legislative Council recommended abolition of the Leeward Islands Federation as a preliminary to the new Federation of the West Indies. The Leewards union, designed to save money, in fact proved expensive as well as unpopular, and survived only six years longer.

A remarkable Kittitian, Robert Bradshaw, employed at sixteen years of age as a machinist in the local sugar factory, was early active in the St Kitts' Workers' League, and by 1943 had become its vice-president. In 1940 and 1943 the League won all five elective seats in the Legislative Council and three years later returned each of its candidates without opposition. These labour representatives pressed strongly, both in the Council and in the columns of the *Union Messenger*, for adult suffrage and constitutional reform.

In 1943 Mr Bradshaw formed the St Kitts-Nevis Trade and Labour Union of which he became president, and in 1946 founded the St Kitts Labour Party as an offshoot of the union. In the general election of that year he was returned to the Legislative Council and was also appointed a member of the Executive Council. He found a stalwart ally in Caleb Azariah Paul Southwell, a Dominican by birth, who had been successively a teacher, policeman, and clerk in the St Kitts' sugar factory. In 1947 Mr Southwell became vice-president of the St Kitts-Nevis Trade and Labour Union and five years later was elected to the Legislative Council.

In Antigua a former Salvation Army captain, Vere Cornwall Bird, in 1940 founded the Antigua Trades and Labour Union. Encouraged by a series of successful strikes, this union established a political committee. In 1940 and 1943 it won three of the five elective seats in the Legislative Council and in 1945 returned trade unionists to all of these. Its organ, the *Workers Voice*, steadily advocated increased autonomy and universal adult suffrage. By the early 1950s the union claimed a membership of some 17,000 of the island's 22,000 wage earners. In 1951 it persuaded the sugar industry to establish a Joint Industrial Council to discuss matters which might cause industrial disputes. The following year it obtained substantial wage increases for labourers in sugar and cotton fields, dock workers, porters, and printers.

In most of the Leewards and Windwards elections held in 1951 under new constitutions returned a majority of labour candidates. The Antigua Labour Party, formed by Mr Bird to contest the election, won all eight seats in the Legislative Council: four by acclamation, owing to a boycott by conservatives. Bird himself was returned and in January 1952 was appointed to the Executive Committee. In Montserrat William Bramble, president of the Montserrat Trades and Labour Union and leader of the Montserrat Labour Party, was returned in February 1952 to one of the five elective seats on the Legislative Council.

POLITICAL ADVANCE IN THE WINDWARDS: 1924-56

When Britain first acquired Dominica, St Vincent, Grenada, and Tobago, these islands were given constitutions of the old representative type like those of settlement colonies such as Jamaica, Barbados, and the Bahamas, instead of the crown colony system usually imposed on conquered territories. St Lucia, acquired later, was, like Trinidad, ruled from the outset as a crown colony. By 1843 franchise restrictions on its free people of colour had been removed, and, until elective seats were abolished towards the end of the nineteenth century, increasing numbers of this group managed to meet the prescribed income or property qualifications. In 1924, in accordance with Major Wood's recommendations, the Legislative Councils of Grenada, St Vincent, St Lucia, and Dominica obtained a minority of elected members. Steady pressures for more self-government led in 1936 to new constitutions for the Windwards, with more elected members in their Legislative Councils.

In Grenada a branch of the West Indian National Party of Trinidad was founded in 1944. During the next year T. Albert Marryshow, a member of its Legislative Council and one of the earliest and most effective advocates of regional federation, was chosen chairman of the Caribbean Labour Conference at Barbados. In St Lucia George Frederick Lawrence Charles, a former commission agent, joined the St Lucia Workers' Co-operative Union in 1948 and in 1949 became its general secretary. With its support he founded the St Lucia Labour Party and assumed the presidency of both the party and union.

Continued agitation for political reform by labour organizations and political parties in the Windwards bore further fruit in 1951. Universal adult suffrage was introduced and qualifications for membership in the Legislative Councils were altered from property or income requirements to sufficient proficiency in English to permit active participation in their proceedings. Each island had an Executive and a Legislative Council and an Administrator who headed the local government and was responsible to the Governor of the Windwards. Thus for the first time these Legislative Councils had an elected majority, as they were composed of two official, three nominated, and eight elected members, presided over by the Administrator who had a casting vote. The Executive Councils consisted of the Governor or Administrator, two officials, one nominated unofficial, and three elected members of the Legislative Council, chosen by it and removable by a two-thirds vote of the Council.

The Governor was advised by the Executive Council, but empowered to act against its advice. As the elected members could be outvoted on the Executive Council but considered themselves entitled to criticize the government, clashes between them and the executive continued. Local politicians were dissatisfied with their constitutional progress compared with that of the larger colonies. Resentment continued until 1956, when both the Windwards and Leewards obtained ministerial government.

In the elections of October 1951 George F.L. Charles of St Lucia won a seat, as did Ebenezer Joshua of St Vincent. Mr Joshua, a former school teacher, had worked in Trinidad with Uriah Butler, and from 1938 to 1951 served as chairman of Mr Butler's union. After being defeated in the Trinidadian elections of 1950 he returned the next year to St Vincent, where he successfully contested a seat with the backing of the United Workers' and Ratepayers' Union, led by G.H. Charles. The union and its supporting party captured the eight elective seats on the Legislative Council.[17] Shortly afterward, because of a disagreement with Mr Charles, Mr Joshua resigned from this union and in 1952 formed both the People's Political Party and the supporting Federated Industrial and Agricultural Workers' Union, a bargaining agency for sugar workers.

Eric Matthew Gairy of Grenada, once an elementary school teacher, later held a clerical post in Trinidad and subsequently helped to organize oil workers on the Dutch island of Aruba. He returned in 1949 to Grenada where in 1950 he founded the Grenada Manual and Mental Workers' Union, later called the Grenada Trades Union. He became president-general of this organization and of an allied party which he formed soon afterward, the Grenada United Labour Party, commonly known as GULP. Under his leadership this body initiated a number of strikes against the island's cocoa and nutmeg planters.

In February 1951 members of his union were involved in arson, looting, and riots in which three people were killed. The Governor called in British troops, declared a state of emergency, and imported police from other West Indian territories. Mr Gairy was arrested and detained for eleven days in Grenada's dependency of Carriacou. As with Mr Bustamante in Jamaica, detention apparently enhanced Mr Gairy's political glamour. In the elections of September 1951 his party won six of eight elective seats in the Legislative Council. Mr Gairy, who was among the successful candidates, became a member of the Executive Council. His career continued to be turbulent. Within a few weeks he was fined for obscenity; in 1952 he was suspended from the Legislative Council for abusive language to his fellow members; and in 1954, by overstaying his leave, he lost his seat on the Executive Council. Later in that year he was suspended for disrupting the legislature. In the Dominican election of 1951 five of eight elective seats were won by the Labour Party led by Edward Le Blanc.

In the Windwards and Leewards, as in Jamaica and Barbados, parties originally developed from the labour movement and were closely linked with trade unions. In the small islands, however, the early leaders were of a type very unlike Norman Manley and his associates in Jamaica or Grantley Adams and Hugh Springer in Barbados. Self-made, hard-headed, and with little formal education, they made their reputations in the labour movement.

Dominica's first such organization was the Dominica Trade Union, founded in 1945 by Christopher Loblack with help from a British adviser. This was a comprehensive union including estate labourers, waterfront workers, carpenters, masons, and civil servants. The Roseau Workers and Peasants Union, 1951-4, was a sugar workers' organization founded by W.G. Brown, who in 1951 was returned to the Legislative Council with the largest majority of any elected member. In 1954 he was deported to Bermuda, because he had played a major role in an island-wide sugar strike contravening an agreement between the union and the Sugar Manufacturers' Association.

Except in St Kitts most small-island labour leaders had not been employed as workers in the industries whose unions they led, yet it was as trade unionists that they rose to political prominence. This was almost inevitable in tiny communities with a very small middle class and few positions of power and prestige. As these Eastern Caribbean politicians came from backgrounds similar to those of their supporters, there was no gulf between them. Their islands' poverty fostered both resentment of the imperial power and financial dependence on it. Over the years it became increasingly clear that the greater self-government which these leaders wanted involved isolation and an extraordinarily difficult attempt to achieve self-sufficiency. While their experience and training scarcely encouraged a broad outlook, economic necessity made them receptive to the idea of British Caribbean union. It was educated men of vision in the larger territories, not small-island politicians, whatever their shortcomings, who ultimately shattered the Federation and with it the dream of West Indian nationhood.

POLITICAL ADVANCE IN BRITISH HONDURAS: 1935-54

The slow pace of constitutional advance in the Eastern Caribbean was paralleled in the United Kingdom's one Central American dependency, British Honduras. It was ruled as a crown colony from 1871 to 1935, when a new constitution was introduced which, with amendments in 1938 and 1945, remained in effect until 1954. This gave the Legislative Council five official and seven unofficial members. Two of the latter were nominated by the Governor and the other five elected by universal suffrage. Policy was determined by an Executive Council over which the Governor presided, and which included the Colonial Secretary, Financial Secretary, and Attorney-General, in addition to four other appointed unofficial members.

All adults were enfranchised, subject to a literacy test and income, property, or rent qualifications. The income requirement was BH $300 a year; the property requirement $96. These stipulations so restricted the suffrage that at the 1936 election fewer than 800 people, or 2 per cent of the population, were registered as voters. A decade later qualifications were lowered and those for men and women made identical. As late as 1948, however, only 2.7 per cent of the population was entitled to vote. Under such circumstances the long-standing dominance of the Legislative Council by business interests remained unaltered. The number of its elective seats was raised to six in 1938, and seven years later the proportion of unofficial to official members increased.

The capital city of Belize was practically destroyed in 1931 by a hurricane in which a thousand people were killed and another thousand injured, while many forests were severely damaged. Two years later, before the town had recovered, it was again devastated, first by fire and then by flood. In return for a substantial British loan for rebuilding the city and developing agriculture, the Legislative Council reluctantly acceded to the United Kingdom's insistence that the

Governor be given reserve powers and colonial finances be controlled by the British Treasury. These stipulations provoked widespread resentment in British Honduras but reduced the power of commercial interests hitherto paramount in the Legislative Council, which could no longer defeat the Governor's proposals.

Opportunities for emigration dwindled when neighbouring Central American republics, seriously affected by the depression, refused entry to British Hondurans. During the 1930s, however, despite acute economic hardship and mounting political discontent, the country escaped the riots and disturbances ubiquitous in other British Caribbean territories.

A Labour Department was established in 1939, when agricultural employees earned an average of $12 a month and domestic servants from $1 to $3 a month, including board but not lodging. There was then neither workmen's compensation nor factory legislation. The General Workers Union, founded in that year, fostered by widespread economic distress, and from 1947 supported by the *Belize Billboard*, within a decade began to achieve successes on the industrial front. By 1953 it claimed a membership of 9500, although workers in Stann Creek had broken away to form the British Honduras Development Union.

The moderately conservative National Party, formed in 1948 with middle-class support, especially from the Legislative Council, was led by Herbert C. Fuller. The following January a People's Committee was established by some dozen people including Philip Goldson and George Price who advocated closer relations with other Central American countries, especially Guatemala. Leigh Richardson joined the committee on his return from Britain in August. A working-class body, it was formed to attack the United Kingdom's devaluation of the British Honduras dollar in 1949. This measure, unanimously opposed by the unofficial members of the Legislative Council, became even more unpopular when it was forced through by the Governor's reserve powers. The People's Committee attempted to win support from the country's diverse ethnic groups, soon extended its criticism to Britain's colonial policy in general, and proceeded to suggest the possible advantages of secession and union with the United States.

In September 1950 the committee transformed itself into the socialist People's United Party, led for the first few months by John Smith, managing editor, publisher, and part-owner of the *Belize Billboard*. Mr Price was secretary, Mr Goldson, editor of the *Billboard*, was assistant secretary, and Mr Richardson, who later became leader, was chairman of its central council. Within a year this party gained control of the elected city council of Belize. A distinct advantage in this predominantly Catholic community was the devout Catholicism of most of the party's leaders. In 1951 Mr Price became president and Mr Goldson secretary of the General Workers Union. Thus from the beginning this labour organization and the People's United Party were closely connected, with the *Belize Billboard*, of which at one time Mr Richardson was part-owner, acting as spokesman for both.

An element of *opera bouffe* was injected into British Honduran affairs in 1951 when the Governor, backed by the Legislative Council, dismissed the Belize city council (which he replaced by a nominated body) for refusing to hang a portrait of King George VI in the town hall. No calculated device could so effectively have increased the party's popularity.

Guatemala claimed part or all of British Honduras because the communication by road or river between Belize and Guatemala City envisaged in the treaty of 1859 had not been established. The United Kingdom denied that it was mainly to blame and argued that when Guatemala became independent in 1821 it had acquired sovereignty, as a successor to Spain, only over territory where the new state in fact exercised jurisdiction.[18] In 1940 Britain proposed that this dispute be referred for arbitration to the permanent Court of International Justice at The Hague or to an independent tribunal, but Guatemala refused.

As British Honduras acquired more self-government and elected leaders increasingly dominated the political scene, their attitude towards Guatemala aroused controversy which early in the 1950s became acute. On 17 June 1951 the *Billboard* published an article contending that there were two roads to democracy: evolution and revolution, of which the latter was justifiable when a country was oppressed, had no alternative means of reform, and revolution had a fair chance of success. The People's United Party hoped to achieve its goal by evolutionary methods but, if these failed, British Hondurans might decide to use other means to establish their right to self-determination and to abolish poverty and exploitation. When on 2 September a similar article appeared, charges of sedition were laid.

Mr Goldson then visited Guatemala, called on its President, and on his return spoke enthusiastically of this expedition in an open square in Belize locally known as 'The Battlefield.' His speech and an article entitled 'Seven Days of Freedom' were published in the *Billboard* on 24 September and 7 October 1951. These stressed his 'splendid impressions' of political and social life in Guatemala which, according to him, respected the rights of its people, unlike the United Kingdom, in whose colony of British Honduras only property owners and wage earners were enfranchised. 'A Green Curtain,' he said, separated free Central America from his enslaved homeland. For a week he had moved among people more advanced in culture, standards of living, and democracy, and had 'breathed the sweet air of liberty.' Although temporarily compelled to live under a dictatorship, he considered himself a free citizen of the world.

On 7 November 1951 Mr Goldson, Mr Richardson, and a colleague were found guilty of publishing seditious articles. Although sentenced to twelve months' hard labour, they were released in July 1952. Imprisonment transformed them, like Mr Bustamante in Jamaica, into popular heroes. From then on, despite internal splits and periodic eruptions of opposing political movements, the People's United Party steadily proceeded from success to success, flaunting blue and white colours which were also those of the Guatemalan flag. In March 1952, with two stalwarts in jail, the party gained three of the nine seats in the Belize City council, in contrast to four won by the National Party and two by Independents.

Two years later the pro-Guatemalan proclivities of the People's United Party led to a British inquiry into alleged contacts between its leaders and Guatemala. Mr Price was said to have accepted money from the Guatemalan consul in Belize towards the costs of his colleagues' defence against charges of sedition. Mr Richardson was alleged to have asked the Guatemalan Foreign Minister to give the party organ, the *Billboard*, more than $5000 and to ensure that the Guatemalan consul in Belize (whose recall had been requested by the British government) was succeeded by someone whom the People's United Party could trust.[19]

Continued pressure for political advance resulted in 1954 in the introduction of adult suffrage on a simple literacy test and in a new constitution. This replaced the Legislative Council by an Assembly with a three-year term of office. It was composed of nine elected members, three *ex officio* members, and a Speaker and three unofficials nominated by the Governor, who retained certain reserve powers. The policy-making Executive Council included the Governor as chairman, three officials, and six others chosen by the Assembly: four from its elected and two from its nominated members. In the general election of April 1954 the People's United Party (abbreviated as PUP), campaigning on a platform of anti-colonialism, independence, and socialism, won eight of the nine elective seats. It thus gained a conspicuous victory over the pro-British National Party, which advocated a gradual increase in autonomy and participation by British Honduras in the projected Federation of the West Indies.

In the autumn of 1954 the Secretary of State for the Colonies empowered the Governor to give unofficial members of the Executive Council responsibility for steering through the Legislative Assembly the business of certain departments and speaking on their behalf in the Council. To three of the elected People's United Party members he assigned the portfolios of natural resources, public utilities, and social services, and the following year, at the party's request, allotted them additional quasi-ministerial functions.

POLITICAL AND LABOUR ADVANCE IN BRITISH GUIANA: 1943-53

British Guiana's constitution was amended in 1943 to provide a majority of unofficial members in the Executive Council and elected members in the

Legislative Council. Two years later an adult franchise was introduced, subject to literacy and reduced property and income qualifications which were finally removed in 1952. By 1945 the territory had the most effective and lively system of local government in the British West Indies, based on village councils. During that year Dr Cheddi Jagan, an East Indian dentist, became treasurer of the Manpower Citizens' Association.

Between 1938 and 1950 some thirty-five trade unions, with a combined membership of over 15,000, were registered. Almost one-third of these belonged to the Manpower Citizens' Association. Thirteen were affiliated with the British Guiana Trade Union Council, founded in 1941 by a leading radical, Jocelyn Hubbard, who became its general secretary. By 1952 fifteen unions with more than 11,000 members belonged to the council, while another six, with 4000-odd members, composed the Federation of Unions of Government Employees.[20]

A Political Affairs Committee to educate members of the Manpower Citizens' Association on public affairs was formed in 1946 by Dr and Mrs Jagan. Two years later Mr Hubbard and Mr Ashton Chase established a new sugar workers' organization, the Guiana Industrial Workers' Union, as Dr Jagan considered that the sugar companies had come to dominate the Manpower Citizens' Association. Rivalry between the two unions was a major cause of a series of strikes from 1948 to 1953.

Because of the Second World War the first elections under the new constitution were delayed until 1947, when both Dr Jagan and his wife stood as Independents. Mrs Jagan was unsuccessful, but her twenty-nine-year-old husband was elected for Central Demerara. Two years later he became president of the Sawmill Workers' Union and until 1953 retained his seat in the Legislative Council. To the Executive Council the Governor nominated four members of the Labour Party founded in 1945 by an East Indian, Dr J.B. Singh, and led by Hubert Critchlow of the British Guiana Labour Union.

Dr Jagan was briefly a member of the short-lived Labour Party, which in 1950 joined with the Manpower Citizens' Association to form the Peoples' Progressive Party. He became leader, his wife (elected in that year to the Georgetown Municipal Council) general secretary, and a prominent African lawyer, L.F.S. Burnham, chairman. The *Bulletin*, journal of the Political Affairs Committee, rechristened *Thunder*, was the party's official organ. The new group's rise to prominence was at first furthered by collaboration between Dr Jagan and Mr Burnham, who became president of the British Guiana Labour Union. Their joint endeavours managed to attract to the People's Progressive Party support from both East Indians and Africans. Had this interracial co-operation endured, British Guiana's subsequent history might have been very different.

A commission on constitutional review, appointed in 1950 by the Secretary of State for the Colonies, rejected proposals by the People's Progressive Party for cabinet government, universal suffrage at the age of eighteen, a unicameral legislature, and restriction of the Governor's functions. The commission advocated instead a ministerial system, an adult franchise at twenty-one, abolition of property qualifications for candidates, a House of Assembly with twenty-four elected and three *ex officio* members, a half-nominated and half-elected upper house, and an executive or Court of Policy composed of three official and seven elected members. It also proposed that the Governor, while advised by the Executive Council, should retain extensive reserve and veto powers.[21] While not all of these recommendations were accepted, the most important — adult suffrage, a more representative legislature, and a measure of ministerial responsibility — formed the basis of a new constitution introduced in 1953.

RELATIONSHIP BETWEEN UNIONS AND PARTIES

Peculiar to the West Indies is a quasi-fusion of unions and parties, the result of historical and constitutional developments in the region. When the first trade unions were founded, only a tiny fraction of the population could vote and Britain governed by crown colony rule. Effective political parties were impractical when the franchise was severely limited and Colonial Office control paramount.

The early unions strove for social and economic advance. The Moyne *Report* advocated encouragement of labour organizations, which developed rapidly after 1940 and were instrumental in achieving a wider franchise and an increased measure of self-government. The growth of political parties was long retarded by a limited suffrage, rudimentary trade unions, and widespread illiteracy. As the experiences of the 1930s abundantly demonstrated, such circumstances, coupled with appalling social conditions, led almost inevitably to violence. An enlarged electorate and a greater degree of political autonomy finally made effective parties possible.

Inadequate opportunities for implementing public opinion and securing constitutional reform long tended to transform criticism into sedition. In time, however, the movement for self-government fostered the rise of politicians supported by unions voicing both political and industrial discontents. Labour organizations emerged, not only as collective bargaining agents, but as political pressure groups expressing both old grievances and new nationalist fervour. By the end of the 1930s it could truly be said that the Caribbean labour movement was on the march. In developing countries, said Senator Frank Walcott of the

Barbados Workers' Union, labour organizations could not afford the luxury of political isolation, but must identify themselves with political parties which supported their aspirations.[22]

Trade unions are the most important but not the only significant pressure groups in the West Indies. Among other bodies which have helped to mobilize public opinion on political and social questions are East Indian organizations in Guyana and Trinidad, and co-operatives, teachers' and agricultural associations, employers' federations, and chambers of commerce. The influence of the press has been enhanced by the fact that many islands have only one newspaper. Where, as in Grenada, this has been taken over by the government, freedom of the press is largely illusory.

Everywhere in the West Indies, as a commission of enquiry noted of British Guiana in 1949, 'politics are the all-absorbing concern of the people and trade unionism ... has reversed the natural pattern by developing the political before the industrial aspects of labour organisations. There have thus been examples of "personalities" founding unions with an eye more to political gain and cheap publicity than to the real benefit of the worker.'[23] Scoring a political point has sometimes seemed their paramount desire, even when this affected labour adversely. Union members tend first and foremost to be political followers of the man who leads the party they support. 'Most trade unions,' another British report noted, 'have remained more political than industrial in outlook, and ... labour leaders are apt to devote a disproportionate amount of time to political considerations.'[24]

In the absence of enough scholarships to secondary schools the vast majority of West Indian unionists receive only a sketchy primary education. Except in the Leewards and Windwards this has made it very difficult to develop from within the rank and file personnel competent to hold responsible union posts. Under such circumstances trade unions are apt to become institutions designed less to benefit the workers than to produce votes for middle-class politicians.

Parties, on the other hand, often appear more interested in industrial than in political questions and are peculiarly sensitive to union pressures. The common description of a labour party as the political arm of the trade union movement is in few places more apposite than in the British Caribbean, where almost all parties at least profess to be labour-oriented. The bulk of their support is necessarily derived from desperately poor unskilled workers who in every territory form the majority of the population.

Although the twin development of parties and unions has often been described as an awakening of labour, its real strength came from the awakening of powerful leaders, rather than of the followers whom they commonly made little effort to educate. The average West Indian trade unionist, commented a local journal, did not awake but emerged, 'as the dormouse in Alice in Wonderland emerged from the teapot without wakening up.'[25] Indeed it may be questioned how far, except perhaps in Barbados, there has as yet developed an informed labour movement with a practical grasp of economic realities.

The conflict common in most countries between such realities and pressures for higher standards of living has in the Commonwealth Caribbean been particularly acute.[26] Demands for better wages are seldom related to the productive capacity of workers or the prosperity of industry, while labour relations are embittered by the fact that many employers are white and most employees black. Despite valiant efforts by the University of the West Indies, in the relative absence of adult education most Caribbean unions have not developed a tradition of responsibility, nor has this been encouraged by their leaders. Frequent wild-cat strikes meet little public disapproval.

Centuries of rule as dependencies inevitably bred an irresponsibility not easily discarded when unions and parties finally developed. The very fact that the Colonial Office encouraged the growth of trade unions tended to make some West Indians consider them alien institutions: an outlook fostered in the larger islands by the gulf between middle-class labour leaders and the agricultural labourers who formed the bulk of trade unionists. With few opportunities for education or advancement the majority of workers have had little prospect of improving their conditions. Yet if British Caribbean unions have normally made few efforts to educate their members, they have provided valuable training for politicians and helped to achieve peaceful political progress.

The West Indian labour movement has been weakened because scanty wages have kept union dues low and difficult to collect, with the result that funds for strike pay are seldom available. Yet this problem is mitigated by several factors: the majority of workers earn part of their livelihood as small peasant proprietors; many receive financial assistance from common-law wives; and relatives in the country frequently bring food to hard-pressed urban kinsfolk. While in most western countries men have families to keep, in the West Indies they are often supported by nominal dependants. Many names on union registers are those of non-paying members. Devotion to the leader, not payment of dues, is the usual requirement for membership, and capacity to retain such allegiance the acid test of a leader.

By 1952 the labour scene was rapidly changing, partly as a result of Colonial Office encouragement of both trade unions and social legislation. In the British West Indies there were then about seventy unions (in comparison with twenty-eight in 1939), boasting a total membership in the neighbourhood of 180,000, and some twenty-six employers' organizations. Departments of Labour, with statutory powers of inspection, had everywhere been established, while most territories had labour advisory boards, employment bureaus, and Whitley Councils. Arbitration was less common than conciliation, for which the majority of colonies made some provision.

All Commonwealth Caribbean territories had fairly adequate labour legislation, except for workmen's compensation schemes which varied greatly from one island to another. All regulated working conditions of women, children, and young people, and the larger, partly industrialized islands had introduced factory acts.

Factory legislation, imposing health and safety requirements, was encouraged by a Colonial Office despatch of 6 November 1939 to the governments of all British dependencies. This asked them to examine local provisions in the light of the United Kingdom Factories Act of 1937. The first modern measure of the sort in the Caribbean was enacted in 1940 by Jamaica. Between 1941 and 1948 the other British West Indian territories passed similar acts, made effective by provisions for inspection and penalties for infringement. Although not universal, minimum wage laws were common by the 1950s, but no colony could afford to provide health or unemployment insurance or collected accurate labour statistics. Small old age pensions, on an extremely stringent means test, were available in Trinidad, Barbados, and British Guiana. In Antigua, St Kitts, Trinidad, Jamaica, and British Guiana collective bargaining had become the usual method of determining wages on sugar estates. Throughout the area trade unions had been freed from liability for actions in tort and peaceful picketing had become legal. A British West Indies industrial court recommended by the Moyne *Report* had not been established, partly because of fear that such a body might retard the development of collective bargaining.

Despite improved labour conditions there were riots in 1947 among the Jamaican unemployed and Trinidadian oil workers. In Trinidad the Governor proclaimed a state of emergency, forbade public meetings, and imposed a curfew in the districts affected. Although in 1948 sugar workers struck in Antigua, St Kitts, and Trinidad, most wages had risen and the industrial outlook was brighter. By 1950 the majority of territories had an adult franchise and legislatures with elected majorities. Barbados, Jamaica, and Trinidad had all secured semi-responsible government.

The largely moribund British Guiana and West Indian Trade Union Congress was revived in 1944. In 1945, at a meeting in Barbados attended by delegates from Surinam as well as from most British colonies, its name was changed to the Caribbean Labour Congress. In 1947 Grantley Adams was chosen president, Norman Manley and Hubert Critchlow vice-presidents, and Richard Hart of Jamaica general secretary. A new constitution opened membership to trade unions, co-operative societies, and socialist parties throughout the British Caribbean.

Like other attempts at regional collaboration, the endeavour to develop an effective West Indian labour movement proved difficult. The Caribbean Labour Congress, which supported socialism, independence, and federation, finally split as a result of friction between its Marxist and non-Marxist wings, and in 1952 was disbanded. Two years later it was succeeded by the Caribbean Area Division of the Inter-American Regional Division of the International Confederation of Free Trade Unions, popularly known as CADORIT. This body, representing the principal trade unions of Surinam and the British West Indies (with the conspicuous exception of Jamaica's Bustamante Industrial Trade Union), fosters regional activities and co-operation. Its criticism of the close connection between unions and political parties has, however, not succeeded in altering this well-established pattern and may have weakened CADORIT's influence.

As has been seen, most political parties in the Commonwealth Caribbean have depended on trade unions for electoral and financial support. The chief exception is Trinidad's People's National Movement. Parties have long been the subordinate partners in this distinctively West Indian alliance, characterized by interlocking directorates and close co-operation. Since the line between parties and unions is normally narrow, if not imperceptible, trade disputes tend to turn into party quarrels. This encourages inter-union rivalry and wild-cat strikes which weaken the labour movement and waste scanty funds that might be more constructively employed.

'Solidarity forever' can scarcely be the theme of unionists forced by party affiliations into bitter opposition. Workers usually decide what labour organization to join, not on the basis of its stand on rates of pay, hours of work, or fringe benefits, but on its political views. Most favour the one which supports the party of their choice. Often, however, they do not consider themselves obligated to vote for the party to which their union is affiliated. In a conflict between union loyalty and political expediency labour leaders normally opt for the latter.

Many West Indians defend the practice of combining a union and party on the ground that its advantages outweigh its liabilities.[27] Others consider this quasi-fusion a long step towards authoritarianism, and attack the political trade union as 'a monster unknown elsewhere. The workers never thought of it: it is the result of the efforts of middle-class leaders ... anxious to speed up the redemption of labour by political action. In other cases the leaders thought more of political power than of unionism as a moral and intellectual force. In either case the effects have been unfortunate for the West Indies.'[28]

Businessmen critical of the integration of parties and unions contend that strikes are more often indicative of a leader's power than of poor relations between employers and employees. 'I share the opinion of many leaders in industry and commerce,' observed the president of the Jamaica Employers' Federation, 'that the greatest single handicap to progress, prosperity, and a secure and satisfactory way of life in Jamaica is the unfortunate integration of the trade unions with the two main political parties.'[29] Whatever the weaknesses of such an alliance, it is unlikely to be severed until economic conditions in the islands are conspicuously improved.

West Indian employers believe that in labour disputes their position is seldom fairly presented. When insular administrations interfere in such disagreements, they do so not as impartial arbiters but as representatives of one section of the workers. Moreover in the Caribbean, as in Australia and New Zealand, governments are among the largest employers of labour. Hence, in any industrial crisis, a Trinidadian alleged, an employer is 'forced to appeal from Caesar to Caesar with the certain knowledge that the scales are weighted against him at every stage.'[30] West Indian businessmen, confronted by the growing strength of labour, in 1960 formed at Antigua a consultative committee on industrial relations, from which the Caribbean Employers' Confederation later sprang.

A potentially dangerous aspect of the union-*cum*-party pattern is the concentration of industrial and political power. This tendency is, however, counteracted by the fact that economic power is often still wielded mainly by white businessmen whose once preponderant influence on local politics has almost vanished. While West Indians are bitter about the continuing influence of expatriate firms, this separation of economic and political control fosters the distribution of power and thus helps to keep it responsible.

Unsuccessful strikes encouraged unions in the Caribbean, as in Britain and Australia, to pursue their goals by political means. Another reason for the link between labour and parties is that union leadership or support has usually offered aspiring politicians the easiest and often the only path to political power and preferment. Concentration on political rather than industrial issues, however, makes it difficult for labour to play its normal role and equally difficult for union-dominated parties to act as genuinely national institutions based on cohesive political programmes. The majority of Jamaicans who vote for the People's National Party, for instance, are no more convinced socialists than the supporters of the Jamaica Labour Party are unequivocal enthusiasts for free enterprise.

It is notoriously difficult to organize farm labourers. Yet in the West Indies, where many people are employed on large estates, agricultural unions, especially among sugar workers, developed early and quickly gained strength. With a largely unskilled population both parties and trade unions tend to be comprehensive bodies composed of people in a wide variety of occupations. Especially in the larger territories they cut across class lines, attracting support from lawyers, doctors, teachers, and journalists, as well as from manual workers. This helps to mitigate social cleavages in eminently class-conscious societies. In Barbados and Jamaica, despite obvious tensions, whites and non-whites have long lived and worked together. Hence they find a sense of national identity easier to achieve than do many people in the Eastern Caribbean. It was no accident that these two islands were leaders in the movement for self-government. Familiarity with a modicum of democracy whetted their appetite and sharpened their demand for more.

LEADERSHIP

Because of the close relationship between unions and parties it is common for West Indians to combine tenure of high office in a party with senior status in one or more labour organizations. In the small islands the premier or prime minister often also leads the principal trade union. Alexander Bustamante long provided a conspicuous example of this practice in Jamaica. There Noel Nethersole headed both the Municipal and Parochial Workers Union and the Machado Employees Union, while at the same time serving as president of the Maritime Union of Jamaica, the Government Printing Office Employees Union, and the Postal and Telegraph Workers Union. Florizel Glasspole (later Minister of Education in Mr Manley's government) was at various times president of the Jamaican United Clerks' Association, the Jamaican Printers and Allied Workers' Union, and the Government Hospitals and Prisons Employees Union, as well as secretary of the Municipal and Parochial Workers Union and the Machado Employees Union.

In Barbados and Jamaica union leadership often came to be regarded as a profession for light-skinned or coloured members of the small educated élite who emerged as leaders of the black working-class majority. Norman Manley, Grantley Adams, and Hugh Springer all stood for political and economic development and better living standards for the mass of their fellow-countrymen. Yet these men of middle-class background, without practical experience as workers in the unions they dominated, were inevitably divorced in tastes and temperament from the bulk of their supporters. Under such circumstances to keep in close touch with the rank and file was very difficult for anyone without unusual capacity for attracting personal allegiance.

Even when leadership of a union and of a party was formally divorced, the connection in fact was often close. Hugh Shearer, who headed the Bustamante Industrial Trade Union after Sir Alexander's retirement, was related to Bustamante and sometimes accused of subservience to him, while Mr Manley's son Michael led the National Workers' Union which supported the People's

National Party. Both later became political leaders of their respective parties and Prime Minister of Jamaica. Unions, the *West Indian Economist* remarked acidly, 'serve as a system of control of the masses by the intelligentsia at the expense of the propertied classes.[31] The comment applies less aptly to the Eastern Caribbean than to the other territories, despite the rise of middle-class leaders in the Windwards during the 1960s.

In the West Indies, as elsewhere, achievement of power has a sobering effect. Men vocally extreme in opposition may in office often become transformed by respectability and pride of place. Translation to the seats of the mighty brings prestige and prosperity which set the élite apart from the rank and file. Such assets its members naturally have little inclination to relinquish.

In Trinidad, where racial and religious divisions long delayed the growth of autonomy, unions developed several decades before representative government. There, as in the Leewards and Windwards, most were at first, and many are still, led by unskilled workers, not middle-class professional men. Trinidad is the one Commonwealth Caribbean territory where control of labour organizations is not considered essential by politicians and where parties flourish without supporting trade unions. Yet in this island also individual statesmen have sometimes sought to use unions to further their own political careers. The racial divisions of Trinidad and Guyana explain the fact that their labour bodies, unlike many others in the region, tend to be organized vertically rather than horizontally and are often politically independent.

Since all West Indian parties advocate better education, more social welfare, and improved economic conditions, and since party discipline is weak and splinter groups are common, it has usually been difficult to establish a two-party system based on distinctions in policy. The one-party system long prevalent in the Leewards has elsewhere in the area proved unacceptable because of the strength of parliamentary traditions. Effective leadership of an unsophisticated electorate is likely to depend more on a forceful personality gifted in oratory, rabble rousing, and flamboyant techniques, than on a practical platform based on coherent principles. While many West Indian party leaders have come from the middle class, their success commonly owes more to a distinguished career in the trade union movement than to a professional reputation at, for example, the bar.

Under a crumbling crown colony system parties developed primarily as instruments for harassing the executive in a contest between rulers and ruled. Early West Indian politicians saw themselves as tribunes of the people battling ancient exploiters: as indispensable men who had to do everything and assume all responsibility. To the mass electorate many represented themselves almost as saviours.

Leaders in office at the time of independence acquired a halo remarkably resistant to tarnish. Flushed with success and aided by the tradition of authoritarian rule during the colonial period, some fostered a cult of personality, and among their cabinet colleagues achieved a position far more commanding than that of first among equals. Politicians often construed strong leadership to include crushing incipient opposition. Some found it easy to claim a monopoly of patriotism and hard to practise the arts of compromise, tolerance, and persuasion basic to democracy but little fostered by centuries of dependence.

Before independence or quasi-autonomy was attained, political parties in the Commonwealth Caribbean tended to be conservative. This may seem surprising, because the appeal of radicalism is predominantly to the disadvantaged: a category which comprises the majority of West Indians. Yet, despite widespread poverty and stock blood-and-thunder utterances by many local politicians and young would-be members of the intelligentsia, before the 1970s the lack of genuine radicalism was marked.

Equally conspicuous was the absence of distinctive party principles. The chief function of slogans such as 'the man with the plan' or 'the party with a purpose' seems to be to distract the electorate's attention from the fact that neither plan nor purpose emerges with clarity from the enshrouding mists of rhetoric. Whatever the slogan, it is likely to be presented as a panacea. Caribbean leaders, observed an astringent Trinidadian, 'babble about independence and democracy as if it were a kind of medicine or pill that they as doctors administered and thereby cured the population of a disease called colonialism.'[32] Separated by few distinctions in policy, West Indian parties have commonly united behind picturesque leaders disinclined to encourage possible rivals by sharing effective power with their colleagues. Such circumstances accentuate the natural ambition of politicians in whose minds the desire for personal advancement and the well-being of their country are often inextricably mixed.

Sir Arthur Lewis, speaking of Africa, once dismissed as a stereotype the view that peoples struggling for autonomy are likely to support a single charismatic leader. Movements for independence, he pointed out, are frequently led by different men often sharply at odds with each other.[33] The West Indies, however, have had few bitter struggles for autonomy. Some, indeed, have shown little eagerness to have it thrust upon them without an accompanying golden handshake. The multiplication of political parties in West Africa during the years preceding independence had few parallels in the Commonwealth Caribbean, except in Trinidad, although the larger territories certainly produced a variety of rival politicians.

As the practice of referring to a party as Mr Gairy's or Mr Burnham's party indicates, the real strength of West Indian parties lies in the personality of their leaders. To the ill-educated majority what governments have done or hope to do seems to appear relatively unimportant. It is men, not measures, all the way, with most policies emanating from the leader. Caribbean parties are seldom united and agree on few common principles. Yet by the 1970s there were indications of discontent with this state of affairs, especially among the young and better educated. In Trinidad, which has never had a strong opposition based on a stable two-party system, a demand arose for putting policies before leaders and for more participation by the rank and file in shaping party programmes.

West Indian party conventions demonstrate the enthusiasm of the faithful and officially approve proposals and strategy previously determined by the leaders. Like their American, Australian, and Canadian counterparts, Caribbean parties commonly lack research groups and receive little such candid and disinterested advice as the Fabian Society offers the British Labour Party. The absence of political ideas fosters the rise of demagogues and the sport of follow the leader. The vacuum created by the lack of ideas remains relatively inconspicuous in communities which, in the twentieth century as in the days of slavery and plantocracy, often continue to associate political power with privilege rather than responsibility. In many territories the passing of colonialism has meant less the development of responsible and genuinely representative self-government, than the transfer of power from the old white élite to a new and darker-skinned ruling class.

Ordinary people, accustomed to having someone else do their thinking for them, are frequently easy prey to political charlatans. Leaders lavish with impossible promises can rest easy in the knowledge that emotional appeals are usually far more effective than rational argument. Such circumstances, especially in the Leewards, where political opposition has developed slowly, often place a premium on the less attractive qualities of aggressive and authoritarian politicians. Where, as in the small islands, party leaders were long drawn exclusively from the workers, their first middle-class rivals found themselves at a distinct disadvantage.

Nurtured on opposition, the majority of West Indian politicians rose to prominence by attacking colonial rule and those who administered it. Party politics were originally based on distrust of and opposition to colonial governments. When autonomy arrived, this outlook continued under independence. However natural, it did not make for either good administration or good citizenship. It was tragic for West Indian unity that such attitudes survived the colonial period and were adapted to the federal scene, where they bedevilled the islands' relationships with each other and with their national government.

4

The federal idea

Federalism seems at first glance an obvious solution to the problems of territories singly too small, poor, or isolated for economic self-sufficiency and political independence. Promising union without unity and variety without fragmentation, it holds out the inducement, especially alluring to colonies, of gaining status through membership in a new and greater entity. It offers a prospect of meeting common social, economic, and political problems more effectively through co-operation and of replacing parochialism, without loss of local distinctiveness, by a national outlook based on faith that the whole is greater than the sum of its parts.

Yet federalism is almost always a second best, in the sense that it is chosen only when unitary government is impossible. Cheaper and more flexible, the latter provides fewer opportunities for political bickering. Communities which elect federalism, it has been said, must pay for their decision in the hard currency of constitutional problems. All federations are at best a gamble; their success largely depends on their people's capacity for tolerance and compromise. They have sometimes been considered peculiarly appropriate for poor communities on the principle that, while the strong may afford to disagree, by every dictate of common sense the weak are well advised to dwell together in unity. Precept, however, is notoriously easier than practice, and the course of federations, as West Indians learned to their cost, has seldom run smooth.

EARLY FEDERAL PROPOSALS IN THE WEST INDIES

For almost three centuries some form of closer association has been propounded as a solution to British Caribbean problems. Such proposals originally emanated, not from West Indians, but from Englishmen impressed by the probable economies of unified administration. The usual attitude of the islanders was early illustrated, towards the end of the seventeenth century, when Barbadian planters rejected a Jamaican plan for a joint expedition against the pirates then infesting the Leewards, on the ground that they would not expend one shilling to save their little northern neighbours.[1]

When the Lesser Antilles were first colonized by England they shared a common government administered by the Governor of Barbados. In 1671 at their own request they were divided into two groups, the Leewards and Windwards, under two governors, with Barbados as the seat of government. Three years later Sir William Stapleton, Governor of the Leewards, called a conference to discuss the political union of Antigua, St Kitts, Nevis, and Montserrat.[2] Although their representatives opposed this suggestion, he summoned members of their assemblies and councils to meet in 1678, 1681, and 1682 in a General Assembly at Nevis. The delegates refused, however, to agree to being represented in England by one agent, to vote funds for recurrent expenses, or to enact uniform laws. They showed, in fact, an already well-defined sense of local insularity which with the passage of time grew no less pronounced.

St Kitts in 1683 requested exemption from laws passed by the General Assembly and permission to be governed by enactments of its own legislature. Six years later a separate legislature was provided for each island, with a common General Assembly for all the Leewards. The latter body met frequently from 1690 to 1705, when an act defining its powers vis-à-vis those of the territorial legislatures was passed. This secured to every island its own laws and customs and empowered the General Assembly and General Council to legislate for the Leewards as a whole. Yet in fact the General Assembly was never effective and held no meetings between 1711 and its last session in 1798.[3]

The Leewards were divided in 1816 into two parts: one composed of Antigua, Barbuda, and Montserrat, and the other of St Kitts, Nevis, Anguilla, and the British Virgins. In 1833 they were again united under one governor, with Dominica added to the group. Almost forty years later, in 1871, the local legislatures agreed to a loose federation, but with little enthusiasm, as each feared losing status. Under this arrangement the Leewards formed one colony with six presidencies: Antigua (with Barbuda), Nevis, St Kitts (with Anguilla), Dominica, Montserrat, and the British Virgins. The total was reduced to five twelve years later when St Kitts, Nevis, and Anguilla were amalgamated into one tripartite colony with the seat of government at St Kitts, which thereafter remained the dominant partner.

Each presidency had wholly nominated executive and legislative councils. The unofficial members of these legislatures elected some of their own number to a

General (or federal) Legislative Council in Antigua, composed of ten nominated (six official and four unofficial) and ten elected representatives with jurisdiction over specified subjects. The legislative councils of the presidencies retained local autonomy and exercised concurrent jurisdiction, provided they did not contravene federal acts. The General Legislature had no power to tax and its expenses were defrayed by highly unpopular contributions levied on each constituent unit. An ordinance of 1924 provided for election of four unofficial members to the Legislative Council of Dominica, which in 1940 was transferred from the Leewards to the Windwards, with which by geography, history, and religion it was more closely affiliated.

Thirteen years after its formation, the Leewards federation was described as a 'costly impediment to good government.'[4] With no independent revenue, it was a singularly weak union whose only solvent member was St Kitts. There was some justification for the islands' belief that their dissimilar problems required different treatment, and for the unpopularity of the federation. 'It has been so brought about and so manipulated and managed,' C.S. Salmon, a former President of Nevis, complained at the end of the 1880s, 'that it has thrown discredit upon the time-honoured name of Confederation. It is a Government powerless in itself to do any good, but which has developed great capacities for hindering any good being done by the several parts ... The islands lost their little local governments and got nothing in return, except a special tax to keep on foot a useless Governor [and] a staff of officials to help him.' Salmon advocated, instead, a federation of all the British West Indies, including the Bahamas, British Guiana, and British Honduras, to enable the peoples concerned to work out their own salvation and to remove the anomaly of expecting each tiny island to support a separate government. The so-called confederations of the Windward and Leeward islands he considered mockeries, since the only visible things abolished were their local governments which cost nothing. Nowhere in the world, he protested, was anything like the same proportion of public taxes eaten up by salaries as in the fifteen colonies of the British West Indies with their seventeen governors and administrators.[5] During the next seventy years similar views were expressed in most of the Leewards.

When in 1763 Grenada, St Vincent, Dominica, and Tobago were ceded to Britain, they were briefly joined, together with the little Grenadines, as the Southern Caribbee islands, under the Governor of the Windward Islands with headquarters in Grenada. Because of strenuous complaints from the first three that they also were entitled to separate assemblies, however, this experiment in unitary government was abandoned. In 1767-8 each little island successfully insisted on acquiring its own legislature, although administrative union continued for a brief period under a common governor for all four. Dominica secured its own governor in 1771, as did St Vincent six years later. Grenada and Tobago continued to be united for administrative purposes until 1783, when the latter was ceded to France. All traces of administrative union then vanished and no attempt was made to revive it at the end of the Napoleonic Wars when Tobago again became British.

A French commentator suggested in 1852 the likelihood of the ultimate fusion of the British Caribbean territories. 'They might well,' he suggested, 'unite in confederation, joined by common interest, and possess a merchant fleet, an industry, arts and a literature all their own. That will not come about in a year, nor in two, nor perhaps in three centuries but come about someday it shall, for it is natural that it be so.'[6]

In the last three-quarters of the nineteenth century the Colonial Office tended to consider federalism a sovereign specific for a variety of ills. It usually overlooked both the views of the peoples concerned and the fact that such associations inevitably create new problems without necessarily solving old ones. To a succession of British governments and officials some form of union seemed sensible for a handful of West Indian islands, many no more than twenty or thirty miles long. Yet the islanders dreaded that their interests would suffer if their individual governments were abolished.

Their fears were well founded. Dr David Lowenthal has pointed out that, although Nevis and Montserrat have approximately the same area and population, the roads, water supplies, electricity, air transport, and hospital services of Nevis are inferior. On most of these facilities twice as much is spent in Montserrat because it has its own responsible government. Nevis has been particularly resentful of being linked with St Kitts and Anguilla, as until 1882 it was a separate member of the Leewards and for some time the seat of the central government. So long as one unit 'attracts an external subsidy,' commented Dr Carleen O'Loughlin, 'to abolish that administration would be to kill the goose that lays the golden egg.'[7]

Among early British enthusiasts for West Indian federation was Viscount Goderich, Secretary of State for the Colonies in the second quarter of the nineteenth century. Forced by local opposition to abandon the federal union he preferred, in 1833 he linked most Eastern Caribbean territories in two administrative unions under separate governors. That of the Leewards has already been discussed. The second group was formed by Barbados, Grenada, St Vincent, and Tobago which, as the Windward Islands, were joined under one governor resident in Barbados. Trinidad and St Lucia were added two years later. Trinidad obtained its own governor and government in 1842, but administrative union of the Windwards continued for another forty-three years.

Union rather than federation of the West Indian territories, with the possible exception of Jamaica and British Guiana, was proposed in 1839 by Herman

Merivale. The next year federation of the whole group was advocated by Sir William Colebrook, then Governor of the Leewards. A federal union of Barbados and the Windwards, proposed in 1871 by the Colonial Office, was bitterly opposed by all these islands and in particular by Barbados. Its Governor, Sir John Pope Hennessy, vainly supported the plan, which he thought would help the labouring majority of Barbadians. 'Your Lordship can scarcely be surprised,' he wrote apologetically to the Secretary of State, 'that the minor islands do not feel disposed to place themselves so completely under the domination of Barbados, which has not acquired for itself a reputation of a generous and cosmopolitan spirit of legislation.'

Barbados' 250-year-old Assembly was outraged at the prospect of reversion to crown colony status. The white planters who controlled it feared losing their abundant labour supply, since sugar workers favoured federation partly because this offered free migration to other islands. The business community also feared being asked to give financial assistance to the poorer Windwards. The Barbados House of Assembly curtly informed Sir John that it did not intend 'to consent to become one of a political Federation of islands.'[8] The quarrel between the Governor and the Assembly resulted in the anti-confederation riots of 1876 and subsequent abandonment of the project.

A proposal by a royal commission in 1882 to have a common governor for the Windwards and another for Barbados was adopted in 1885, when the seat of government in the Windwards was transferred back to Grenada. Four years later Tobago was detached from this group and linked with Trinidad in an administrative union. As a result of bitter local opposition plans for federating Grenada, St Lucia, and St Vincent were also abandoned. St Lucians objected to the capital being in Grenada, Grenadians disliked a federal treasury, and Vincentians emphasized their antagonism by stoning the Lieutenant-Governor and Acting Attorney General. Even the suggestion of a common Chief Justice for Grenada and St Vincent so outraged the latter territory that in 1891 a warship was sent to help maintain order. The three islands consequently remained under one governor but were otherwise independent of each other. Each retained its own executive and legislative councils and fiscal autonomy, save for loans or grants-in-aid provided by the United Kingdom.

Baron H. de Worms stated in the House of Commons in 1891 that the British government had no intention of federating all its West Indian colonies.[9] Three years later Sir Robert Hamilton, chairman of a royal commission appointed to enquire into conditions in Dominica, recommended linking the Windwards in an administrative union.[10] He also proposed withdrawing Dominica from the Leewards Federation, but almost half a century elapsed before this island was finally attached to the Windwards in 1940. The West India Royal Commission of 1897, chaired by Sir Henry Norman, a former Governor of Jamaica, tentatively suggested closer relations between Barbados and the Windwards, but opposed federation of all the British West Indian territories under a common governor and doubted whether such a union would effect any economies.[11]

Unitary government for the whole British Caribbean was again advocated at Westminster on 2 August 1898, and supported five years later by Sir Norman Lamont.[12] The alternative of confederation under a single governor general, with individual administrators and legislatures in the various colonies, was proposed as particularly opportune at a time when imperial federation was being widely discussed. West Indians, optimists argued, were loyal and ardent imperialists who would welcome such a scheme, provided it recognized the islands' right to control their own finances. If imperial loans were required to help defray the expenses of confederation, these might be considered a reasonable contribution to the well-being of peoples whose forefathers had been forcibly taken as slaves to the West Indies with the approval and encouragement of British governments.[13]

Union between St Vincent and Grenada was broached in 1905, but both islands were opposed, although Grenada then showed some enthusiasm for fusion with Trinidad and Tobago. During that year the Secretary of State for the Colonies, Alfred Lyttelton, told the House of Commons that the United Kingdom considered federation of all the British Caribbean territories an ultimate objective, but hoped this might come about naturally from increased regional co-operation.[14] From then on successive British governments advocated federalism as the best solution for the region, if and when local public opinion was ready to support such a scheme.

Meanwhile the Colonial Office tried to encourage insular co-operation. The usual reaction of West Indians was flatly to reject any form of union. As the English historian Froude observed after visiting the Caribbean in the 1880s, federation was 'no sooner understood than it was universally condemned.' In consequence all these proposals were tactfully shelved by the Colonial Office. There were some, however, like Lord Rothermere, who argued that the British West Indies must federate or be annexed to the United States. A former American Secretary of the Treasury, William McAdoo, suggested in 1920 that they might be transferred to the United States in satisfaction of Britain's indebtedness to it: an idea which neither then nor later received any serious consideration.

As early as 1907 a *Times* correspondent proposed free trade and possible amalgamation with Canada. An anonymous article in the *Fortnightly Review* suggesting that the British West Indies be exchanged for the Philippines provoked an indignant reply from Sir Norman Lamont. He approved of free trade with Canada and reflected (like Canadians half a century later) on 'how vastly the work would be simplified if the Federated Dominion of Canada could deal direct with a Federated ... West Indies.' The real solution for the area's problems, he contended, lay in new men, new minds, and new methods.[15] Sir Norman later argued that a West Indies federation should be entitled to a seat at imperial conferences, and that unification of civil services in the British Caribbean would be a strong consolidating influence and assimilation of tariffs an even stronger one. In each colony, he believed, thoughtful men considered the time ripe for a federal union which safeguarded local institutions.[16]

There was clearly no dearth of remedies proposed for West Indian ills. In the next half century opinions similar to those cited were frequently reiterated and ingenious new permutations and combinations hopefully suggested. Until the 1940s, however, the Caribbean colonies themselves showed no strong inclination towards closer union. 'The people of one island,' wrote a pessimistic Jamaican advocate of federation, 'know little or nothing, and care less about the products, customs, resources, religion, or law of a sister colony. ... They view the migration of the inhabitants of one ... to another as a foreign element, and proceed to set up barriers for their exclusion.'[17]

Before the First World War C. Gideon Murray, a former Administrator of St Vincent who later served in the same capacity in St Lucia and eventually became Governor of the Windwards, advocated federal union, under one governor, of the Leewards, Windwards, Barbados, Trinidad, and British Guiana.[18] Early in 1918 the Barbados Chamber of Commerce recommended prompt and serious consideration of federating the British West Indian colonies, as did the Trinidad Chamber of Commerce later in the same year.[19] Shortly after the war ended Sir Samuel Hoare, who had business interests in British Honduras, urged appointment of a high commissioner for the West Indies, including British Honduras, Jamaica, and the Bahamas.[20] Sir Edward Davson, president of the Associated Chambers of Commerce in the West Indies, suggested a less ambitious scheme: a West Indian council with a permanent secretariat, to prepare material for conferences on which common action should be based.[21]

THE WOOD *REPORT*'S VIEWS ON FEDERATION

The Under-Secretary of State for the Colonies, Major E.F.L. Wood, considered the views of Sir Edward Davson and Sir Samuel Hoare somewhat ahead of public opinion: a belief confirmed by his visit to the British Caribbean in 1921-2. On his return he stressed the liabilities of the islands' physical and psychological isolation and cited difficulties encountered by Canada in trying to arrange a mutually preferential tariff with ten separate West Indian governments. The full paraphernalia of administrative machinery in a collection of little territories seemed to him top-heavy and expensive, while provision for interchange of civil servants, doctors, and teachers would benefit all. Although he thought more unity and co-operation highly desirable, he yet believed that practical and political objections made federation impossible at that time. In January 1922 the West Indian colonies declined even to attend a conference to discuss the possibility of closer co-operation. The difficulties of geographical separation were accentuated by political distinctiveness, diverse languages, religions, and traditions, and the absence of a spirit of unity.

Any effective federation clearly had to be supported by West Indians. In Major Wood's opinion the best way to discourage such support was to suggest that an alien imperial power wanted to coerce reluctant colonies into union. The existing loose association of the Windwards was disliked by St Lucia and St Vincent, if only because the seat of government was in Grenada. The sole combination the Under-Secretary then considered possible was joining Trinidad to the Windwards. Such a union he deemed inadvisable unless both parties wanted it, and of this he was wisely dubious. The Governors of Trinidad and the Windwards, at the instance of the Secretary of State for the Colonies, in 1923 discussed closer association between these islands, but with no result.

The Leewards could scarcely be cited as an argument for union when in each there was a movement for secession. Although Major Wood believed attempts should be made to overcome insular prejudices, he concluded prophetically that 'establishment of West Indian political unity is likely to be a plant of slow and tender growth.' His views were supported by Sydney Olivier, a senior member of the Colonial Office, with long experience in the British Caribbean. 'It is to be hoped,' he wrote, 'that this authoritative pronouncement will lay this superficial and futile prescription to rest for a generation at least. No major West Indian Colony would tolerate being governed from any one of the others.'[22]

As the Wood *Report* emphasized, sharp differences of opinion on federation divided the British West Indies. Dominica was the only Caribbean colony where both the Chamber of Commerce and the rest of the community urged abolition of the Leeward Islands Federation. In certain territories the apparent wastefulness of multiplying local legislatures and the prospect of saving money through some form of union appealed to the small group of white businessmen. Yet the Trinidad Chamber of Commerce, which in 1918 had championed the idea of federation, later voiced strong objections to it. The latter stand was supported by planters in some British Caribbean colonies and by many ordinary people, although in 1924 the Associated Chambers of Commerce in the area advocated an inter-island customs union.

The United Kingdom and its Caribbean dependencies viewed the prospect of federation very differently. Most political parties and trade unions led by black and brown West Indians had no interest in financial economy and saw nothing to commend closer union, unless this proved the only road to their cherished goal of self-government. The majority of local politicians were naturally reluctant to relinquish the prospect of power and prestige for which they had struggled and for the first time saw almost within their grasp. The more authority they attained in their own islands the less willing they became to share or lose it.

Among distinguished exceptions were T. Albert Marryshow of Grenada, Cecil Rawle of Dominica, and Captain Cipriani of Trinidad. At the British Guiana and West Indies Labour Conference of January 1926 the Trinidad Workingmen's Association advocated federation and dominion status for all the British West Indian colonies. During this year a loosely organized West Indian Federal Labour Party was founded at a conference in St Lucia.

FEDERALISM AND SELF-GOVERNMENT

The movements for self-government, nationalism, and federation were intimately linked. To most West Indians the chief argument for closer union was as a shortcut to autonomy. The fact that federalism necessarily involves some diminution of independent action by its constituent parts was generally recognized only after the islands had agreed to federate.

On the initiative of L.S. Amery, Secretary of State for the Colonies, predominantly white representatives of the British West Indian territories discussed federal union at London in 1926, without conclusive results. They agreed, however, to establish an advisory Standing Conference, meeting at eighteen-month intervals alternately in England and the Caribbean. The first (and only) session was held in 1929 in Barbados, where all the British colonies in the region, except Bermuda, were represented.

Limited union was advocated later in the year by unofficial members of the Executive and Legislative Councils of Antigua, who petitioned for federation under one governor of the Leewards, Windwards, and Trinidad. They were influenced by financial difficulties occasioned by the stock market crash of that autumn, which produced a serious economic crisis in the sugar industry. In 1930 Dominica urged federation of the Windwards and Leewards as a preliminary to a wider union of all the colonies. Similar proposals were put forward by the West Indian Sugar Commission and by Mr Marryshow of Grenada, who asked for a royal commission to investigate both federation and increased self-government for the British Caribbean territories.

The Labour Colonial Secretary, Lord Passfield, in 1931 told the Governors of Trinidad, the Windwards, and the Leewards that he intended to appoint a commission to examine the possibility of closer union and co-operation. An unofficial conference met early in 1932 at Roseau in Dominica. Organized by the Dominica Taxpayers' Reform Association, attended by representatives from Antigua, Dominica, Grenada, Montserrat, St Kitts, and Trinidad, and dominated by Captain Cipriani and Mr Marryshow, it recommended federation of all British islands in the Eastern Caribbean, including Barbados and Trinidad. This meeting designed, according to one speaker, to 'lay the foundation stones of West Indian nationality,' drafted a federal constitution and formed the West Indian National League, with headquarters at Grenada, to further joint political action on common problems of British territories in the area.

The delegates attacked crown colony rule as a wasteful, inefficient, and discriminatory system which denied opportunities to the governed, stifled popular initiative, and was based on complete indifference to local public opinion. 'Powerless to mold policy,' declared the report of the conference, 'still more powerless to act independently, paralysed by the subconscious fear of impending repression and bereft of constructive thought, the West Indian politician has hitherto been inclined to dissipate his energies in acute and penetrating but embittered and essentially destructive criticism of the government on which, nevertheless, he has waited for the initiation of all policies intended to benefit his people, and which he has expected to assume the full responsibility for all necessary decisions.'[23]

A Closer Union Commission appointed by the Colonial Office in accordance with Lord Passfield's promise visited the Eastern Caribbean from November 1932 to February 1933. Its *Report* stressed the deep-seated divisions even among islands administratively linked as one colony. Each cherished its own individuality and, while paying lip-service to federation, insisted that this must not involve absorption in a larger unit or destruction of local distinctiveness. Each clamoured for more voice in managing its own affairs, particularly financial matters, and contended that this would produce economies. Some Dominicans wanted both federation and self-government. Others, including members of the black and brown majority, were strongly opposed to increased autonomy.

The Windwards, more politically conscious than any of the Leewards except Dominica and preoccupied with local problems, showed little enthusiasm for any type of closer union. Ignoring the worldwide depression, they argued that control over their own affairs would have prevented or mitigated their economic difficulties, which most representatives attributed to the shortcomings of crown colony government.

Trinidad, far more prosperous than the Windwards and Leewards but with sharp racial cleavages, had always found Tobago a financial liability. Closer association with other territories, which might involve additional commitments and costs, it opposed so strongly that the commission saw no point at that time in discussing the matter further with Trinidad. Federation of the Leewards and Windwards also appeared impractical, partly because this would involve a common tariff and no island was willing to relinquish its right to collect customs duties. Various witnesses made it clear to the commissioners that any type of closer union was unacceptable unless it could effect economies in administration.

The commissioners nevertheless recommended uniting the Windwards and Leewards into one colony with a single governor for the whole group and separate administrators for the individual islands to preserve as much local autonomy as possible. By welding several territories into one political whole they hoped to encourage in the Eastern Caribbean the concept of a unified West Indies, and thus to take the first step towards federation or closer association of all the British Caribbean territories.[24] West Indian governments, however, when asked to estimate the cost of uniting the Windwards and Leewards, reported that instead of saving money this would probably involve spending some additional £6000 each year. As Trinidad, Grenada, St Kitts, and Antigua flatly rejected the scheme and debates in the other Legislative Councils revealed wide differences of opinion, no action was taken.

Yet the idea of a broader federation was fostered by the burgeoning Caribbean trade union movements. In 1938 the British Guiana and West Indies Labour Conference presented to the Moyne Commission a proposed federal constitution for the British West Indies drafted by Grantley Adams of Barbados, who shared the enthusiasm for federation of Mr Marryshow and of Captain Cipriani who had just died. At this meeting the conference changed its name to the Caribbean Labour Congress. Support for federation by working-class leaders in the various colonies thereafter helped to strengthen the movement for union and West Indian nationality. A spirit of nationhood at last seemed destined to triumph over long-standing insularity.

Despite disagreement on details almost every witness who appeared before the Moyne Commission favoured some form of closer union. Public opinion had changed sharply since 1922, when the Caribbean colonies had not only opposed federation but refused even to discuss increased co-operation. Underlying the new spirit of unity, however, lay great diversities of interest, especially between the large and small islands. Although the Moyne commissioners believed that combining all British territories in the area into one political entity was the 'ideal to which policy should be directed,' because of insular antagonisms they thought the time not yet ripe for a general federation. As a small-scale, practical test of what closer association might accomplish, they advised uniting the Windwards and Leewards under a strong central government.[25] These islands, however, were no more enthusiastic than before about the proposal.

Delegates from the Windwards and Dominica, meeting at St Lucia in 1939, advocated federating for certain purposes, with each island retaining its local legislature and control over its own finances. Although many political circles in the British West Indies retained a lively interest in federation, which between 1942 and 1944 was often debated at Westminster,[26] wartime pressures postponed further serious consideration.

In the 1930s, as later, most local support for a British Caribbean nation came from West Indians educated abroad, who sometimes overestimated the breadth of vision among the mass of people who had never left their own small islands. Early in the 1940s an outstanding Trinidadian, Dr Eric Williams, argued that federalism was indicated 'not only by economic considerations but by every dictate of common sense.' Only popular governments in the various British territories, he believed, could introduce the political federation essential to future progress. Economic union of all the West Indies — British, American, French, and Dutch, together with the independent republics — he then, as later, saw as the goal. 'The Caribbean, like the whole world,' he prophesied, 'will federate or collapse.'[27]

By that time pressures for federation were no longer based mainly on the white planters' interest in economy or on Britain's administrative convenience, but on black and brown West Indians' desire for more control over their own affairs. In this change of attitude the rise of trade unions and political parties was of cardinal importance. 'How to reconcile effective federal control with the decentralisation demanded by sheer distance,' a distinguished Guyanese lawyer commented, 'is, perhaps, the fundamental problem.'[28]

Although constitutional discussions were halted during the war, the geographical separation of the territories was profoundly modified by the advent of air travel. National consciousness was fostered by the regional approach of the Caribbean Commission, the Colonial Development and Welfare Organisation, the Regional Economic Committee, the Federated Chambers of Commerce of the West Indies, and the Caribbean Labour Congress.

From discussions about West Indian federalism Jamaica long stood significantly aloof. As there was no direct communication by sea between it and the other British Caribbean territories, their peoples knew little or nothing about each other. No Jamaican representative attended either the Roseau Conference of 1932 or the Labour Conference six years later, although in 1938 Norman Manley supported the idea of federation. Early meetings on the subject were confined to Eastern Caribbean leaders, who usually did not propose including Jamaica, where the matter received scarcely any serious consideration until 1944, when the annual conference of the People's National Party strongly advocated federalism.

In that year the Jamaican Legislative Council also supported federal union of all British West Indian territories as a prerequisite for economic and social development as well as for independence. It urged the island's government to ascertain the attitude of other Caribbean colonies, with a view to requesting the imperial authorities to establish a federation. The Progressive League of Barbados also reaffirmed its former support of federal union.

In the British House of Commons various members argued that the time for West Indian union was ripe and that the Colonial Office should take a strong lead. The Secretary of State, Mr Oliver Stanley, replied that the United Kingdom's policy was 'the greatest integration the people of those islands themselves want ... The one thing that might delay or even in the end entirely destroy that prospect would be to force a decision too early.'[29] This policy, reiterated by his predecessors and successors, was steadily adhered to by subsequent British governments.

Delegates from the Windward Islands discussed the Moyne *Report* at Grenada in January 1945. They recommended federation of the Windwards and Leewards, but no action was taken as the question of a wider union intervened. In March the Secretary of State for the Colonies sent all West Indian governors a despatch pointing out that federation was the aim of British policy and suggesting that the matter be debated by each local legislature. He stressed the difficulty of complete independence for very small areas and the greater economy and efficiency of large-scale units. The United Kingdom, he believed, should try to foster a sense of Caribbean unity through joint services, communications, and conferences, and should work towards federation whenever public opinion in the colonies was favourable. The more immediate goal of responsible government in the British West Indies should not obscure the larger project of federalism. As financial stability (not necessarily economic self-sufficiency) was essential for complete autonomy, it would be important for any federation to show that it did not require recurring outside financial aid. The ultimate aim of such a union would be full internal self-government within the Commonwealth. The Secretary of State emphasized that the United Kingdom had no desire to impose federalism against the wishes of any large section of the West Indian community. The impetus for political unity must, in its opinion, come from within, not from without, the region.[30]

The Caribbean Labour Congress, meeting at Barbados in September 1945, brought together West Indian political and labour leaders, including Grantley Adams of Barbados, Hubert Critchlow of British Guiana, Richard Hart of Jamaica (who spoke both for the Jamaican People's National Party and St Kitts), T. Albert Marryshow of Grenada, and Albert Gomes of Trinidad. This was the first time that Jamaica was represented at a conference of the Caribbean Labour

Congress to which Mr Manley, as president of the People's National Party, nominated Mr Hart. The ominous absence of any representative from the ruling Jamaica Labour Party was largely explained by Mr Bustamante's cool relations with Eastern Caribbean governments.

This meeting discussed at length and unanimously approved the Colonial Office despatch. Mr Hart argued that the only way to create stable and viable communities was to develop the British West Indies as one economic entity, and that the only means to this end was to establish a federation able to exert unified control.[31] Fifteen years later Jamaican spokesmen were to put forward diametrically opposite contentions.

Early in February 1947 a Conference on Closer Union of the Windward and Leeward Islands, attended by members of the legislatures concerned, met at St Kitts. It advocated a Caribbean federation with a strong central government and a capital in Grenada.[32] This plan again was superseded by proposals for wider union. Two weeks later the new Secretary of State for the Colonies in the British Labour administration, Mr Creech-Jones, circulated another memorandum to West Indian governors, pointing out that his predecessor's 1945 despatch had been debated by the legislatures of all the British Caribbean colonies, including the Bahamas. Both Houses of the latter group of islands declined to consider any form of closer association with the West Indies or to attend a conference to debate it. The other legislatures expressed willingness to discuss the idea.

Mr Creech-Jones proposed that each colonial legislature (with the Windwards and Leewards regarded as two) should appoint three delegates, accompanied by financial advisers, to a conference at Montego Bay, to which four British members of the Caribbean Commission should be invited as observers. The most important reason for this meeting was the apparent impossibility, under modern conditions, of self-government for small and isolated communities. In contrast, a united Caribbean nation of well over two million might reasonably hope for genuine autonomy. While a unitary rather than a federal form of government might be logical and advantageous, it was very doubtful, as Mr Creech-Jones tactfully observed, whether British West Indian opinion was ready for such a solution. The colonies were divided by history, race, and disparities in constitutional development and natural resources. All, however, were accustomed to parliamentary institutions and had well-developed political traditions. As all cherished the right to control their own local affairs, the extent to which they were prepared to modify or transfer any of their powers to a central authority was crucial.

If federation were approved, the Colonial Secretary then considered it essential that the central government should be financially independent, although the United Kingdom would for a time provide some assistance to islands which had received grants-in-aid. Customs union he thought the one reform most beneficial to all the territories, as existing tariff barriers seriously restricted inter-colonial trade and lowered living standards throughout the area. A federal union, on the other hand, offered a prospect of improved shipping, postal, wireless, cable, and broadcasting services.[33]

THE MONTEGO BAY CONFERENCE

A week before the Montego Bay Conference the Caribbean Labour Congress held a meeting in Jamaica from which Mr Bustamante was again conspicuously absent. Grantley Adams was elected president of the congress, which approved a revised version of his proposal for federation. This plan made a substantial contribution to subsequent discussions at Montego Bay. The congress also urged constitutional reforms leading to self-government in all British West Indian territories.

Norman Manley of Jamaica, an outstanding member of the congress, although not present, sent a letter stating his views. 'What do we as a people,' he asked, 'look for in the court of history? Are we satisfied to be obscure and small nonentities in a world in which only larger groupings have ... [a] chance of survival and success? I put first, and ... above all other things, the desire to see a West Indian nation standing shoulder to shoulder with all other nations of the world.'[34]

The Montego Bay Conference held in September 1947 to discuss closer association of the British West Indian territories was attended by twenty-two delegates from all the colonies, as well as by representatives of the Colonial Development and Welfare Organisation and the British sector of the Caribbean Commission. Mr Bustamante represented Jamaica, while Mr Manley was present as a member of the Caribbean Commission. Mr Creech-Jones, in the chair, expressed hope that the members would approach their task as representative West Indians. 'Federation,' he said, 'has been a dream, something long hoped for ... I doubt if any of us would seek to prostitute the idea ... for narrow political ends.' Many British Caribbean problems could, he believed, be tackled effectively only by some wider association. While federalism need not subject any territory to the domination of any other, it yet required surrender to a central government of ultimate authority on certain major issues.

Although in the Jamaican House of Representatives Chief Minister Bustamante had previously supported union, at Montego Bay he was distinctly lukewarm about a 'federation of paupers,' which he dubbed a British device for preventing self-government and keeping the colonies in bondage. He wanted to be 'master in his own house' and argued that the United Kingdom should

guarantee continued financial assistance as long as the new nation needed help. With considerable justification he contended that West Indians had no conception of the true meaning of federation in which, without self-government, he saw few advantages. Before the discussions ended, however, he was describing Mr Creech Jones as the 'father' of a conference which in a brief period had achieved wonders.

Mr Manley, in contrast, pointed out that the Jamaican House of Representatives had already accepted the principle of a federal union. He believed that there was a large and growing sentiment in its favour and that the West Indies were destined for nationhood. He hoped they could free themselves from the most dangerous of all vested interests, which might prove the greatest obstacle to their common aspirations: that of ambition in power. He appealed to his colleagues to forget the lure of security, influence, and position in their own territories and to grasp the wider opportunity offered by a larger objective. 'It would be an irony,' he added, 'the like of which history has never known, that a community with that ambition of nationhood, having been offered this chance of amalgamation which is its only hope of a real political destiny, were to refuse that offer. Dare we refuse it and condemn ourselves and our generation for all time at the bar of history? I say that we dare not!' If, he concluded, West Indians refused to leave their boats and 'get into that larger vessel, which is able to carry us to the goal of our ambitions, I say without hesitation that we are damned and purblind and history will condemn us.'[35]

Albert Gomes of Trinidad also warmly supported federation, stressing the encouragement that abolition of customs duties would give to industrialization and interterritorial trade. W.A. Crawford of Barbados expressed a view voiced by almost every speaker when he advocated federation because 'it gives us the opportunity to liquidate once and for all every vestige of colonialism.' His colleague, Grantley Adams, emphasized two major Caribbean problems: the absence of comprehensive social security legislation and the lack of regional planning. He believed delegates should do everything possible to hasten the advent of West Indian nationhood, which alone would make possible common action on national issues.

J.B. Renwick of Grenada agreed with Mr Adams that returns from customs duties and income taxes should form the sources of federal revenue. Grenada's annual per capita income, he pointed out, was then as high as Jamaica's and its public debt considerably less. These figures were capped by the Antigua delegate, V.C. Bird, who stated that his island's per capita revenue was £7.2 as compared with £5.9 in Jamaica, while Antigua's public debt was £1.65 in contrast with £6.8 in Jamaica. Representatives from most of the small islands warmly approved federation as economically and politically advantageous to all the colonies.[36] British Guiana alone dissented from the general enthusiasm for union.

Almost all non-governmental organizations which presented submissions to the conference also favoured federation. Among these were the Caribbean Labour Congress, long a leading proponent of the project, the Caribbean Union of Teachers, which since its establishment in 1935 had consistently advocated federalism, and the Federation of Civil Service Associations in the Caribbean area. The latter body, founded in 1944, urged the advantages of a unified civil service throughout the British territories, the appointment of West Indians wherever possible, and the transfer of public officials from one colony to another.

Many delegates urged more local self-government as a necessary prerequisite for successful federalism. The most constitutionally advanced territories feared retardation of their progress through union with the more backward. Others thought federation would itself prove the best means of furthering autonomy. The majority considered federal union and increased control over their own affairs as closely linked objectives.

Yet the conference passed a resolution supporting political development of the units as 'an aim in itself ... in no way subordinate to progress toward federation.' This clearly opened the way to a race among the islands for the prize of independence and suggested that federation might not be a necessary preliminary. Another even more disastrous resolution supported in principle a federation in which each unit retained control over all matters not specifically assigned to the national government. Thus from the outset a weak centre and strong periphery were enshrined as basic aspects of the new state.

AFTERMATH OF THE MONTEGO BAY CONFERENCE

The Montego Bay Conference appointed a Standing Closer Association Committee to consider the form of a federal constitution and judiciary, common customs and tariff policies, unification of currency, and assimilation of laws in the various units.[37] Chaired by Sir Hubert Rance, head of the Development and Welfare Organisation, and composed of seventeen West Indians chosen by their local legislatures, this committee met in November 1948 in Barbados, in March 1949 in Trinidad, and in July and October 1949 in Barbados and Jamaica. Early in 1950 it issued a report describing federation as an economic and political necessity. This recommended federal union of all the British West Indian colonies, including British Guiana and British Honduras, with a capital in Trinidad, and drew up a draft constitution providing for a weak national government, residual powers vested in the units, and a federal supreme court and public service commission.

The fiscal subcommittee of the Montego Bay Conference advocated full customs union among the British Caribbean territories, whether a federation was formed or not. It believed that from the outset the central government should have one major and independent source of revenue over whose collection it should have complete control. The subcommittee also proposed that after the establishment of the federation British Treasury grants to the West Indies should be given to the national government for allocation to the constituent units. Unfortunately the latter recommendation was eventually accepted and the former two rejected.

While the proposed federal constitution was roughly modelled on that of Australia, their similarities have often been exaggerated. Both gave residual powers to the units or states, but in Australia authority gravitated to the centre because the national government had paramount powers over taxation. In the West Indies, by contrast, absence of any independent power to tax necessarily produced a remarkably weak national parliament.

The federal legislature recommended by the Standing Closer Association Committee was bicameral, with a fifty-member House of Assembly to be elected on an adult franchise and a nominated Senate (with a one-year revisionary power) composed of two members from each territory except Montserrat, which would have one. In order to avoid domination by the most populous units, it was suggested that membership in the lower house should not be based strictly on population. The proposal was that, of the fifty seats in the national House of Representatives, Jamaica should have sixteen, Trinidad nine, British Guiana six, Barbados four, Montserrat one, and the remaining units two each.

While federal revenues were to come mainly from customs duties, the national government was obligated to return to the units some 75 per cent of sums thus raised. Power to levy an income tax was placed on the concurrent legislative list, with the proviso that during the first five years this should not be exercised by the central government. Policy would be determined by an Executive Council of State, containing some officials but a majority of elected members drawn from and responsible to the House of Assembly. The Governor General would preside at meetings of the council and have discretionary, reserve, and veto powers over defence, finance, public order, and external affairs.

The Standing Closer Association Committee further recommended that for the first two years the United Kingdom should make the federation an annual grant approximately equal to the financial assistance given during the preceding five years. It believed that independence within the British Commonwealth was the legitimate political objective of West Indians. Since real, as distinct from formal, autonomy implied independence of outside financial aid, the region's economy should be developed as rapidly as possible. In the committee's opinion this could only be achieved through a federal government entrusted with important responsibilities and power, especially over economic affairs. Full dominion status must await achievement of financial solvency. These proposals were based on the conviction that, while independence for small islands was a mirage, an autonomous federation was practicable.[38]

Commissions on unification of the civil service and on customs union reported in 1949 and 1951 respectively.[39] The latter strongly advocated the earliest possible establishment of a customs union among all British West Indian territories except the Virgins, Turks, Caicos, and Caymans. Excise and export duties should, it thought, be left for the time being to the constituent units. Although the yield from import duties then provided some 30 per cent of the islands' gross revenues, the commission optimistically considered customs union both politically practical and economically desirable. Obstacles to free trade within the area and to a common tariff against goods imported from abroad were in its view few, and the desire for fiscal and economic union general.

The Holmes *Report*, equally enthusiastic about unification of public services, suggested that this might be introduced before a federation was formed. It hoped thereby to achieve greater interchangeability of public officials, despite the problems posed by salary differentials among the more and less prosperous territories. Most posts, both senior and junior, were then held by West Indians, although governors and colonial secretaries were still almost always British members of the Colonial Administrative Service. Among the exceptions was Sir Errol dos Santos, an able coloured West Indian who during the Second World War served as Colonial Secretary in Trinidad. By 1950 less than 300 of the more than 1300 civil service positions in the British Caribbean with salaries of £600 or over were filled by expatriates, of whom many were technicians.[40]

When the reports of the Standing Closer Association Committee and the commissions on customs union and the public service were considered by the territorial legislatures, sharp differences of opinion became evident.[41] In Trinidad Dr Patrick Solomon advocated rejection of the proposed federation, although he supported immediate regional co-operation and federal union at some future date. The costs of federation seemed to him too high in relation to its probable benefits. He objected to a national constitution which, without providing independence, would establish an undemocratic, because wholly nominated, Senate, a Council of State including appointed officials, and a Governor General with powers inconsistent with real cabinet government.

Many East Indians in Trinidad also opposed federalism, because they feared this would weaken the position currently assured them by their numbers. Albert Gomes, on the other hand, urged acceptance of the Rance *Report*, on the grounds that its critics suggested no preferable alternative and that rejection would definitely postpone federation. Without union, he believed, the British West Indies could not achieve independent nationhood. Others criticized the financial proposals, fearing that loss of customs revenue would cause deficits in some territories.

Sir Hubert Rance, recently appointed Governor of Trinidad and Tobago, concluding the debate, said he had no wish to influence the legislature one way or the other. He emphasized that the United Kingdom did not want to force federation upon anyone, but simply invited West Indians to decide their own future. The Legislative Council of Trinidad and Tobago finally approved the *Report* on 31 July 1951, by nine votes to six.

In Jamaica a resolution to accept it was moved by Donald Sangster, then Minister of Social Welfare and a leading member of the Jamaica Labour Party government. Although his island might achieve dominion status alone, he believed it had a responsibility towards the smaller territories which could not hope to do likewise. Federalism offered some economic advantages, but, in view of the heavy initial costs, he urged that during the first fifteen years the United Kingdom be asked to defray any additional expenditures. He doubted the wisdom of depriving individual islands of experienced leaders by making members of the federal parliament ineligible to hold seats concurrently in local legislatures. Later events abundantly justified his hesitation on this point.

The leader of the Jamaican opposition, Mr Manley, agreed that this island, with its long tradition of political leadership in the British Caribbean, should support the proposed federation, which he considered the shortest road 'to our political ambition of nationhood in the West Indies,' as well as the best means of combatting poverty and facilitating economic planning. He believed, however, that the Rance *Report* gave too little real power to the national government, which in his opinion should be able to impose direct taxation. A successful federation, to his mind, required more adequate finances: a view he was subsequently to repudiate.

One speaker criticized nomination by the Governor General of senators and certain members of the Executive Council. Another attacked federalism because the United Kingdom, which he considered chiefly interested in economic exploitation of the colonies, favoured it. Premier Bustamante declared that for years he had supported federation as the best route to self-government for the West Indies. He advocated modifications in the Rance *Report*, however, and increased financial assistance from Britain, lest Jamaica be left to support the poorer islands of the Eastern Caribbean. Both Jamaican parties attacked the Governor General's proposed reserve powers, veto, and right to dismiss members of the council and, under certain circumstances, to act without its advice. They also objected to the United Kingdom's being empowered to legislate by orders-in-council for the new state.

Yet, when the debate concluded on 4 August 1951, the Jamaican House of Representatives unanimously reaffirmed its approval of federation and of the Rance *Report* as a basis for further discussion. It requested the Secretary of State to hold a conference of West Indian representatives to consider financial aspects of federal union. A joint committee of the two Jamaican Houses was appointed to consider the Rance proposals in detail. The following month the Legislative Council announced its agreement with them.

On 5 November 1951 the Barbados House of Assembly with certain reservations confirmed its acceptance of federalism. It supported unification of British Caribbean public services, but objected to permitting the national constitution to be amended by the Queen-in-Council. Mr Adams pointed out that the Governor of Barbados had no reserve powers. He disliked the idea of giving these to the Governor General of the new federation, lest it be 'not much more than a glorified Crown Colony.' He also questioned the advisability of locating the national capital in Trinidad. Despite the approval of their Assembly Barbadians did not conceal their hesitation about a union certain to be dominated by Jamaica, which they considered relatively backward politically.

The *Report* was unanimously approved by all the Windwards except Grenada, where it was opposed by Mr. Marryshow. For forty years a leading supporter of federation, he wanted the new state to be self-governing from the outset. If autonomy could not be achieved at once, he believed it should be promised within five years. He also thought that a general election should be held in Grenada on the issue of joining the federation. Despite his opposition the *Report* was endorsed by an eight to three vote in the Grenada legislature, with the official members abstaining. Unofficial members in St Vincent supported the proposals by five votes to none, with one abstention. In the Leewards the Legislative Council of St Kitts unanimously accepted the *Report*, as did that of Antigua after a ten-minute debate. Montserrat also approved the plan with the qualification that it, like the other islands, should have two senators.

The British Virgins decided against joining a West Indian federation, owing to their close economic and geographical ties with the American Virgins. They also feared that a central government responsible for grants-in-aid to the poorer territories might be less sympathetic towards their needs than the United Kingdom. They wished, however, to be closely associated with the federation and to continue to receive the technical and administrative services and advice they had hitherto obtained from the Leewards.

British Honduras, far away in Central America, was unenthusiastic about the Rance *Report*, and its Legislative Council eventually concluded that it would be premature to commit the colony to joining a British West Indian federation. Its doubts sprang from the country's remoteness from other Caribbean territories. Its nearest West Indian neighbour, Jamaica, was over six hundred miles away, while the distance from Belize to Barbados was greater than from London to Moscow. Like Barbados, it dreaded domination by Jamaica and Trinidad. Like British Guiana at that time, it feared an influx of immigrants from the islands. Its People's United Party thought the United Kingdom wanted to force British Honduras into federation, although the Governor, Sir Ronald Garney, explained that neither His Majesty's government nor he himself had the least desire to influence the decision. The issue was clouded by Guatemala's claim that federalism should be postponed until its dispute with the United Kingdom about the boundaries of British Honduras had been settled.

The British Guiana legislature, after a two months' debate, also rejected federal union with the other West Indian colonies. Some members argued against the economic burden of having to assist the smaller islands. Many dreaded free migration, while others considered prospects of a 'continental destiny' in South America more natural and alluring than alliance with the British Caribbean. Certain East Indians disliked the idea of joining a federation with an overwhelming preponderance of blacks, especially as their own rising birth rate was likely to give their racial group a majority in British Guiana within fifteen years. Dr Cheddi Jagan, however, moved an unsuccessful amendment to support a federation to which dominion status was promised. His Peoples' Progressive Party unsuccessfully advocated a constituent assembly to draft a new federal constitution.

Two advances towards further regional co-operation occurred in 1951. The Eastern Caribbean dollar was adopted as a common unit of currency by British Guiana, Trinidad and Tobago, Barbados, and the Leewards and Windwards. The governments of the various British West Indian territories established the Regional Economic Committee with headquarters in Barbados and closely associated with the Development and Welfare Organisation. Its function was to encourage common action on public finance, communications, trade, and exports. This committee conducted studies of regional problems and served as a valuable advisory body until 1957, when its responsibilities were transferred to the Pre-Federal Organization. Above all it accustomed West Indians to co-operate for the benefit of the whole area.[42]

Enthusiasm for closer association within the British Caribbean and for West Indian unity reached its height at Montego Bay. The extent of agreement achieved there was never recaptured. In the sober light of day practical obstacles loomed steadily larger. Even leading public men in the various territories knew little of each other, while most ordinary West Indians had never left their own islands. Air fares were high and communications by sea indirect and infrequent. Federation of itself promised no solution for the acute social and economic problems of the region. Countering the common-sense argument for free trade was the indubitable fact that all the colonies derived an important portion of their revenue from customs duties. Yet some West Indians, like Australians sixty years earlier, believed that the tariffs they had erected against each other served mainly as a reminder that they had created artificial barriers where none should exist.

To Eastern Caribbean delegates the decision at Montego Bay to support federation represented a major stride towards a cherished goal. To Jamaicans, however, it meant commitment to a largely undiscussed project with far-reaching implications for their country. Even from the point of view of the small islands the situation had altered drastically in the previous quarter century. Interest in federation during the 1920s and 1930s sprang mainly from determination to transfer political control from white planters and merchants to popularly elected dark-skinned West Indians. By 1947 this process had been largely accomplished.

The advent of adult suffrage in Jamaica, Trinidad, and Barbados, coupled with a much extended franchise in the Leewards and Windwards, had transformed local legislatures and executive councils into bodies usually chosen and dominated by West Indians. While the Montego Bay Conference can fairly be described as the high-water mark of faith in federation, constitutional advance in one territory after another had already indicated that legislative union might not, as had earlier been assumed, be a *sine qua non* for self-government. Federation was long considered an essential means to insular autonomy. From 1947 on it could be and increasingly was viewed as more likely to thwart than hinder full responsible government.

All British Caribbean politicians wanted greater autonomy for their own islands and disliked yielding any significant powers to the centre, especially to a federation less independent than Jamaica. The most prosperous territories, still poor by western standards, anticipated more economic liabilities than assets from closer association and were understandably reluctant to assume the additional burden of supporting the Leewards and Windwards, most of which had long required grants from the United Kingdom to balance their budgets. Jamaica, Trinidad, and Barbados, the most advanced politically as well as the richest, were determined not to decline to the level of the less advanced.

Federalism seemed more likely to increase than reduce already high administrative costs, although on this point there were differences of opinion. In January 1953 the Comptroller for Development and Welfare, G.F. Seel, circulated to West Indian governors and administrators a despatch on financial aspects of the proposed union. This pointed out that the major new expenses would be an initial capital outlay for national government buildings and recurrent costs for the federal parliament, civil service, and headquarters staff.[43]

Administrative charges could be cut only by reduced establishments in the various units. Such reductions, apparently inconsistent with increased control over their own affairs, were unacceptable to even the smallest and poorest territories. West Indians hoped that Britain would help to meet necessary additional expenses by generous financial aid to the new federation. Some, ignoring regional pressures for union, thought the United Kingdom supported federation mainly in order to evade costly responsibilities which it should be prepared to honour. Many believed that it owed them a living, or at least very large subventions over an indefinite period, as partial amends for the centuries when African slaves enabled white planters to amass huge fortunes.

Yet despite doubts and qualifications all the British West Indian legislatures except British Guiana, British Honduras, and the British Virgins eventually supported federation. They hoped a wider Caribbean market would foster industrialization. Population pressures seemed to demand freedom of movement within the area, while competing tariffs were clearly uneconomic. International stature could be achieved, trade agreements negotiated, and much needed capital more easily attracted by a united West Indies than by an archipelago of separate islands.

When all the arguments were balanced, the two which tipped the scales were common bonds of anti-colonial sentiment and desire for self-government. These in turn had been fostered by the social conditions which provoked the passionate protests of the 1930s. The effective movement for federalism was spawned by the troubles of that disastrous decade, which clearly demonstrated the weakness of unorganized workers in isolated communities. It sprang also from the circumstances of the Second World War, which both in the United Kingdom and its dependencies produced permanent and far-reaching changes of opinion on imperial policy and the future of colonies.

Significantly, only a handful of far-sighted public men were moved by genuine enthusiasm for a united nation. Yet successful federations must be based on a desire to co-operate under a common government. At no stage in the West Indian negotiations was such a desire conspicuous. If union was the shortest road to independence, British Caribbean leaders thought in 1947 that the prize was worth the price of submerging ancient rivalries and attempting to dwell together in unity. Few fully realized that the price also included some sacrifice of local autonomy. Federalism was widely viewed as a means to two incompatible ends: complete independence, both for the national state and its component units. Herein lay the seeds of much misunderstanding and ultimately of failure.

5

Political developments, 1953-8

The eleven crucial years from the Montego Bay Conference to the establishment of a united West Indies were dominated by two interacting and at least partially conflicting ambitions: federalism and self-government. Achievement of the latter goal steadily eroded earlier enthusiasm for the former.

In April 1953 a conference at London discussed, and with certain modifications approved, the *Report* of the Standing Closer Association Committee, commonly known as the Rance *Report*.[1] This was the first such meeting at which the West Indian members (drawn from all the territories which supported a federal union) represented legislatures wholly elected by adult suffrage. The Colonial Secretary, Oliver Lyttelton, again emphasized that the United Kingdom had no wish to impose its own views but would approve any type of federation the islands desired. Grantley Adams later told the Barbados Assembly that nothing had been forced on the delegates by the Colonial Office, which had stressed that it was for West Indians to create their own constitution.[2]

The Rance *Report* had proposed that movement of persons within the Federation should be subject to concurrent jurisdiction, but that, in the event of conflict, federal legislation should prevail. This recommendation was not accepted in 1953 at London. There it was agreed that, while the preamble to the constitution should note the desirability of the greatest possible freedom of movement of people and commodities within the area, the national government should have exclusive power to legislate on such matters, subject to certain provisos. These were that, while no national law should restrict migration for economic reasons, both federal and unit legislatures might control it on grounds of health or security. One of the two delegates from Trinidad and Tobago objected to this compromise and signed the report subject to a reservation on the issue.

As previously noted, Trinidad had long been the one territory which attracted large numbers of migrants from other islands. By 1946 one-tenth of its population came from elsewhere in the British Caribbean: mainly from the neighbouring Windwards. Although the most prosperous of the territories, Trinidad had its own problems of unemployment and inadequate resources. Its determination to regulate the influx of people seeking work was early apparent. This played a major role in making an effective federal constitution impossible and ultimately contributed to the downfall of the union. While Trinidadians saw freedom of movement as a threat to their standards of living, Barbados, with the highest population ratio in the area, considered such movement essential. In 1953, as a result of pressure from the Eastern Caribbean, the latter view prevailed.

Largely because of Trinidad's objections, however, the United Kingdom convened a conference on immigration problems at Port-of-Spain in March 1955. Delegates agreed that migration within the Federation on grounds other than health or security should not be a subject of exclusive federal jurisdiction, as recommended two years earlier, but of concurrent jurisdiction, with the proviso that, unless approved by both houses of the national parliament, unit legislation on the matter should cease to have effect five years and three months after the establishment of a federation.[3] The recommendations of this conference were subsequently adopted by all the West Indian legislatures concerned.

The Secretary of State for the Colonies agreed at the 1953 conference that during its first decade Britain would give the new state financial assistance equal to the average grants-in-aid received in the previous five years by the Leewards and Windwards, while further help might be anticipated from the Development and Welfare Fund. The United Kingdom also undertook to contribute £500,000 towards the cost of the national capital. The most important constitutional changes made in London concerned the number of seats in both houses of the federal legislature, residence qualifications for members, the distribution of powers between central and unit governments, and the amending process in which West Indians were given a greater voice.

These modified recommendations for a British Caribbean Federation were then referred back to the West Indian governments, except those of British Guiana and British Honduras which, although represented by observers at the 1953 conference, had decided that they did not wish to join the union. A revised version of the plan propounded in 1953 was approved by all the West Indian legislatures, although Mr Grantley Adams and Dr Eric Williams in particular considered the proposed federal constitution too colonial in character and the powers it gave the national parliament too restricted. Indeed Mr Adams complained that such a weak federation would be little more than a glorified crown colony.

Both Jamaican houses unanimously supported the plan and urged its prompt implementation. Mr Bustamante's doubts at Montego Bay seemed to have been transformed into enthusiastic advocacy. In 1954 he announced his intention of fighting for federation because he considered Jamaica's interests interwoven with those of her neighbours. 'We should federate,' he declared, 'we must federate, we are going to federate.'[4] Below the surface, however, there were significant differences of opinion. 'Some local leaders,' wrote a perceptive Jamaican journalist, 'would do everything in their power to prevent the emergence of Federal solidarity, or any other kind of solidarity, since they prosper in their little world of West Indian individualism.'[5]

FISCAL, CIVIL SERVICE, AND JUDICIAL COMMISSIONS

In the spring of 1955 the United Kingdom appointed three commissions to examine the fiscal, civil service, and judicial aspects of the proposed union. The Fiscal Commissioner, Sir Sydney Caine, agreed with the Standing Closer Association Committee that it was essential for a national government to have its own direct sources of finance and not to depend completely on contributions by constituent territories. The conference at London in 1953 proposed that the federal government retain only 15 per cent of customs revenues, instead of the 25 per cent suggested by the Rance Committee. Sir Sydney estimated that the income from this 15 per cent could not be relied on to ensure national solvency and commented that he knew no precedent for a federal government returning to its constituent units as much as 85 per cent of the yield from customs duties. The distribution of powers proposed in London would have produced an unusually weak and limited central government, entrusting more than normal executive responsibilities to the units.

Sir Sydney questioned the wisdom of prohibiting the national government from levying an income tax during its first five years and of making it responsible for administering grants-in-aid formerly allocated by the United Kingdom. Federal-unit relationships, in his opinion, might well be strained, as the small islands would resent being denied the degree of autonomy enjoyed by their more prosperous neighbours. From the beginning, he suggested, the federal government should rely for revenues on consumption taxes on motor spirits, cigarettes, and liquor, and later be enabled to levy an income tax. Since it was unanimously assumed that the Federation would support the University College of the West Indies, he advised including higher education in the subjects assigned to exclusive national legislation. In his opinion the central government should be given power to delegate jurisdiction to the units and to appropriate funds for activities such as advisory and research services, designed to promote the general well-being of the country, although it might not have the right to legislate on these matters.[6]

The Civil Service Commissioner, Sir Hilary Blood, presented recommendations on the transfer of functions from unit to national control, the organization and structure of the central public service and departments of state, and terms and conditions of service for public employees. He advised federalizing as promptly as possible such existing organizations as the British Caribbean Meteorological Service and the Trade Commissioner Services. The national government, in his view, should provide research, advice, consultation, and leadership on common problems of economic development in the various islands. The federal civil service, although modest in size, should be of high quality. To ensure obtaining the best staff available he advised appointment of a national Public Service Commission.[7]

The Judicial Commissioner, Sir Allen Smith, recommended establishment of a national Supreme Court, staffed by learned, experienced, and strictly impartial judges. The plan approved at London in 1953 provided for the appointment of judges by the Governor General with the assent of the Minister of Justice. Sir Allen shared the dissatisfaction widely expressed by West Indians about giving the Minister of Justice a voice in the nomination of judges. To avoid any suspicion of political or other improper influence, he recommended that, until the Federation attained dominion status, judges should be appointed at the discretion of the Governor General, but that if those proved unacceptable they should be appointed by him after consultation with the Prime Minister.

He further proposed that the federal Supreme Court be comprised of a chief justice and not less than three judges and have original jurisdiction in such matters as suits to which the Federation was a party and disputes between units. It should, he believed, normally sit in the national capital, but when hearing appeals from courts of the units and any affiliated territories should as far as practicable sit in the jurisdiction from which the appeal came. This had been the practice of the West Indian Court of Appeal, slated to be dissolved on the formation of the federal Supreme Court. Except on constitutional questions, a right of appeal to the Privy Council should, he thought, lie from federal Supreme Court decisions. All existing rights to appeal direct to the Privy Council from any unit courts should be abolished.[8]

CONFERENCE ON BRITISH CARIBBEAN FEDERATION, 1956

The *Reports* of the three commissioners were published in December 1955, and in the following February another conference on British Caribbean Federation met at London, with delegates from the United Kingdom, all the islands which had agreed to join, and observers from British Guiana and British Honduras. Among the representatives were Mr Marryshow of Grenada, Mr Gomes of Trinidad, and Mr Manley, newly elected Chief Minister of Jamaica. By this time federation had been discussed by four commissions and three conferences and debated on five occasions by the legislatures of the British West Indian colonies. General agreement had been reached on the form a federal union should take. The purpose of the 1956 conference was to make final decisions, within the framework determined, without having to refer these back to the individual legislatures.

The Secretary of State for the Colonies, Lennox Boyd, pointed out that federation would help the West Indies to achieve self-government within the Commonwealth. This meant not only that the United Kingdom would relinquish its power, but that the new state could 'stand on its own feet economically and financially,' pay for its own administration, and assume responsibility for defence and international affairs. In modern times, however, no country was independent in the sense of being completely self-sufficient. Mutual aid was a principle of the Commonwealth, and there was no reason why some members should not help others, as in the Colombo Plan. Mr Bustamante later lamented the failure to extract from the United Kingdom a firm promise of 'millions of pounds' as the price for the West Indies' consent to federate.

The 1956 conference agreed that the British Caribbean delegates should form themselves into a Standing Committee on Federation, chaired by the Comptroller for Development and Welfare, to prepare the federal organization and draft a constitution. It expressed hope that British Guiana, British Honduras, and the British Virgin Islands would eventually decide to join, and a clause was added to the constitution to provide for their entry.

In 1957 the Standing Committee on Federation submitted a resolution to the Secretary of State for the Colonies pointing out that the union would begin 'with an inherited situation of poverty and unbalanced and inadequate economic development.' Hence it asked the British government to give the new Federation prompt and substantial aid of at least £100 million, plus an equal sum for the second five years of its life. West Indian ideas about the financial assistance which could be expected from the metropolitan power were influenced by their needs, their belief that Britain had a moral obligation to them, envy of the United States' massive contributions to Puerto Rico, and inadequate appreciation of the United Kingdom's critical economic position after the Second World War.

Their views on the matter differed sharply from those of Britain, which then still adhered to the traditional concept that the acid test of colonies' readiness for self-government was their ability to become financially self-supporting.

Although the islands' demands may have been unrealistic, their needs were undeniable. While the United Kingdom was not prepared to accede to West Indians' financial desires, it promised to double its capital grant to the Federation from the £500,000 offered in 1953 to £1,000,000. It refused, however, to give the new state the loan of £2,000,000 requested by Mr Manley.

Certain changes were made at the 1956 conference in the Plan for a British Caribbean Federation put forward in 1953. The preamble was revised to include statements that freedom of worship should prevail throughout the Federation, that the economic circumstances of the region demanded an integrated trade policy, and that as quickly and as far as possible internal free trade should be established. It was decided to establish a Committee on Trade and Tariffs to report to the federal government on the economic and financial problems involved and to work out plans for a customs union.

The conference restored the ban, removed in 1953, against a member of a unit legislature holding a seat in the national parliament and vice versa. Any such member elected to either federal house must, it was agreed, resign his former post within three months. In the political circumstances of the British Caribbean this proved a singularly unfortunate decision, as it discouraged the ablest local statesmen from seeking federal office. Mr Manley, aided by delegates from St Lucia and Antigua, succeeded in winning support for it against strong opposition, especially from Mr Adams and Mr Eric Gairy of Grenada. Many people in the United Kingdom also thought the decision unwise, but on this as on other matters deferred to West Indian majority opinion.

The delegates agreed in principle to establish a Loans Council to co-ordinate borrowing by national and unit governments. During the first five years the federal government would obtain revenue from profits on the issue of currency and from a mandatory levy on the units. It would also assume responsibility for losses on currency issues, formerly a liability of the territories. The national parliament would have concurrent legislative power to impose excise and customs duties, but in this early period any sums so raised would be deducted from the mandatory levy. This decision effectively debarred the central government from access to revenue from customs duties.

The federal exclusive legislative list was enlarged to empower the West Indies parliament to establish and regulate national agencies to advise or otherwise aid any territorial government or authority upon request. The University College of the West Indies was placed on this list, although higher education in general, including professional and technical training, was assigned to the concurrent list.

Two changes went far towards meeting West Indian complaints that the proposed federal constitution was too colonial. The composition of the Council of State was changed to exclude official members, but the Governor General would nominate three officials to attend meetings of the council and participate in its debates. The Secretary of State assured the delegates that the need for attendance by these officials would be reviewed periodically and that when the Governor General thought this no longer required the provision might lapse. It was further agreed that the Governor General should consult unit Governors before making appointments to the federal Senate. He retained a general power to reserve bills.

The conference decided that Supreme Court judges should be appointed by the Governor General after consultation with the Prime Minister. The court would be itinerant, holding hearings in six places – Barbados, British Guiana, Jamaica, one of the Leewards, Trinidad, and one of the Windwards—and would normally hear a case in the nearest centre. Although the federal Supreme Court, with both civil and criminal jurisdiction, would serve as a court of appeal from Supreme Courts of the units, local appellate courts might be retained if the territories so desired. Except under unusual circumstances and by leave of the federal Supreme Court, no right of appeal would lie from the Supreme Court of a unit to the Privy Council.

Despite certain minor additions to federal jurisdiction the changes made at the 1956 conference further detracted from the exiguous national powers previously proposed by substituting a mandatory levy from each territory for the previous provision that the Federation receive a stated fraction of customs duties collected by the units. It was also barred from imposing an income tax during the crucial first five years. Moreover, during the fifth year the federal government's right to impose an income tax was to be reviewed. The proposed Loans Council, which would have strengthened the central government, was never established.

The last paragraph of the conference's report noted that the representatives of the British Caribbean colonies were unanimously agreed 'on this historic occasion that our countries should be bound together in Federation.'[9] The report was signed on 23 February 1956, a date kept during the lifetime of the union as a national holiday known as Federation Day.

Dr Eric Williams, leader of the newly established People's National Movement of Trinidad, had recently voiced his conviction that in the West Indies federalism was plain common sense and any federation better than none. Whether it were more or less costly, more efficient or less efficient, it was inevitable, he said, 'if the British Caribbean territories are to cease to parade themselves to the twentieth-century world as eighteenth-century anachronisms.'[10]

THE FEDERAL CAPITAL SITE AND CHAGUARAMAS

The location of the federal capital was long the subject of acrimonious debate. The *Report* of 1950 had recommended Trinidad as the site, but the smaller islands objected on the ground that this would increase the inevitably large influence of the richest territory. Grenada, proposed as an alternative in 1953, was ultimately rejected, partly because of St George's lack of various facilities, including convenient access by sea or air.

As the British Caribbean leaders could not agree, they accepted the Colonial Secretary's suggestion that a three-man commission of non-West Indians be appointed to make recommendations. Chaired by Sir Francis Mudie, in 1956 it suggested as the three most suitable sites, in order of preference, Barbados, Jamaica, and Trinidad. Except in Barbados this proposal aroused widespread resentment.

Trinidadians were especially irritated by the reasons given for placing their country third: 'the instability of that island's politics and the low standard accepted in its public life.' Trinidad, the *Report* observed with more frankness than tact, 'is less politically advanced than either Jamaica or Barbados, in that up to now it has had no Chief Minister and no clear-cut political parties with established programs ... The political future of Trinidad seems to us uncertain because of the traditional fragmentation of parties and the racial cleavage which exists there.'[11] During the campaign preceding his election in 1956 Dr Williams had attacked the corruption of Trinidadian politics as dishonest and immoral. He was outraged, however, by similar criticism from outsiders and regarded himself as a symbol and guarantee of the island's political stability.

Jamaica, only slightly less aggrieved at not being the first choice, was not placated by the explanation that it was too far away and too aloof from the Eastern Caribbean. 'There is considerable movement between the islands in the eastern half of the Federation,' the *Report* noted, 'but little between these islands and Jamaica ... In the east far more is known about life in the United Kingdom than about life in Jamaica ... Similarly in Jamaica very little is known about the islands in the east. Jamaicans, when they go abroad, go to Britain, the United States, or Canada and only very occasionally to the other islands of the British West Indies. The two halves of the Federation are widely separated by more than water. It will be one of the tasks of the Federation to bring them together, but this will not be easy, and may well take a long time.'[12]

The small islands were almost equally annoyed by the commissioners' observation that 'great harm would be done to the Federation if for the first ten or fifteen years of its existence, the capital were something between a dead-end and a construction camp.' One reason for preferring Barbados was that it was smaller than Jamaica or Trinidad, whose size and wealth were bound to give them an influence in the new union which, if either was to become the seat of government, might be overwhelming. Yet Barbados was unacceptable to the other territories, if only because its colour discrimination was uniquely offensive. Jamaica and Trinidad were determined that one of them should have the capital. To all but Jamaicans the argument of Jamaica's remoteness made sense. The commission's strictures on Trinidad settled the issue in that island's favour.

The Standing Committee on Federation, after considering the *Report* of the Federal Capital Commission, agreed in February 1957 that the new state should be called The West Indies and that the capital should be in Trinidad. A subcommittee to examine sites met at Port-of-Spain in April of that year and discussed the report of a committee established by the Trinidad government which suggested seven possible locations in the island. The subcommittee recommended Chaguaramas, one of the areas leased in 1941 by Britain to the United States in exchange for destroyers much needed by the United Kingdom at a critical stage of the Second World War. This proposal was accepted by the Standing Committee on Federation, which requested the United Kingdom's support on the matter. The British government accordingly consulted the United States which, however, regretted its inability to release the naval base.

Although as colonials West Indians had had to accept American bases in their territories, many considered that no self-respecting autonomous nation could be expected to do so. Chaguaramas, an eighteen-square-mile tract of land seven miles from Port-of-Spain, had the only good beach conveniently accessible to the Trinidadian capital's large population. Apart from this beach most of the area was originally an undesirable swamp, drained and developed by the United States at a cost of more than $3 million.

The Chief Minister of Trinidad and Tobago, Dr Eric Williams, objected in 1957 to the insistence of the Standing Committee on Federation that Chaguaramas should be the site for the federal capital, because before its election to office in the previous year his party had promised to honour all international obligations, including the agreement on American bases. At that time he acknowledged that this base was vital for Trinidad's defence. Large sections of the Trinidadian press and public thought the Americans should not be asked to withdraw. Yet for Dr Williams to dissent from the Standing Committee's decision to ask the United States promptly to relinquish all its holdings at Chaguaramas would clearly have placed him in a very difficult political position.

At meetings in London during July 1957, attended by representatives of the United States, the United Kingdom, and the Standing Committee on Federation, Dr Williams reversed his stand, attacked the agreement on bases as immoral, and demanded that the United States withdraw from Chaguaramas. An announcement by the Secretary of State for the Colonies that the United Kingdom would no longer support this request was denounced by both Dr Williams and Mr

Manley as an insult to Trinidadians, West Indians, and the federal government. Tensions between the Trinidad administration and Sir Grantley Adams were increased by his statement that Chaguaramas was genuinely needed as an American base and that the federal government would refrain from any stand which might render defence of the western world more difficult.

West Indian delegates to the London meetings insisted that they wanted the capital in Trinidad and considered Chaguaramas the only suitable site there. Although the conference unanimously accepted the need for an American naval base in the Caribbean, the West Indians did not agree with the Americans that for strategic and economic reasons this base must remain at Chaguaramas. Trinidad's offer of an alternative site on the island was rejected by the United States. A joint commission of technical experts, chaired by Sir Charles Arden-Clarke representing the United Kingdom, met from January to March 1958 in Port-of-Spain. This advised that no other site on the island would be possible for the capital without the expenditure of between $2 million and $4 million.[13]

When in June of that year the United States offered to review the Chaguaramas agreement within a decade, Sir Grantley announced the federal government's approval. Neither Dr Williams nor Mr Manley forgave him and his cabinet for taking this decision without prior consultation with them. If, said Dr Williams, the United States refused to give up Chaguaramas, the Trinidadian government might have to acquiesce, but the matter would remain 'a running sore.'

In this protracted controversy the real issue was prestige rather than the peculiar desirability of Chaguaramas as a capital site or the scarcity of other suitable locations in Trinidad. Many West Indians considered it unbecoming for their new nation to have a large area close to its capital which was alien soil on which they could not tread freely. They strongly resented the fact that one 'foreign' power, the United Kingdom, had leased some of their land to another without consulting the people who lived there.

At the London conference in 1941 on leasing to the United States bases in Bermuda, Newfoundland, and the West Indies, the colonies concerned had been represented by their respective governors. Most of these had attacked the agreement, but to no avail. Especially critical was Sir Hubert Young, then Governor of Trinidad and Tobago, who argued that if a base in Trinidad was essential, it should not be at Chaguaramas, because of the peninsula's importance for the future development of Port-of-Spain.

Other Caribbean governors warned that granting ninety-nine year leases to the United States was almost certain to create conflict with nationalist movements in the British West Indies. When the agreement was finally concluded, the

American ambassador to the United Kingdom commented: 'The rights and powers it conveys are ... probably more far-reaching than any the British Government has ever given anyone over British territory before. They are not used to giving such concessions and on certain points they have fought every inch of the way.'[14]

Most West Indians showed little sympathy for the fact that, although no country would welcome a foreign base on its soil, the United Kingdom's wartime need for destroyers was urgent. Many regarded the arrangement as simply one more milestone on the long road of imperial Britain's sins against its Caribbean colonies. While it was finally decided that the federal capital should be located in Port-of-Spain, the future of Chaguaramas remained unsettled.

THE BRITISH CARIBBEAN ACT, 1956

On 2 August 1956 the parliament at Westminister passed the British Caribbean Act to establish a federal union among the ten territories. The constitution was semi-colonial in that it did not provide full internal self-government. Executive authority was vested in the Queen, represented by a Governor General empowered to disallow and reserve bills. He was required to act in accordance with the advice of the Council of State unless he believed the public interest demanded that he consult the Prime Minister, who was to be elected by the House of Representatives. In an urgent case the Governor General might act without consulting the council, but must as soon as possible tell it what he had done and why. Her Majesty-in-Council (in practice the Governor General) was authorized, if necessary, to legislate for the Federation on defence, external relations, and questions of financial stability. On such matters the Governor General might act contrary to the advice of the council or the Prime Minister only if he had first obtained approval from the Secretary of State for the Colonies.

The Council of State, which advised the Governor General and served as the principal instrument of public policy, was to be composed of the Prime Minister and ten other ministers appointed by the Governor General on the advice of the Prime Minister. At least three were to be senators and the remainder members of the House of Representatives. No member of an executive council or legislature of any territory would be qualified for appointment as a minister. The Governor General was not obligated to assign to any minister responsibility for defence, for auditing the accounts of the Federation, or for the appointment, dismissal, or control of public servants.

The Senate, the upper house of the federal legislature, was composed of nineteen members nominated by the Governor General, after consultation with the governor of the territory concerned, who would normally act on the advice of his ministers. Senators would serve for five years, regardless of any dissolution of parliament. Two were to be appointed from each of the nine largest units and one from Montserrat in order to give roughly equal representation to the islands, whose wide variations in population meant that the smaller ones would necessarily be outvoted in the lower house. The Senate might delay non-financial bills for not more than a year.

The House of Representatives was allotted forty-five members elected by universal adult suffrage: seventeen from Jamaica, ten from Trinidad and Tobago, five from Barbados, one from Montserrat, and two from each of the other territories. Procedure in both houses was modelled on that at Westminster. Eight senators and seventeen members of the House of Representatives would constitute a quorum, provided four of the latter represented different territories. Money bills might be introduced only in the House of Representatives and be discussed only with the consent of the Council of State. The maximum life of the federal legislature was set at five years, with at least one session to be held each year.

Provision was made for delegation, by mutual consent, of national powers to the territories and of territorial powers to the Federation. The central parliament was given authority to legislate on subjects on an exclusive legislative list. The most important of these were borrowing monies for federal purposes, defence, the provision of financial or advisory assistance, the establishment and maintenance of federal agencies and institutions for research, exchange control, national libraries, museums, the University College of the West Indies, immigration into and deportation from the Federation, the central public service and public relations, and income tax on emoluments paid from national funds to senators, members of the House of Representatives, or federal public servants.

Both national and unit legislatures were empowered to make laws on matters on a concurrent legislative list, with federal legislation prevailing in case of conflict. Among the most important subjects on this list were industrial development, trade and commerce, civil aviation, atomic energy, conciliation and arbitration of industrial disputes, trade unions, meteorology, banks and banking, borrowing of money by the government of any territory, census and statistics, criminal law and procedure, currency and coinage, prisons, shipping, and telegraph and telephones.

Control of movement of persons between units was also placed on the concurrent list, subject to articles 49, 50, and 51 of the constitution. These provided that after five years territorial legislation on the subject would lapse if not approved by both houses of the national legislature. In other words, from 1963 the federal parliament would have exclusive jurisdiction over this matter.

Customs and excise duties were similarly placed on the concurrent list, subject to articles 94 and 95. These required the national government during the first five years to give back to the units any excise taxes collected by it in excess of BWI $9,120,000 a year: the total amount of the mandatory levy the units were obligated to pay the Federation. This sum was approximately one-seventeenth of Trinidad's annual budget.

Income and profits taxes were also subjects of concurrent jurisdiction, with the proviso that for the first five years the central legislature might not impose them. Finally, postal services were placed on the concurrent list, subject to article 97, which provided that for the first five years after establishment of a national postal system the federal government should pay each territory the amount of its average postal revenue. The reason for this somewhat unusual requirement was that in the smaller islands yields from the sale of postage stamps represented a considerable fraction of public revenues.

Residual powers were assigned to the units, which were given jurisdiction over subjects not included in the exclusive federal legislative list, although on subjects in the concurrent legislative list they shared jurisdiction with the central parliament. Stripped of legal verbiage, the limitations on national powers meant that the federal government, during the critical first five years, had no power to tax and was specifically debarred from the most lucrative types of revenue: imposts on customs, income, and postal services. It had only two sources of funds: profits on the issue of currency and mandatory contributions from the territories. Of these contributions Jamaica was to pay 43.1 per cent, Trinidad and Tobago 38.6 per cent, Barbados 8.5 per cent, and the remaining seven territories less than 2 per cent apiece, Montserrat's allocation being 0.27 per cent.

The national constitution could be amended by Her Majesty-in-Council. It was agreed that within five years of the Federation's establishment there should be a conference of delegates from the central government, each constituent unit, and the United Kingdom to review the constitution.

Provision was made for a Public Service Commission, composed of a chairman and from two to four other members, serving for a three-year term, and appointed by the Governor General. A federal Supreme Court, presided over by a Chief Justice, was to be established, with the composition agreed upon at the 1956 conference. The Governor General would appoint the first Chief Justice on instructions from the Secretary of State for the Colonies and later incumbents at his own discretion, after consultation with the Prime Minister. The Supreme Court was given original jurisdiction in proceedings between the Federation and a territory, between one territory and another, between the Federation and an officer or authority of a territory, and, if requested, in interpreting the national constitution. The national legislature was empowered to confer appellate jurisdiction on the Supreme Court in cases of appeals from any superior court of a territory, unless local legislation provided that decisions by its own superior court should be final.

FEDERAL PROBLEMS

In a phrase later quoted against him by political opponents, Norman Manley in 1957 described the West Indian union as 'the most improbable historical venture that one can imagine.' Yet, guided by its motto – to dwell together in unity[15] – he looked to the future of the Federation with supreme confidence as 'the greatest adventure of our people in our time.' In the past decade, he observed, West Indians had begun to examine their foundations and background, to discover themselves and their common heritage. Despite marked diversities between different islands, he believed they were united by the strongest possible bond: an underlying similarity of outlook. Their common history had produced multi-racial communities whose people were learning to live together in harmony and to look on divisions as insignificant. Jamaica and Trinidad, in his view, had a responsibility to help the smaller and weaker islands.

All were then agreed that federation was the best, and for many of the smaller territories the only, path to independence and dominion status. They hoped to transcend the limitations of the old colonial economy and, through the larger opportunities offered by unity, to fashion a society which could provide for the British Caribbean peoples the basic elements of a decent life. It was not, Manley admitted, a strong federation. West Indians had agreed to enter into matrimony, but had hedged the contract with so many safeguards and stipulations that he could only pray that by some divine providence it would in due course produce offspring. Nevertheless, he concluded, 'have no fear about our success if we walk with strength and patience and wisdom.'[16]

The fact remained, however, that after a decade of discussion West Indians had fashioned a union too weak to accomplish much and hence vulnerable to attack as an expensive and useless luxury. Each territory objected to contributing more than the barest minimum to national revenues. Some federal expenditures represented a transfer of previous financial commitments, such as those for the University College, shipping services, and overseas commissions in the United Kingdom and Canada. They amounted in 1958 to some BWI $4,785,000, which would have had to be paid even if there had been no federation. If these amounts were subtracted, Jamaica paid about BWI $2,175,000 for federal costs and Trinidad and Tobago about $2,413,000.

The maximum sum which might be raised from the mandatory levies plus profits on the issue of currency amounted to a little over BWI $10 million, one-seventh of which was absorbed by expenses for the university. Thus, even before the new state came into being, it was already clear that national ministers would be frustrated by lack of adequate funds to implement any comprehensive programmes.

Throughout the protracted pre-federal discussions the most difficult problems were the sources of national revenue and common tariff and immigration policies. Jamaica was as unwilling to lower its relatively high tariff, which produced a considerable proportion of its revenues, as was Trinidad to allow free entry to West Indians from other units. As the largest territories refused to yield the powers they cherished most, there was no common coinage or postage and no provision for a customs union or for migration at will from one island to another.

Most federations have suffered from an imbalance of power among their component units, from disparities in size, population, and natural resources, but in none has the distribution been so heavily weighted with such unfortunate results as in The West Indies. Jamaica and Trinidad between them accounted for seven-eighths of the population and three-quarters of the wealth. Their influence was naturally commensurate. Jamaica, the largest and second richest territory, contained just over half the inhabitants of The West Indies. Montserrat had only 0.5 per cent.

In no other federation had half the population, and therefore half the political strength, been thus concentrated in one unit. This lopsided distribution of power created much difficulty in obtaining the compromises necessary for a healthy national state. The smaller and poorer territories were understandably fearful of domination by the twin giants, Jamaica and Trinidad. In 1958 Jamaicans earned almost three times as much as Leeward and Windward islanders. The transfer of even a tiny fraction of the incomes enjoyed in Trinidad, Jamaica, and Barbados, it was cogently argued, would transform living standards in the smaller islands.[17]

The allotment of seats in the federal House of Representatives involved a marked departure from the principle of representation by population. With one seat for Montserrat, Jamaica was mathematically entitled to 110, Trinidad and Tobago to 55, and Barbados to 16. This would have created an unwieldy and needlessly expensive lower house. In 1956 the territories accepted the view of the Standing Closer Association Committee that distribution of seats should be related to population, but not strictly or mechanically. Considerations such as financial stability, economic development and productivity, and the need for reasonable representation for the less populous units were also given weight. By a compromise it soon regretted, Jamaica accepted seventeen of the forty-five seats, because this concession appeared necessary if there was to be any federation.

The Leewards and Windwards, with only 15 per cent of the total population, obtained almost 30 per cent of the seats. Yet their spokesmen sometimes accused the two larger islands of taking all and giving nothing. He would rather see his island a province of Canada, declared one forceful politician, than part of a West Indian union which offered St Lucians opportunities inferior to those in the big territories.[18]

Most people in the British Caribbean had little real interest in federation. The union was brought about largely through the efforts and enthusiasm of a small group of educated middle-class politicians and public servants with widely divergent views but a common determination to achieve independence and a common conviction that they could do better for their islands than a distant and neglectful imperial power.[19] These political leaders made few attempts, before or after union, to explain to their citizens what federation involved or to seek their support for the national state. Of the many problems confronting the new country, least attention was devoted to the most urgent and difficult: the need to develop among its scattered and heterogeneous peoples a real sense of unity and loyalty to the Federation.

In the lengthy discussions which preceded federation hard bargaining was more conspicuous than genuine enthusiasm for a united West Indies. Doubtless this was natural. As Benjamin Franklin observed at the Philadelphia Convention of 1787, 'when you assemble a number of men, to have the advantage of their joint wisdom, you inevitably assemble with those men all their prejudices, their passions, their errors of opinion, their local interests, and their selfish views. From such an assembly can a perfect production be expected?'

It was ultimately disastrous for the British Caribbean that the idealism and co-operative spirit of Montego Bay had largely vanished before the Federation came into being eleven years later. During this decade pro-federal sentiment often seemed simply to coast along on the impetus existing in 1947. By 1958 little momentum was left and the islands appeared almost taken aback by the agreements to which they had committed themselves. The explanation for this change of attitude lay in the political and economic developments which occurred in the protracted interval.

INDUSTRIAL AND POLITICAL ADVANCE IN JAMAICA: 1952-8

Early in 1952 the Jamaican People's National Party expelled, on grounds of communist activities, four prominent left-wing leaders of the Trades Union Congress: Kenneth Hill, one of the founders of the party who was then mayor of Kingston; his journalist brother, Frank, long a conspicuous radical; Richard Hart, an attorney who was secretary of the Caribbean Labour Congress; and Arthur Henry, a well-known trade union official. As a result of this party split the connection of the Trades Union Congress with the People's National Party was severed and not renewed until 1964.

Ken Hill promptly founded a one-man radical organization, the National Labour Party. He later joined the Jamaica Labour Party but eventually returned to the People's National Party fold. Richard Hart established a Marxist group, the People's Educational Organization, which co-operated with Ferdinand Smith's Federation of Trade Unions. This was soon succeeded by another radical body, the West Indian Freedom Movement, and subsequently by the Jamaica Socialist Party. The purge strengthened Mr Manley's position by removing possible rivals and, by its clear rejection of communism, providing an effective rebuttal to his opponents' allegations that the People's National Party was tainted with Marxism.

Another group, the Farmers' Federation, formed in 1953, was led by Robert Kirkwood, a prominent white sugar-estate owner who a decade earlier had launched the short-lived Jamaica Democratic Party. Although this new body tried to win votes from small proprietors as well as large planters, it had little success and soon disintegrated.

Shortly after the split with the Trades Union Congress, the People's National Party, conscious of its need for a supporting labour organization, founded the National Workers' Union. Noel Nethersole was president, Florizel Glasspole general secretary, and Kenneth Stirling supervisor. One of their assistants was a young journalist, Norman Manley's son Michael, who became the union's sugar supervisor, charged with endeavouring to entice sugar workers away from the Bustamante Industrial Trade Union. He later led the National Workers' Union and in 1972 became Prime Minister of Jamaica.

This new body established branches in various parts of the island and soon achieved considerable success among unskilled Jamaican labourers, most of whom had formerly supported the Bustamante union. Although the majority of its officers were professional or business men, they were elected to their posts. Thus from the outset the National Workers' Union, unlike its rival, provided a measure of democratic control.

The Jamaica Labour Party also ostensibly moved in this direction. In 1951 its constitution was altered to provide an island-wide General Council, a central executive, local branches, and constituency committees and executives. Claiming to represent all classes in the community, the party stressed its belief in the rights of both labour and capital, concern for the workers' welfare, faith in social legislation, rejection of socialism, and friendliness towards Britain and the United States.[20]

Industrial bargaining in Jamaica was complicated by the existence of three labour bodies, all of the comprehensive, industrial, non-craft-union type. Every trade unionist belonged to the Bustamante Industrial Trade Union, the National

Workers' Union, or the much smaller and less important Trades Union Congress. In the absence of legislation requiring workers to choose one union to represent them, employees in certain industries, especially cane and citrus, often divided their allegiance. Employers thus sometimes found themselves obliged to bargain with all three unions. Newer industries, such as bauxite, had only one, the National Workers' Union (affiliated with the steelworkers' unions in Canada and the United States), because these firms insisted that employees select by majority vote the organization of their choice.

Figures on comparative wage rates were seldom available, since West Indian governments hesitated to collect and publish such statistics, lest these be used by political opponents to show how little insular administrations had done to increase prosperity. Trade union membership was also difficult to estimate accurately, as each of the two larger unions claimed as supporters more than half the organized workers. It was said in 1956 that some 13 per cent of all workers in Jamaica were union members, as opposed to 29 per cent in Trinidad, where about one-quarter of labourers belonged to the Oilfield Workers' Union.[21] Nor were figures on union membership necessarily reliable guides to party preferences. Some Bustamante Industrial Trade Union members voted for the People's National Party and some National Workers' Union members for the Jamaica Labour Party. Neither party could be sure of receiving electoral support from every member of its affiliated union.

All three unions found dues difficult to collect and did not develop the practice, usual in the United Kingdom and many other parts of the Commonwealth, of allocating a certain fraction to political parties. During election campaigns each union gave financial assistance to the party it supported, but the amount was determined by union officials on the basis of what they thought their organizations could afford. Members were asked neither for their views on the matter nor for special political contributions.

Sir Hugh Foot (later Lord Caradon) was appointed Governor of Jamaica in 1951. With the possible exception of Lord Olivier, he proved the most popular holder of this office in the island's history. His liberal opinions on colonial policy were well known before he went to Jamaica, and from the time of his arrival he encouraged the movement for greater autonomy.

By an order-in-council of 1953 ministerial government was introduced by changing the constitution to give the Executive Council eight (as opposed to the former five) elected members, chosen by the House of Representatives from among its own number. For the first time this gave elected members a majority on the council, where the Attorney General and Colonial and Financial Secretaries continued to serve as nominated officials. Thereafter the Chief Minister was appointed by the Governor with the approval of the House. On the recommendation of the Chief Minister he appointed the other seven elected members to various portfolios. The Chief Minister was empowered to recommend dismissal of a minister, and the House of Representatives, by a majority vote of all its members, to recommend dismissal of the Chief Minister.

At the same time the Governor's authority was increased to allow him to use his reserve powers without the consent of the Executive Council. Control over finance, the police, the judiciary, and external affairs continued to be exercised by officials, not elected representatives. These innovations produced almost full responsible government but did not go far enough completely to satisfy Jamaican public opinion.

In the island's general election of January 1955 three-quarters of the electorate voted. Federation was not an issue, as both parties supported it. The People's National Party was returned to power with eighteen seats and 50.5 per cent of the popular vote, as opposed to fourteen seats and 39 per cent of the vote for the Jamaica Labour Party. In the course of that year Mr Bustamante was awarded the consolation prize of a knighthood.

Mr Manley, leader of the opposition since 1949, became Chief Minister. Mr Glasspole and Mr Nethersole resigned their union posts on becoming Ministers of Labour and Finance respectively. The former, who also acted as Leader of the House, later became Minister of Education. Mr Manley adopted the practice of holding a conference of all elected ministers to decide on action in the Executive Council. By operating as a cabinet this group automatically reduced the power of official members.

Further constitutional advances were inaugurated by various orders-in-council. In 1955 the number of elected legislative members was increased to nine. In the following year provision was made for election of an Acting Speaker of the House of Representatives and an Acting President of the Legislative Council. The requirement of two nominated official members on the Legislative Council was removed and the minimum number of unofficials increased by two. The new upper house was thus composed of not less than twelve unofficials in addition to the Colonial Secretary, Financial Secretary, and Attorney General.

The Executive Council was replaced in October 1957 by a Council of Ministers, ten of whose twelve members were drawn from the House of Representatives, while the remaining two were unofficial members of the Legislative Council. These replaced the Colonial and Financial Secretaries, leaving the Attorney General as the sole remaining official. Responsibility for internal security was transferred to an elected minister. Under this new dispensation the Chief Minister normally summoned and presided over meetings of the Council of Ministers. The Governor retained the right to call and chair special meetings, but appointed ministers on the recommendation of the Chief

Minister. The Legislative Council was then composed of the Attorney General and sixteen unofficial members nominated by the Governor, while the House of Representatives had thirty-two elected members, including an elected Speaker.

The People's National Party had fought and lost the elections of 1944 and 1949 on the issues of self-government, socialism, mitigation of class distinctions, and public ownership. By 1955 autonomy was largely achieved, and it was apparent that socialism and public ownership tended to frighten rather than attract most voters. Democratic labour parties elsewhere in the Commonwealth had similarly discovered that it was difficult to define socialism and inexpedient to translate its more radical principles into action. No longer, as in the 1930s, did nationalization seem an infallible panacea for a multitude of ills. Recognizing the electorate's obvious lack of enthusiasm for radical change, Mr Manley largely replaced his previous advocacy of socialism with the innocuous slogan of economic development.

During the election campaign of 1955 he undertook not to nationalize any industries, and after he became Chief Minister he said little and did nothing about introducing socialism. His new concentration on economic and agricultural development, obtainable goals calculated to win popular support, indicated an increased understanding of practical realities. Tourism, agriculture, and industry all advanced under Mr Manley's government, but the gradual erosion of his strength among the working class was illustrated seven years later when the referendum on the Federation went against him.

The constitution of the People's National Party provided for election by the annual conference of the president and four vice-presidents. Since the party's inception, however, Mr Manley was invariably re-elected as president, usually by acclamation. The positions of vice-president, by contrast, were often closely contested. Party affairs were administered by the National Executive Council which met monthly. This large body was composed of party officials, members of the legislature, twenty-five members chosen by the annual conference, and ten representatives from the National Workers' Union, in addition to one or two from each constituency organization. An Executive Committee, which met weekly, determined policy and strategy. It included the leader, party officials, four members of the House of Representatives, eleven others chosen by the National Executive Council from among its own ranks, and three delegates from the National Workers' Union.

Although Mr Manley and his principal colleagues all wanted cabinet government for Jamaica in order to control internal administration, they were scarcely a united team. The attempt to organize the People's National Party more democratically than the Jamaica Labour Party made it more subject to factional rivalries and splinter groups, while the wide range of its supporters, from illiterate agricultural labourers to educated professional people, detracted from its homogeneity. Sharpest dissension occurred on the issue of federation. In particular, Wills Isaacs, the powerful Minister of Trade and Industry, long openly opposed Jamaica's participation in the union. Until temporarily silenced in 1960, he continued to express his criticisms both in public and in private. Other cabinet ministers and many members of the People's National Party agreed with him.

Mr Manley was subsequently attacked for making little effort until 1960 to foster Jamaicans' enthusiasm for the Federation. Division on the question within the party and even within the cabinet was undoubtedly a major reason for his failure to do so. This difference of opinion accentuated his natural absorption in Jamaican affairs and in consolidating his own political position. Yet, however understandable, his failure to cultivate public support for the Federation was to prove disastrous.

On a visit to the neighbouring island of Puerto Rico he was impressed by what 'Operation Bootstrap' had accomplished under conditions not unlike those of Jamaica, where he himself assumed the portfolios of Agriculture and Development in addition to the responsibilities of Chief Minister. His government promptly passed a Land Appropriation Act and proceeded to buy a number of large estates which it subdivided among small peasant proprietors. Through the good offices of the United Nations' Technical Assistance Administration, George Cadbury (formerly chairman of the Economic Advisory and Planning Board of Saskatchewan) was lent to the Government of Jamaica as economic and social adviser, to establish a central planning organization. In 1956, a year after its inception, this body was incorporated as a separate unit in the newly established Ministry of Development, with direct access to Mr Manley. The Planning Unit made a number of studies on health, education, agriculture, and industrial development. The average per capita annual income in Jamaica was then BWI $510, as compared with $612 in Trinidad and $283 in the other British islands. During the next five years the economic gap between the two wealthiest and the poorer territories steadily widened.

At the time of the Montego Bay Conference Jamaica produced no minerals of major significance and had no important industries. Ten years later it had become the world's principal source of bauxite, whose export began in 1952. The development of this industry was mainly responsible for the facts that from 1952 to 1958 Jamaica's national income more than doubled and from 1952 to 1961 its exports increased by some 250 per cent. In 1951 agricultural products accounted for more than 90 per cent of its earnings abroad. A decade later 10 per cent of the total domestic revenue of almost £60 million a year was obtained from royalties and taxes on bauxite, which had become the island's largest earner of foreign exchange. Sugar, rum, and molasses then produced 25 per cent of domestic revenues, bananas about 8 per cent, and citrus, coffee, cacao, pimento, and ginger another 8 per cent.

From 1952 to 1962 the value of Jamaica's manufactured goods quadrupled. By 1960 industry had supplanted agriculture (which still employed half the wage earners) as the chief contributor to the gross national product. In the course of this decade over seventy factories were built. Production and exports tripled, giving the island an annual rate of economic growth of eight per cent: the fastest in the world during this period. These developments were fostered by the Pioneer Industries Act of 1949 and the Jamaica Industrial Development Corporation, established in 1952 and complemented by the Small Businesses Loan Board and the Development Finance Corporation.

Between 1951 and 1960 Colonial Development and Welfare allocations to Jamaica, coupled with British grants-in-aid, amounted to some £7 million. The tourist industry expanded into a major source of American and Canadian dollars. The combined result of all these events was to transform Jamaica from an underdeveloped to a developing country. Its business community, already paying one of the world's highest tax rates, was appalled at the prospect of additional levies to support a federal government and of reduction in the tariff (the highest in the British Caribbean) which produced a large fraction of the island's revenue.

By 1958, when the Federation was established, the Jamaican economy bore little resemblance to that of 1947. Bauxite accounted for a considerable portion of public revenues, industrialization was well underway, and agricultural development was actively encouraged by the government. During this decade Jamaica's political and economic advance was so striking that many thought membership in a federated West Indies likely to produce more loss than gain. Central control over economic development appeared likely to interfere with the inducements which this island offered prospective manufacturers. At Montego Bay Jamaica had seemed a major breeding ground of West Indianism. A decade later its nationalism had become Jamaican nationalism, not a sense of West Indian nationhood.

INDUSTRIAL AND POLITICAL ADVANCE IN TRINIDAD: 1953-6

Developments in Trinidad and Tobago during the same period were also impressive, despite uneasy labour relations. In 1953 its government invited F.W. Dalley, who six years earlier had surveyed trade union organization and the industrial scene in Trinidad, to pay a return visit to discuss progress and examine labour conditions. His terms of reference did not mention communism, but it was well known that the government was concerned about the spread of Marxist views in certain unions. The Trade Union Council, which included two of the major labour organizations, was affiliated with the communist-dominated World Federation of Trade Unions, and the President-General of the Oilfield Workers' Trade Union, John Rojas, who had recently visited countries behind the iron curtain, had publicly expressed his admiration for the Soviet system. The Trinidad government had been particularly concerned by the association of the Oilfield and Federated Workers' Unions with the West Indies Independence Party, founded in 1952 and allegedly communist-inspired. Its major tenets were abolition of British rule, faith in a mixture of socialism and peasant proprietorship, and a demand for immediate self-government.

Mr Dalley's report to Mr Albert Gomes, Minister of Labour, Industry, and Commerce, suggested that Trinidad had very few dedicated communists, many more fellow-travellers, and others who, while denying communist connections, certainly adopted Marxist tactics.

The differences between the two largest industries, oil and sugar, were significant. The former was well organized, provided its employees with many amenities and good apprenticeship programmes, and appointed large numbers of Trinidadians to senior posts. In the sugar industry, by contrast, employers but not workers were well organized, trade unions were not recognized, and there was no collective bargaining or satisfactory machinery for remedying grievances. Such sugar workers' unions as existed were weak and divided by internal rivalry and jealousies. From 1945 to 1948 the All-Trinidad Sugar Workers' Union had been recognized by the manufacturers but almost broken through threats of intimidation and violence by Uriah Butler and his followers. In 1954 this body and the sugar industry labour unions agreed to federate (three smaller unions having withdrawn from the industry) under the presidency of Bhadase Maraj, a member of the Legislative Council.

Mr Dalley considered the unwillingness of the Sugar Manufacturers' Federation to recognize the amalgamated union most unwise. Unless employers as well as the government encouraged constitutional collective action by workers, unionists would be forced to resort to other means, and neither they nor their leaders could be blamed for extreme views and irresponsibility. The slowness with which barracks-type housing was being replaced on the sugar estates was particularly unfortunate in view of the acute housing situation in Trinidad.

In most government departments adequate labour relations machinery then existed, Whitley-style joint committees were functioning, and unions were recognized. Civil servants complained, however, that even when agreements were reached, there was no guarantee that these would be implemented within a reasonable period. Mr Dalley supported the demand of the Civil Service

Association for arbitration in cases of disagreement about salaries and conditions of work.

Employers in various industries were regrettably reluctant to recognize trade unions. Yet they could hardly be expected to negotiate willingly with labour leaders convicted of dishonesty, with those 'who call on their followers one day to throw their employer into the sea and on the next demand collective bargaining; or with those ... striving to use the union for unconstitutional and undemocratic purposes.' Although the government and public opinion could help by encouraging responsible and democratic trade unions, in the long run effective remedies had to come from labour organizations and their members, through greater regard for constitutionality by the leaders and education of the rank and file.[22]

No one could accuse Mr Dalley, a distinguished and veteran British trade unionist, of hostility towards labour. Consequently his strictures on certain unions' irresponsibility, misappropriation of funds, and occasional recourse to violence and intimidation were the more effective. His terms of reference applied only to Trinidad and Tobago, but his comments were pertinent throughout most of the British West Indies.

On a motion by the Trinidad legislature a Constitution Reform Committee, composed of unofficial members of the Legislative Council and other leading citizens, was appointed by the Governor, Sir Hubert Rance, in January 1955. Its majority report, presented in September of that year to the new Governor, Sir Edward Beetham, was accepted with only minor amendments by the local government and later by the Secretary of State for the Colonies. The changes proposed were effected by an order-in-council of June 1956.

This introduced a new constitution creating the office of a Chief Minister, to be elected by the Legislative Council, who was to lead the government in the Executive and Legislative Councils. In both these bodies the number of official members was reduced from three to two by substituting an elected Minister of Finance for the Financial Secretary. The single nominated member of the Executive Council was replaced by an elected minister, and the one appointed member by an elected Speaker. The number of ministers was increased from five to eight and the elected members of the Legislative Council from eighteen to twenty-four.

These changes produced an Executive Council composed of the Governor as chairman, the Colonial Secretary and Attorney General *ex officio*, the Chief Minister, and seven other ministers elected by the Legislative Council. The latter body included the same two officials and five nominated unofficials, in addition to twenty-four elected members. The new Legislative Council elected as its first Speaker, not one of its own number, but a retired judge. Provision was made for appointment of parliamentary secretaries and an advisory Public Service Commission and Police Promotions Board.

Trinidad's first really effective party, the People's National Movement, was founded in January 1956 by Dr Eric Williams. He became its political leader, Dr Patrick Solomon deputy leader, and a well-known Trinidadian cricketer, Learie (later Sir Learie) Constantine, chairman. Dr Williams, affectionately known to his supporters as 'the little doctor,' was a graduate of Oxford, where he took a brilliant degree, sometime Professor of Political and Social Science at Howard University in Washington, and a former staff member of the Caribbean Commission.

Among public men in the British West Indies he was outstanding in intellectual and political ability. A man of immense energy and unrelenting capacity for hard work, he wrote much of his party's weekly organ, *The Nation*, and while holding the country's highest political office found time to edit documents on West Indian history and write books on the development of his people and party. The quality of his public addresses earned their locale the soubriquet of the University of Woodford Square. The defects of these virtues, according to his opponents, were chilly self-satisfaction, ruthlessness, arrogance, and contentiousness. A scholar, but also a politician who could stoop to conquer, he promptly won the devotion of followers unperturbed by his allegedly authoritarian tendencies.

Although Dr Williams and the majority of his supporters were black, the People's National Movement was avowedly inter-racial. It emphasized party discipline and political education for its members, self-government and independence, equal rights for women, improved social services, economic development, attraction of overseas capital, and encouragement of private enterprise. Its constitution provided for many local party groups throughout Trinidad and Tobago, smaller numbers of larger constituency associations, a general council, and an annual convention. The People's National Movement originally supported a strong Federation of the West Indies with a capital in Trinidad, and made this a major issue in the election campaign of 1956. Once in office, however, the party was not always prepared to sacrifice insular interests to those of a united British Caribbean.

At the general election of September 1956, at which over 80 per cent of voters cast their ballots, the People's National Movement, founded only eight months before, secured support from a wide economic cross-section of the community and won 43 per cent of the popular vote and thirteen of the twenty-four elective seats in the Legislative Council. Dr Williams became the first Chief Minister of Trinidad and Tobago, leader of its first party government, and Minister of Finance, Planning, and Development. Of his eight cabinet ministers, five were black, two East Indian (one Hindu and one Moslem), and one white. Of two parliamentary under-secretaries, one was Chinese. Dr Williams's small majority in the Legislative Council was opposed by many East Indians, the Catholic Church, and much of the press.

Shortly after the election a majority of the eleven opposition members (of whom seven were Indian) combined to form the predominantly East Indian Democratic Labour Party, chaired by Victor Bryan and led by Bhadase Maraj, former leader of the People's Democratic Party. When in March 1960 the latter resigned because of ill-health, he was succeeded by Dr Rudranath Capildeo, a barrister and former staff member of the University of London, who was then principal of Port-of-Spain's Polytechnic Institute. On entering politics he resigned this post but later rejoined the teaching staff of the University of London while continuing to serve as leader of the opposition in Trinidad.

A month after the new government took office the Secretary of State for the Colonies agreed to include among the five nominated members of the Legislative Council two People's National Movement members selected by Dr Williams. His administration devoted major attention to economic and industrial development. A five-year plan envisaged expenditure of nearly BWI $250 million (almost all raised locally) for such undertakings as roads, schools, hospitals, fisheries, water supplies, and expanded rural electrification. The Industrial Development Corporation, established in 1958, offered various incentives to prospective manufacturers. This active programme, coupled with increased revenues from the oil industry which had long made Trinidad the wealthiest territory in the British West Indies, stimulated local nationalism. So also did Dr Williams' unusual emphasis on political education of the people. In a series of public addresses he expounded his party's programme, criticized colonialism, attacked the American base at Chaguaramas, analysed federation, and detailed the shortcomings of his political opponents.

POLITICAL ADVANCE IN THE EASTERN CARIBBEAN: 1954-8

At the general election of 1956 Grantley Adams's Labour Party was again returned to power in Barbados, with fifteen of the Assembly's twenty-four seats. Two years later the island achieved government by a cabinet, chaired by the Premier, which controlled internal affairs and met without the Governor. The full Executive Committee might still, however, be convened at the request of either the Governor or the Premier, while a nominated Chief Secretary retained responsibility for internal security and personnel aspects of the public service.

In the smaller colonies political advance was more tardy. After the elections of 1954 some departmental responsibilities were assigned to elected members of the legislatures. In 1956 Antigua, St Kitts-Nevis-Anguilla, and Montserrat obtained new constitutions. In the first two territories the Legislative Council was composed of the Administrator and thirteen other members of whom two were *ex officio*, three nominated, and eight elected. The Executive Council included the Administrator as President, two *ex officio* members, one nominated member of the Legislative Council appointed by the Governor, and four elected members of the Legislative Council. Thus there was a majority of elected members in both the Legislative and Executive Councils, with the latter recognized as the principal instrument of policy. A ministerial system was introduced when three elected members of the Executive Council were appointed as ministers. The Montserrat Legislative Council also obtained a majority of elected members (five instead of eight as in Antigua and St Kitts). Its Executive Council, however, was composed of the Administrator, two official, one nominated, and two elected members.

To their intense satisfaction the Leewards were finally defederated on 1 July 1956, when the General Legislature was abolished and the presidencies reverted to their former status as separate colonies. During that year the four Windward Islands also obtained new constitutions with ministerial systems similar to those of the Leewards.

With the advance of self-government and highly organized political parties, Independents and whites were progressively eliminated from most insular legislatures. The Grenada election of 1957 removed the last Independent elected member, as T. Albert Marryshow, long an Independent, had earlier joined the People's Democratic Movement. In the St Vincent election of the same year, however, Mr Joshua's victorious People's Political Party faced an opposition composed of several Independent members. In St Lucia an able barrister, John Compton, who in 1954 had been returned as an Independent, became leader of the Labour Party, despite the electoral handicap then almost unknown in the smaller islands, of being a university graduate.

A party system developed slowly in Dominica, where in 1951 five of eight elective seats were won by the Dominica Labour Party led by Edward Le Blanc. Four years later West Indian traditions were shattered when a revived Labour Party based on trade union support was founded by Mrs Phyllis Allfrey, a white woman born in the island. A middle-class group, the Dominica People's National Movement, was founded by a coloured lawyer, Clifton A. Dupigny. In October 1957 the Dominica Labour Party, under the presidency of Mrs Allfrey, was admitted to membership in the West Indies Federal Labour Party. A similar affiliation was unsuccessfully sought by Franklyn Baron, Dominica's Minister of Trade and Industry, for his newly formed Independence Party. Although there were no clearly marked doctrinal differences between this group and Mrs

Allfrey's, the latter was more homogeneous and probably considered by the Federal Labour Party more stable.

In 1947 all the participating territories hoped to gain solid advantages from federalism. During the eleven years between the Montego Bay Conference and the establishment of the Federation, however, political and economic development modified former enthusiasm and increased doubts about the merits of union. At first supported by leading West Indians as the shortest route to self-government, federalism was gradually viewed by many as the chief obstacle in its way. The more autonomy the territories obtained, the less willing they became to surrender any portion of it and the less convinced that union offered the only road to independence. Each political advance strengthened local feeling and the insularity fostered by centuries of isolation. The economies of the units were for the most part competitive rather than complementary. While each wanted to broaden and diversify its exports, only the larger territories could do so without regional planning and central direction. There was nothing simple or logical about federation in the British Caribbean, where it was faster to fly from Kingston to New York than to Port-of-Spain.

Trinidad feared that free migration would encourage an influx from neighbouring islands. Almost all East Indians, who formed one-third of Trinidad's population, were opposed to a federal union in which they would compose only a tiny racial minority. Jamaica suspected that federalism would delay its own progress towards self-government, hamper the development of new industries, and force a reduction in its lucrative tariff. Nor did it welcome the idea of absorption in a national state at the outset less independent than Jamaica itself.

Both Jamaicans and Trinidadians believed that their own critical economic problems demanded first consideration and were alarmed by the prospect of replacing the United Kingdom as subsidizers of the small islands. This argument at first appealed even more strongly in Jamaica than in Trinidad, which was linked by geography, if by little neighbourly sentiment, with the Eastern Caribbean.

The smaller islands welcomed the prospect of customs union, free migration, and extension of the co-operation fostered since 1952 by the Regional Economic Committee. They scarcely hoped to attain autonomy individually. Yet they feared that in a federation dominated by the large territories their interests might receive less consideration than was shown them by the United Kingdom.

None of these apprehensions was altogether unfounded. West Indians' unfamiliarity with each other made it difficult to develop a consciousness of unity and a genuine loyalty to the new nation. Yet in many ways the Caribbean islands appeared more ready for autonomy than other British colonies. They valued the familiar institutions and practices of parliamentary democracy, prided themselves on impartial courts, and possessed a competent civil service and judiciary largely staffed by their own nationals. By 1955 all six Chief Justices in the British Caribbean were West Indian, in contrast with two in 1946.

At the Montego Bay Conference in 1947 the islands' formidable problems seemed counterbalanced by at least one conspicuous asset: a developing will for common nationhood. Yet before the Federation was established in 1958 there was already cause for concern. Few if any of the territories were deeply moved by a broad vision of Caribbean unity for which they were prepared to relinquish hard-won gains. It remained to be seen whether the embryonic sense of West Indian nationhood would be strong enough to bind together a Federation which, unlike most such unions, offered few obvious economic advantages and, like all federal states, clearly required sacrifices. Was it an impractical dream of idealists, a luxury too expensive for poor communities? 'How to marry expectation with reality,' wrote Norman Manley in 1955, 'how to create a larger field for ambition, how to overcome the disadvantage of being too small to be heard in a world where silence means stagnation, how to make a real culture and a real unity out of all the richness of our diversity, ... how to overcome distance and poverty and win out against large odds, these are the challenges that Federation faces.'[23]

6

Federation: the first two years, 1958-9

The Federation of The West Indies came into being on 3 January 1958, before national elections were held or a prime minister chosen. Lord Hailes, formerly a British Conservative Party Whip, became Governor General: an appointment attacked in certain quarters. Critics argued that the British government sacrificed the well-being of the Federation in order to give a political plum to a party official. The post, they contended, demanded strong and intelligent leadership and should therefore have been awarded to an experienced and tactful colonial civil servant. Not even limitless tact on the United Kingdom's part, however, could have held the Federation together. West Indians were determined to achieve independence and abolish colonialism as rapidly as possible. They strongly resented the power retained by the British government under the federal constitution. Under such circumstances the appointment of a Governor General who was much more than a figurehead would almost certainly have been bitterly resented. When Lord Hailes arrived in the West Indies at the beginning of 1958 an interim administration was appointed which held office until a permanent government was established on 22 April of that year.

The Federation included ten British colonies with a land area of over eight thousand square miles and a population of some three million people. The constituent units were Antigua (with its dependencies of Redonda and Barbuda), Barbados, Dominica, Grenada, Jamaica (with the Cayman Islands), Montserrat, St Kitts-Nevis-Anguilla, St Lucia, St Vincent, and Trinidad and Tobago. The Grenadines, as dependencies of St Vincent and Grenada, were also included.

Jamaica, with 4,411 square miles and 1,609,800 people, accounted for 51.6 per cent of the Federation's population. Trinidad and Tobago, with over 800,000 people, comprised another 26.5 per cent, while its area and population roughly equalled that of the remaining eight units. Thus the two largest islands had between them more than three-quarters of the Federation's total area and population. Montserrat, the smallest unit, with thirty-two square miles, had only some 14,000 inhabitants.

FEDERAL PARTIES

The first West Indian national party, the nominally socialist Federation of Labour Parties of the British Caribbean, was formed in June 1956. The moving spirits were Norman Manley, leader of the Jamaica People's National Party; Grantley Adams, leader of the Barbados Labour Party; V.C. Bird, leader of the Antigua Labour Party; Robert L. Bradshaw, leader of the St Kitts' Workers League; J.N. France, a St Kitts trade unionist; Eric Gairy, leader of the Grenada Labour Party; Carl La Corbinière, general secretary of the St Lucia Labour Party; and W.H. Bramble, president of the Montserrat Trade and Labour Union. There was no representative from Trinidad, which then boasted some dozen parties of which three were avowedly socialist. Dr Eric Williams's People's National Movement, which attracted much support from the middle class and from Trinidad's large Catholic majority, at first hesitated to join a professedly socialist national party.

The inaugural conference of the Federation of Labour Parties met on 1 September 1956 at St Lucia, when its name was changed to the Caribbean (later West Indies) Federal Labour Party. James Griffiths, deputy leader of the Labour opposition in the United Kingdom and a former Secretary of State for the Colonies, attended this meeting and announced a gift of £5000 over a three-year period from the British Labour Party to the new West Indian party. A small token gift was tendered by Canada's Co-operative Commonwealth Federation. Although British Guiana and British Honduras eventually decided not to join the Federation, they sent delegates to these discussions.

Foundation members were the labour parties of Antigua, Barbados, St Lucia, and Grenada, the People's National Party of Jamaica, the St Kitts' Workers League and Labour Party, and the Montserrat Trade and Labour Union. The Dominica Labour Party joined later in 1956. Mr Manley was elected as leader, Mr Adams, Mr Bradshaw, and Mr Bird as first, second, and third vice-presidents, and Mr La Corbinière as treasurer.

The St Lucia meeting drafted a constitution providing a biennial conference, for which an elected executive council would act between meetings. This council, to convene at least once a year, was to be composed of party officers and seven others elected at the biennial conference. Member parties were required to pledge active support of the trade union movement and of public ownership or control where this would best serve the public interest, and to advocate a society offering equal opportunities for all, regardless of colour, race, or religion. The new party stood for political, economic, social, and cultural progress in the Caribbean area, development and expression of public opinion, and political self-determination in the region.

In May 1957, in order to include Trinidad's non-socialist People's National Movement, returned to power in September 1956, the constitution of the West Indies Federal Labour Party was amended to allow admission of progressive parties and democratic trade unions, whether technically socialist or not. Under this category Dr Williams's Party affiliated with the Federal Labour Party. Leading members of the People's National Movement, however, neither forgot nor forgave their original rebuff.

The West Indies Federal Labour Party (WIFLP) thus originated as a loose combination of the ruling parties in each constituent territory except St Vincent. Associate membership was open to parties in British Guiana and British Honduras, but no provision was made for individual members. Early in January 1958 the WIFLP issued a political manifesto which formed its election platform. This advocated a democratic socialist society, maintenance of close contacts with countries with which the islands had strong cultural and economic ties, encouragement of agriculture and tourism, and establishment of a central bank to expand credit resources throughout the area. Other prominent aims were dominion status within five years for the Federation, full internal self-government in all the units, encouragement of British Guiana, British Honduras, and the Bahamas to join the union, and an international project, similar to the Colombo Plan, for technical and financial aid to the Caribbean.

A week after the formation of the West Indies Federal Labour Party in 1956 Sir Alexander Bustamante announced that the Jamaica Labour Party intended to participate in federal politics. Making the best of two worlds, he explained that he was both 'definitely "Labour" and a believer in private enterprise.'[1] In May 1957 he founded the federal Democratic Labour Party, with a comprehensive programme offering something for everyone. It attacked communism, fascism, and socialism and advocated 'an enlightened ... democratic policy, ... protection of labour, ... social and economic advancement of all classes, and ... encouragement of private enterprise.' Unlike the West Indies Federal Labour Party, the Democratic Labour Party admitted as members both individuals and affiliated parties. Sir Alexander Bustamante was unanimously elected leader; and Ashford Sinanan and Victor Bryan of Trinidad and Ebenezer Joshua of St Vincent were chosen first, second and third deputy leaders. Other members of the executive were Donald Sangster, Mrs Rose Leon, and Morris Cargill,[2] all of Jamaica, and Bhadase Maraj of Trinidad.

Foundation members of the federal Democratic Labour Party were the Jamaica Labour Party, three Trinidad and Tobago organizations (the Party of

Political Progress Groups, the Trinidad Democratic Labour Party, and the Tobago Labour Party), the People's Progressive Party of St Lucia, and a number of individuals. Among the latter were Mr Maraj, leader of the People's Democratic Party of Trinidad, Mr Sinanan of the same party, Roy Josephs, sometime Minister of Education in Trinidad, and Albert Gomes, formerly Minister of Trade and Commerce in that island.

The often confused party situation in the West Indies was especially complicated in St Vincent where by October 1957 applications for affiliation with the West Indies Federal Labour Party had been made by both major parties: Ebenezer Joshua's People's Political Party and Dr Milton Cato's St Vincent Labour Party. The latter was ultimately approved. Mr Joshua ultimately adhered to Sir Alexander's party because he was annoyed at being kept waiting for a decision on his application to join the Federal Labour Party. Despite his reputation for radicalism he then promptly denounced socialism and was rewarded by being chosen third deputy leader at the first annual meeting of the federal Democratic Labour Party.

In November 1957 a group of Trinidadians formed a new organization, the Federal Democratic Party, generally supposed to be inspired by Mr Gomes, who had not received the recognition he considered his due in Sir Alexander's Democratic Labour Party. The predominantly East Indian Trinidad Democratic Labour Party, which contested the 1958 federal election and was affiliated with the national party of the same name, was formed by a combination of several small parties which had contested the 1956 election in Trinidad. Its founder and chairman was Mr Bryan, formerly of the Trinidad Labour Party.

The platform announced at the federal Democratic Labour Party's first annual convention in January 1958 formed its election manifesto. This emphasized West Indian unity, freedom of worship and of speech, encouragement of trade unions, a climate of opinion favourable to both private industry and labour, development of human and economic resources, and expansion of tourism. Like its rival, the party pledged itself to work for the entry of British Guiana and British Honduras into the Federation. It would be disastrous, the manifesto contended, for the new state to be governed by socialists dedicated to public ownership, bureaucracy, and frustrating controls.

While stressing the probable costs of union and eventual dominion status, the federal Democratic Labour Party then considered these responsibilities inseparable from nationhood. Envisaging the need for much financial aid, it promised to press for loans and technical assistance in order to raise standards of living and avoid high taxation. It also urged strengthening existing ties with the United Kingdom, the United States, and Canada, and fostering 'very strong and profitable friendships' with neighbouring countries.[3] The Jamaican origin of the

Democratic Labour Party was apparent not only in the fact that it was founded and led by Sir Alexander, but in its advocacy of early freedom of movement within the Federation, coupled with the caution that rash implementation of a customs union would be unrealistic and dangerous.

The two major national parties were thus headed by the leaders of the government and the opposition in Jamaica. The fact that neither was willing to forsake the Jamaican for the federal scene made their Eastern Caribbean supporters feel uncomfortably like pawns in the game of Jamaican party politics: a position they understandably resented.

Scarcely any common views united the amorphous groups which formed the two major national parties, whose platforms showed few marked differences. The Democratic Labour Party said nothing about full internal self-government for the units, which the West Indies Federal Labour Party advocated. The latter tactfully omitted any mention of the two most contentious issues, freedom of movement and customs union. The FDLP attacked socialism, whereas the WIFLP hoped to create a democratic socialist society but did not elaborate the concept. Indeed few people in the British Caribbean, including members of parties affiliated with the Federal Labour Party, would have been prepared to say precisely what socialism involved.

Mr Manley and Mr Adams described themselves as moderate socialists but in office showed little disposition to implement radical measures. The socialism for which his party stood, Mr Manley told the People's National Party conference in 1957, did not mean nationalizing everything. 'Socialism,' he said, 'is about true equality. That is all.'[4] On winning the Jamaican election two years later he declared: 'Of course we do not intend to introduce extreme socialist measures. Our main purpose is still to encourage the inflow of venture capital for every type of enterprise ... and particularly for the development of industry and tourism.'[5]

Most West Indian parties have been held together more by the personalities of charismatic leaders than the Burkeian principle of agreement on common beliefs. The formation of federal parties as loose insular groupings involved a haphazard combination of strong-minded politicians, often accustomed to autocratic rule over their own territories. Before the Federation was officially launched it was already clear that these alliances would be uneasy and their future dubious.

When Mr Adams announced in 1957 that the federal government would not give grants to non-labour administrations in the islands, the Jamaican *Daily Gleaner* voiced its conviction that 'Mr Manley does not subscribe to any such nonsense.'[6] By the end of that year West Indian journalists were freely predicting divorce on grounds of incompatibility among the partners in both national parties. Rejoicing at the birth of the new state was mingled with the voices of local Cassandras prophesying doom.

CHOICE OF A PRIME MINISTER

A federal prime minister proved unexpectedly difficult to find. In an attempt to avoid or diminish tensions between national and unit loyalties it had been decided that seats in central and insular legislatures could not be held concurrently. Events were to show that such conflicts could scarcely have been sharper, and the spirit if not the letter of the law was transgressed when the same men served as leaders of both Jamaican and federal parties.

From the time of the inaugural meeting of the Federal Labour Party in June 1956 it was freely prophesied that Mr Manley would become the West Indies' first prime minister — a post he could undoubtedly have had if he wished. It was soon apparent, however, that the ablest political leaders preferred to remain in their own islands. 'Can an Adams, a Williams, or a Manley,' asked the *Daily Gleaner*, 'afford to let go the strings of local political machinery and perhaps threaten the structure he has built up over the months and years? Could he maintain control of local politics from a federal capital that may be hundreds of miles distant?'[7]

As Mr Manley had been returned to office only in 1955 and Dr Williams in the following year, their newly assumed responsibilities at home were naturally still uppermost in their minds. Their reluctance to seek national office was accentuated by their islands' striking political and economic development during the previous decade and by the equally striking weakness of the powers allocated to the federal government. The West Indian national stage, unlike that of Canada at the time of Confederation, appeared to offer a more restricted rather than a more important sphere of action. 'It is asking a lot of local leaders,' the *Jamaica Times* remarked presciently on 12 October 1957, 'to abandon the certainty of local power and position for the possibility of a place in a federal government of uncertain authority. Yet only such sacrifices will ever make federation a worthwhile proposition. If talent is to remain in local legislatures, and only the second-raters are to gather at Chaguaramas, then the West Indian Federation will remain weak and ineffective, doomed to failure from the outset.'

As late as the autumn of 1957 the Jamaican *Gleaner*'s political reporter argued that as federation approached it became increasingly clear that West Indians believed its success depended on leadership by Norman Manley: widely respected not only in his own island but in the Eastern Caribbean. Despite the wishes of most Jamaicans that he should remain at home, the *Gleaner* contended that his duty to the new state outweighed his responsibility to Jamaica. Without him as national prime minister, 'the West Indies Federation will lose substance before it ever begins to affect the consciousness of West Indians at large ... It is a sacrifice that he must make or lose for himself and Jamaica, the regard of the rest of the British West Indies ... There are only two alternatives,' the article concluded. 'He can remain Chief Minister of Jamaica, carrying out our own ambitious economic programme to the pleasure of his supporters in Jamaica but to the displeasure of all the people of the Eastern Caribbean. Or he can go into the Federation against the wishes of most Jamaicans and become the historic father of the new nation.'[8]

This view was supported by the *Jamaica Times* in the article previously cited. 'The truth is,' it observed, 'that only Mr Manley has the prestige, the experience, the unquestioned ability to give the first federal government the status it ... needs. Not only his brilliance of mind but his strength of character and his utter integrity raise him to a peak far above other West Indian leaders ... Whatever the ... exigencies of his political situation in Jamaica, Mr Manley should go on to give leadership at the centre.'

He ultimately decided not to do so. Yet until early in 1958 he seemed the most probable and popular choice for federal prime minister, especially as both Dr Williams and Sir Grantley Adams announced that they would not accept the position. In mid-January, however, Mr Manley told a large and cheering party rally that he had decided it was his duty to stay and develop Jamaica so that this island would be on an economic par with Trinidad when the time came to request full independence for the Federation. His determination to remain in Jamaica he considered in the best interests of the new state.[9] Two months later he reiterated his agreement with Sir Alexander Bustamante's view that federal union was essential.[10]

Mr Manley's decision was doubtless influenced by belief that Jamaican politics were more important than national affairs, by a desire to press forward with uncompleted projects in his own island, by coolness towards federation among his supporters at home, and by fear that without him the People's National Party would lose the next Jamaican election. His public explanation was that he could best serve the new union by combatting its enemies in Jamaica. Whatever his reasons, Mr Manley's decision almost certainly predestined the Federation to failure.

Although he remained president of the West Indies Federal Labour Party, his influence on its counsels was permanently weakened by his decision not to seek the national prime ministership. During the previous two decades he had been an outstanding champion of federation. Yet his open preference for insular as opposed to national politics led his Eastern Caribbean colleagues to consider Mr Manley first and foremost a Jamaican nationalist and only secondarily a West Indian. His decision not to 'go federal' accentuated Jamaicans' doubt that their interests would be protected in the new union. It also helped to foster their latent sentiment against federation.

This outcome was foretold on 17 January 1958, by *The Times* (London) which, in a regretful and perceptive comment on Mr Manley's decision, observed that Jamaica seemed the only island strong enough to stand alone. 'Therefore the temptation to drift out of a Federation whose weight is in the Eastern Caribbean will be great. Federation without Jamaica would be meaningless. The surest, probably only means of firmly enmeshing it into Federation is to ensure that the first Federal Prime Minister is a Jamaican.'

Thus even before the first national election the federal government's prestige was lowered by the obvious preference for local politics of the two leading West Indian statesmen: Mr Manley and Dr Williams, who was twenty years younger than Mr Manley or Sir Grantley Adams. Their decision set an example to their colleagues and established a pattern whereby able aspirants for political power were reluctant to leave insular for federal politics. In too many instances the national contest was left to men of second- or third-rate abilities. This struggle between local and central loyalties, with the former prevailing, doomed the Federation from the outset. A distinguished Jamaican or Trinidadian prime minister would almost certainly have been able to win his island's firm allegiance to the new state. As it was, this vital support never materialized. Few Jamaicans or Trinidadians ever really considered themselves West Indians.

Under these unpropitious circumstances the only outstanding public man willing to stake his future career on belief in a united British Caribbean was the convinced federalist, Sir Grantley Adams, long Premier of Barbados and the first Deputy Leader of the Federal Labour Party, who eventually agreed to become Prime Minister of The West Indies. Unfortunately it soon became clear that he lacked sufficient influence to preserve the Federation.

THE FEDERAL ELECTION

The campaign preceding the federal election of 25 March 1958 for the forty-five seats in the national House of Representatives aroused little public interest in the British Caribbean, partly because of the absence of clearcut issues. The only government leaders who stood as candidates were those of Barbados, Montserrat, and St Kitts. As insular parties affiliated with the West Indies Federal Labour Party led by Mr Manley controlled all unit legislatures except in St Vincent, its victory was generally considered assured.

In the event, however, the WIFLP won only twenty-two seats, although these were drawn from nine of the ten territories. Thirteen members of the federal lower house came from the Leeward and Windward Islands and Barbados. The ruling parties in both Jamaica and Trinidad were decisively defeated: in Jamaica by five to twelve and in Trinidad and Tobago by four to six. The extent of ordinary West Indians' concern for their new state was indicated by the size of the polls. Some 74 per cent of the electorate voted: under 26 per cent in

Barbados, and under 54 per cent in Jamaica, as opposed to over 65 per cent in the two preceding Jamaican elections.

The holders of the twenty seats won by the federal Democratic Labour Party headed by Sir Alexander Bustamante came from only three islands: twelve from Jamaica, six from Trinidad, and two from St Vincent. The balance of power was held by one Independent, Mrs Florence Daysh of the Barbados National Party, and two members of Grenada's United Labour Party whose affiliation was at first doubtful. One of the latter was removed from political controversy by being appointed Deputy Speaker. The government's shaky majority was bolstered by the fact that Mrs Daysh, as a Barbadian, was usually willing to support the Prime Minister, who came from Barbados, and had indicated this during her election campaign.

The federal government was also aided by the constitutional provision that senators be appointed by the Governor General after consultation with Governors of the various units, who were required to consult with their Executive Councils. This produced a Senate strongly favourable to the West Indies Federal Labour Party. The upper house also included a number of distinguished and politically neutral members such as Douglas Judah of Jamaica, Dr Cato and Sir Archibald Cuke of Barbados, and T. Albert Marryshow of Grenada. Fortunately for Sir Grantley, the constitution stipulated that at least three of a cabinet of eleven should be senators. It could be argued, however, that the federal upper house was no more genuinely national than the lower, as more than half its members were drawn from territorial legislatures or Executive Councils.

The new Prime Minister was from the outset in the anomalous position of being second-in-command of his parliamentary supporters, since Mr Manley and Sir Alexander, without seats in the national legislature, led the two federal parties. Even the Jamaican press criticized this situation and argued that Mr Manley should conform with accepted political practice by relinquishing to Sir Grantley formal leadership of the West Indies Labour Party.[11]

The opposition parties in Jamaica and Trinidad had won a majority of their islands' seats in the federal House of Representatives. Ashford Sinanan of Trinidad, chairman of the national Democratic Labour Party, assumed the duties of leader of the opposition in the federal lower house. The first deputy leader was Robert Lightbourne of the Jamaica Labour Party, who held a similar post in Jamaica.

Mr Manley's refusal to stand for the prime ministership probably accounted for the fact that the West Indies Labour Party secured only five of Jamaica's seventeen seats in the national lower house. Dr Williams's similar refusal was doubtless the major reason why his People's National Movement secured only four of Trinidad and Tobago's ten federal seats as opposed to six won by the Trinidad Democratic Labour Party, affiliated with the Democratic Labour Party of the West Indies. Most urban blacks in Trinidad supported the People's National Movement in the national election and most East Indians the Democratic Labour Party.

The outcome was that the two largest and most important territories, which between them accounted for 78 per cent of the Federation's population, received less representation in the national cabinet than the small islands of the Eastern Caribbean which, with 15 per cent of the population, returned almost two-thirds of the West Indies Federal Labour Party members. To them the most important cabinet posts were allocated, although the Council of State included members from eight of the ten units.[12]

The dissatisfaction of Jamaica and Trinidad at this situation was not lessened by criticism of the calibre of some members they returned, who were widely dubbed a 'second eleven.' The fact that the leaders of both national parties were Jamaican accentuated the other islands' fear of Jamaican domination without lessening Jamaicans' fears that federalism would affect their island's economy adversely. Jamaicans complained that the national government was bound to be dominated by Trinidad, because the capital was in Port-of-Spain. The majority of opposition members came from the two larger islands which had to bear the chief costs of federation and could expect least economic advantage from it. They had, on the whole, more ability and legislative experience than the government's supporters.

Leading Jamaican public men, including many members of the business community, were already doubtful whether, without adequate communications by sea, the expanded market of a united West Indies would materially aid their manufactures. Although Jamaica was the second wealthiest territory in the Federation, they considered it too poor to afford any measures that might hamper its infant industries and retard its economic growth.

Sir Alexander was able to exercise more control over the Democratic Labour opposition, with its twelve Jamaican representatives, than could Mr Manley over the Federal Labour Party, most of whose members were not Jamaican and therefore not subject to local party discipline. This situation was the more serious because there was little national party organization. During the four years of the Federation's existence the whole West Indies Federal Labour Party never held a formal meeting, apart from annual conferences, because its leading members were scarcely on speaking terms.

National policy emerged less from cabinet discussions than from statements by individual leaders. This was doubtless inevitable, with Mr Manley and Dr Williams without seats in the federal House and party leadership divided between

Mr Manley and Sir Grantley. While the government from the outset was beset by internal divisions, Sir Alexander was at first pre-eminent in the Democratic Labour Party, within whose ranks there was even less pretence of democratic discussion. As time went on, discipline in both national parties became at best weak and at worst non-existent. Members' loyalty to their own islands and local parties was commonly paramount, dwarfing concern for wider issues of central policy. Thus from the beginning West Indian national politics operated in an Alice-in-Wonderland atmosphere of unreality almost guaranteed to strangle the Federation at its birth.

THE FIRST SESSION OF THE FEDERAL PARLIAMENT

Despite ominous tensions behind the scenes the federal parliament in Port-of-Spain was opened with éclat by Princess Margaret on 22 April 1958, amid what then seemed the general enthusiasm of West Indians, the unqualified support of the United Kingdom, and the friendly good will of other members of the Commonwealth. Sir Grantley hailed the advent of the new nation as a climax to the hopes of many generations of men and women inspired by the vision of a united West Indies. Yet once the union was consummated and the first honeymoon period over, it became increasingly apparent that the British Caribbean peoples would find profoundly difficult the attempt to dwell together in unity.

The Federation clearly faced formidable problems. 'It's a boy. A bouncing baby boy,' Mr Marryshow had said in 1956, 'and all that is required now is post-natal care.'[13] The nurture required by a singularly sickly infant proved sufficient to daunt the most devoted founding fathers. And with the exception of Sir Grantley, few West Indian politicians exhibited much devotion to their national state.

Article 118 of the constitution provided for review by a conference *within* five years of the Federation's inception. This proviso, substituted in 1957 for *during* the new state's fifth year, was designed to ensure early achievement of full dominion status for The West Indies. On 26 June 1958, however, within six months of its establishment, the national House of Representatives passed a motion by a Jamaican member of the opposition to hold such a conference within a year. This premature decision, supported by Trinidadian members of the opposition, to reconsider a constitution forged with difficulty over many years, proved disastrous. Although based on an understandable desire to win autonomy for the new state, it reopened all the contentious issues so recently and hardly resolved. Jamaica was already less concerned with dominion status for the Federation than with reduction of its powers.

Sir Alexander Bustamante had been prepared to support federation and head a federal party when the Democratic Labour Party seemed to have a chance of forming the national government. When, however, his party was defeated in the general election, his enthusiasm promptly dwindled. Within a week after the opening of the new parliament he was complaining that Jamaica would get nothing out of 'this messy Federation to which we have been committed by Mr Manley except one thing: taxpayers' money to be sent to Trinidad for no other purpose but ... to improve the economy of the ... small islands and to deplete the revenue of Jamaica.'[14] The traditional function of an opposition is to watch, criticize, and, if possible, control the government. Under Sir Alexander, however, the Democratic Labour Party soon devoted its energies to attacking West Indian union.

Kenneth Hill, the Jamaican member of the federal opposition who had first proposed early revision of the constitution (a move previously supported by the Jamaica Labour Party), declared during the summer of 1958 that this island, which in his view had always led the others politically and economically, should take the lead in ending the 'tragic farce of union.'[15] By September Sir Alexander was announcing that he would prefer to see both the national opposition, which he led, and the Federation destroyed 'rather than have the economy of Jamaica hurt.'[16] Thus before the new state was a year old the growing force of Jamaican nationalism, in 1947 directed against the United Kingdom, was turned against the federal government.

Trinidad, for its part, was equally irritated at coupling free migration among the islands with customs union. Dr Williams saw no reason to give up his territory's right to limit immigration simply because a federation had been established. While for reasons of prestige Trinidad had been eager to obtain the national capital, its location in Port-of-Spain accentuated rivalry between the governments of that island and the Federation. It was inevitable, Dr Williams wrote later, that his strong nationalist ministry should conflict with a weak federal administration situated in its territory and supported by the British Colonial Office.[17] 'It looks,' a Jamaican journalist observed wryly, 'as if Federation is starting to fall apart even before it has got properly stuck together.'[18]

Existing tensions were drastically increased when the Prime Minister, Sir Grantley Adams, told the Jamaican press on 30 October 1958 that, if any island tried to raise new tariff barriers against goods from other territories in the Federation or undertook to protect investors against competition from other parts of the British Caribbean, his government might find it necessary to take action. His administration wanted to levy a national income tax within five years, would certainly do so after that period had elapsed, and could make such a levy retroactive. Unit governments, he warned, should bear this in mind when planning industrialization. Before they extended tax holidays or other concessions to new industries, he suggested that they should consult with the federal government.[19]

The Jamaican *Gleaner* reacted with the headline: 'Adams: Cannot Hope to Continue as Federation Without Control of Own Revenue.' Jamaicans interpreted the Prime Minister's statement as meaning that, when the national government secured the right to levy income tax, this might be made retroactive to the time when the Federation was first established. They neither forgot nor forgave the threat.

Although Sir Grantley was without constitutional sanction for implementing these proposals, the Jamaican government and public took them at face value and were correspondingly indignant. Mr Manley protested vigorously and flatly denied that the federal government could impose an income tax within the next five years or that any such levy could be made retroactive. 'If ever,' he wrote in a public letter to the *Daily Gleaner* on 2 November 1958, 'there should arise any possibility of the Federal Government contemplating policies ... disrupting the economic development of Jamaica, ... [the island] would be forced to reconsider her position in regard to Federation itself.' His concern was understandable. He had no advance knowledge that Sir Grantley intended to make such statements, which were certain to inflame the already mounting opposition to federation in Jamaica, where elections were due within six months.

Sir Alexander Bustamante was no less caustic. He cabled Sir Grantley that he had put nearly every Jamaican against federalism by threatening, with the support of Trinidad's People's National Movement, to impose a retroactive levy unless Jamaica opened its doors wide to customs union. 'If Jamaica is to continue in the Federation,' he declared, 'then the Constitution will have to be rewritten, so that the Federal Government will have no right whatever to impose any kind of taxation upon Jamaica, without Jamaica's prior agreement.' Failing this, it must secede. His country, he maintained, was not getting its money's worth for the £800,000 a year it contributed to the national exchequer. He demanded representation by population in the federal parliament, to increase the number of Jamaican members, if the island was not to withdraw from the union.[20] Even Mr Manley declared: 'No one can compel us to stay if we wish to leave.'[21]

When shortly after the national parliament opened the contentious problem of customs union was raised, the federal opposition bitterly attacked proposed changes. These involved internal free trade and uniform external tariffs. The latter meant lowering rates then levied by some units and raising those of others. Jamaica strongly objected to the prospect of interference with the incentives it offered new industries, including tax-free entry of raw materials. On this matter Mr Manley largely supported the stand of Sir Alexander, his chief political rival.

Despite more than a decade of discussions and conferences the underlying implications of federalism were neither widely publicized nor generally understood by Jamaicans, who were shocked at the suggestion that the union involved some sacrifice of local autonomy. In the Eastern Caribbean also Sir Grantley's statements were widely criticized. In Trinidad, however, they were stoutly defended by Dr Williams, whose support only increased anti-federal sentiment in Jamaica.

Sir Grantley subsequently pointed out to Jamaicans, who complained about paying 43 per cent of federal revenues, that of their £820,000 contribution the major portion was returned to their island. During the Federation's first year 30 per cent of its revenues were allocated to the University College of the West Indies. Among other expenses defrayed by the national exchequer were the upkeep of the West India Regiment, stationed in Jamaica, and the salaries and travel allowances of the seventeen Jamaican members of the federal House of Representatives.[22]

The Trade and Tariffs Commission, appointed in accordance with a decision of the London Conference of 1956 and chaired by Sir William Croft, reported in November 1958. Emphasizing the need for a regional economic policy, it recommended partial free trade and assimilation by 1961 of the varying tariffs levied by the ten territories, with full customs union five years later. A federation without such a union, the commissioners pointed out, was virtually unknown, and wise use of a tariff was essential for necessary industrial development in the whole region. To mitigate the units' loss of revenue they recommended that the islands should be enabled to collect consumption duties or sales taxes on spirits, tobacco, and oil. Another provocative issue was raised by the commissioners' observation that free movement of persons and capital was a natural corollary to free movement of goods.[23]

Customs union had not formed part of the federal agreement because of the opposition of Jamaica, whose tariff was the highest in the area while that of Trinidad was the lowest, although all the territories derived much revenue from such duties. It would have been relatively easy to compensate poorer islands such as Dominica and Grenada for the loss involved, but by no means easy to compensate industrial Jamaica. The latter had agreed in 1957 to Trinidad's wish that industrial development should be included in the concurrent list, so that both the Federation and the islands could legislate on the matter. Jamaica soon regretted this concession and was alarmed at the prospect of an early customs union, although at the conference in 1956 Mr Manley had argued for prompt introduction of internal free trade.

By the summer of 1958 Dr Williams was announcing that his government would not support freedom of movement as soon as possible and freedom of trade as late as possible.[24] Sir Alexander Bustamante declared that he would prefer to see the Federation collapse, rather than have thousands of Jamaicans unemployed owing to dumping of Trinidadian manufactured goods. His supporter, Ken Hill, said Jamaica should lead in abolishing a federation which promised no advantage to ordinary Jamaicans.[25]

In the autumn of 1958, while he was still leader of the national opposition, Sir Alexander attacked the Federation and described as a traitor to his country any Jamaican who supported it. On 23 November the Jamaica Labour Party approved a motion in the federal lower house by one of its members, Robert Lightbourne, for a new national constitution which should outlaw retroactive taxation and federal interference with insular taxes. It advocated reconstitution of the house to provide representation by population. Later unanimously supported by the Jamaican legislature, this proposal was defeated by the federal parliament.

By this time it was clear that both Jamaican parties were agreed that their island should not remain in the Federation unless the changes they wanted were obtained. Mr Manley's conversion to support of a weak federal government cost him much of the liking and respect he had hitherto commanded throughout the Eastern Caribbean. Thereafter he could be viewed more as an antagonist than a supporter of the Federation. Thus it was scarcely surprising that he subsequently lost the referendum of 1960.

A decision to build an oil refinery in Jamaica produced a rift between Mr Manley and Dr Williams, as hitherto Trinidad was the only British West Indian territory to refine oil. The two men were further estranged by their very different attitudes to Sir Grantley's threat of retroactive taxation. Jamaica's insistence on an early constitutional review, before the Federation had a chance to establish itself as a focus for a West Indian patriotism which transcended insular loyalties, practically ensured the downfall of the new nation. The well-publicized bickering of leading federal personalities was scarcely calculated to encourage public confidence or attract public esteem.

Jamaica's attitude towards the Federation provoked sharp criticism in the Eastern Caribbean. A St Lucian journalist described Jamaica as fast becoming the most insular territory. History, he warned, would condemn leaders who did their island a disservice by generating an atmosphere of narrow-mindedness for their own political ends. He urged all enlightened West Indians to support the Federation so that it might fulfil its promise.[26]

Trinidadians virtuously observed that it was a case of Jamaica for the Jamaicans, but Trinidad for the West Indies. They were little better pleased than

Jamaicans, however, when at New York in 1959 Sir Grantley described Barbadians as the most intelligent and industrious people in the British Caribbean, Trinidadians as preferring calypsos to hard work, and 50 per cent of Jamaicans as illiterate.[27] The element of truth in these observations made them no more palatable.

No one, however tactful and efficient, would have found it easy to be Prime Minister of The West Indies. The hard fact was that the federal government had been denied sufficient power or funds to provide many useful services or win the confidence and loyalty of its people. Far weaker and poorer than the governments of either Trinidad or Jamaica, the federal government necessarily suffered by comparison with them.

Yet on the first anniversary of the establishment of the national parliament, Sir Grantley reported with determined optimism and concluded: 'Our future is now in our own hands.' The Federation, he pointed out, had assumed responsibility for the University College of the West Indies, the national shipping service, Overseas Commissions in the United Kingdom and Canada, the Students' Liaison Service in Washington, the West India Regiment, the West Indies Meteorological Service, representation at such meetings as the Commonwealth Economic Conference in Montreal, and certain duties formerly undertaken by the Development and Welfare Organisation and the Regional Economic Committee.[28]

He did not mention that among its most difficult tasks was the allocation to the constituent territories of grants which were formerly administered by the British Treasury and Colonial Office. This important but thankless responsibility brought on the federal government much criticism previously directed against the United Kingdom by certain islands which, like Oliver Twist, were always asking for more. Of the £9 million made available for 1959-64 by the Colonial Development and Welfare Corporation, the federal government proposed to give £1,000,000 to Dominica, £900,000 to St Lucia, £540,000 each to Grenada and St Vincent, £500,000 to Barbados, £250,000 to Jamaica, £150,000 to the Caymans, Turks, and Caicos, and £100,000 to Trinidad and Tobago, retaining £3,240,000 for the Federation. National policy was to grant preferential treatment to the smaller and poorer territories which had most difficulty in attracting loans for development.[29]

The British government also entrusted the Federation with certain responsibilities for international affairs, including the right to negotiate and sign agreements with Venezuela and deal directly with the United Nations Technical Assistance Board. At the request of the units the federal government undertook various surveys, commissioned studies of harbour developments, and provided the services of advisers on such matters as agriculture, fisheries, forestry, housing, health, and marketing. In view of its scanty funds this was a respectable, if modest, list of accomplishments.

The Minister of Finance, Robert Bradshaw of St Kitts, hampered by the difficulties of spreading thin a tiny budget, pointed out that the Federation could only 'crawl along financially.' Without external aid, it had no resources with which to tackle the major task of economic development, especially necessary in the small islands. Trinidad and St Kitts alone exported more than they imported.

'The economic and financial state of the Federation,' he declared, on moving second reading of the 1959 Appropriation Bill, 'demands that all of us as West Indians must learn more, produce more, export more, save more, work harder, invest more, and co-operate more fully ... to establish our nation as a viable political entity in this highly competitive world.'[30] He wished, Sir Grantley commented wistfully, that these words could be engraved on the mind of every West Indian. Mr Bradshaw might have added that the federal government had no funds to develop national resources or to introduce regional social security, health, and labour programmes. Its budget of BWI $11,301,832 for 1959 contrasted sharply with Trinidad's budget of almost $140,000,000 for the same year.

Jockeying for position among leading politicians steadily increased. From November 1958 Mr Manley and Sir Grantley were disputing about national economic policy. By the first week in January 1959 it was rumoured that Mr Manley was thinking of resigning the leadership of the Federal Labour Party. He raised the question of whether Jamaica had the right to secede. Many of his countrymen considered this an astute political gambit which, by playing on the widely held Jamaican conviction that Sir Grantley was anti-Jamaican, might help to swing support away from Sir Alexander in the island's forthcoming elections.

The Daily Gleaner contended that Jamaica's continued co-operation was essential and must be retained. It also argued against increased representation for Jamaica in the national House of Representatives. 'Secession,' it maintained, 'should be a last recourse when all hope for the federal union has fled and men have lost their reason.' Sir Grantley, for his part, declared that Jamaica would not and could not secede.[31]

Dissension within the ranks of the federal opposition came to a head on 22 January 1959, with the resignation of Badhase Maraj. Leader of the Trinidad section of the Federal Democratic Labour Party in the Trinidad and Tobago Legislative Council, he was generally considered the real power behind the scene. Ashford Sinanan, deputy leader of the national opposition, ruled that Mr Maraj had not resigned from the party and was still leader of the Trinidad opposition. He reversed Mr Gomes's suspension from the Trinidad party's executive and announced the formation of a new executive of which Victor Bryan remained a member but was no longer chairman. Mr Bryan was a member of the federal House of Representatives and chairman of the Trinidadian Democratic Labour Party. He promptly countered with the contention that the meeting at which the executive committee of the Trinidad Democratic Labour Party was dissolved and another formed was unconstitutional, and that consequently he remained party chairman.

The result was a split in the Trinidad section of the Federal Democratic Labour Party, with one faction officially led by Mr Sinanan but in fact by Mr Maraj, and the other by Mr Bryan. 'It looks,' observed *The Daily Gleaner*,' as if the whole idea of federalisation of politics in the West Indies can hardly survive Sir Grantley Adams' frequent side-shots at Mr. Manley ... and the shenanigans of the Democratic Labour Party.'[32]

The first meeting of the Regional Council of Ministers was held 12-13 January 1959. Composed of the Chief Ministers of the various units, with Sir Grantley as chairman, the council posed an implicit threat to his cabinet's freedom to determine national policy. This doubtless explained his reluctance to convene it. The sessions proved contentious. As a result of the controversy about Chaguaramas Dr Williams wanted to restrict federal powers over external affairs, although he advocated increasing them in other respects. Mr Manley, for his part, wished to weaken them.

The executive of Trinidad's People's National Movement, meeting at the same time as the Regional Council of Ministers, said it intended to urge that the Federation become independent on 22 April 1960. Its General Council did so in May 1959, when it called for a strong central government, independent within a year. Dr Williams also advocated immediate customs union.

Three days later, on 27 May, the Jamaican government laid before the island legislature its Ministry Paper No. 18. This demanded that the federal constitution be changed to provide representation by population in the lower house, the exclusion from the concurrent legislative list of income tax and industrial development, and a large measure of free trade before gradual inauguration of a customs union. This White Paper, which clearly illustrated the cleavage between Jamaica's and Trinidad's points of view, was unanimously adopted by the Jamaican legislature. To grant its demands would have been to weaken yet further the already weak central government by transferring to the units control over the development of industry, consumption duties, and excise and income taxes. The federal and Eastern Caribbean governments, although appalled at proposals which clearly presaged the collapse of any effective Federation, made little public protest, in order to avoid embarrassing Mr Manley before the imminent general election in Jamaica.

On 11 September 1959 the Legislative Council of Trinidad and Tobago also advocated revision of the federal constitution, but in a diametrically opposite way. It supported a resolution by Dr Williams endorsing 'a strong, independent Federation, vested with the powers and responsibilities pertaining thereto' and instructed the Trinidad and Tobago delegation to the forthcoming Inter-governmental Conference to seek support from other units for amendments to achieve this end and thus enable the Federation of The West Indies to assume its proper place in the Commonwealth and the United Nations.

These proposals, originally framed by a committee of the People's National Movement chaired by Dr Williams, had been approved by a party conference. Presented to the Legislative Council and amplified by the Trinidad government, they formed the basis for his *Economics of Nationhood*, published before the Intergovernmental Conference convened. This document urged full inde-pendence for the new nation as soon as possible, a strong federal government with power to impose any type of taxation, and a more comprehensive exclusive legislative list providing national jurisdiction over such matters as customs and excise duties, education, and national economic policy. Somewhat surprisingly, freedom of movement was included. The document thus advocated far wider central powers than the existing federal constitution permitted. It called for Barbados, Jamaica, and Trinidad to bear the whole cost of the Federation and also to contribute to most of the small islands. Without common allegiance to a national government, it contended, the federal concept would be discredited and the units more divided than before. The whole point of West Indian federation, in Dr Williams's view, was the opportunity it afforded to attempt by united efforts to bridge the widening gap between the more and the less advantaged territories.[33]

The third annual conference of the West Indies Federal Labour Party met on 26 September 1959. It did not, however, discuss what could be done to reconcile the divergent views of Jamaica and Trinidad and Tobago, on the curious ground that this meeting should not take decisions binding on territorial delegates to the imminent Intergovernmental Conference.

CONSTITUTIONAL ADVANCE IN THE UNITS

While the federal government confronted this collision between the Jamaican and Trinidadian points of view and struggled with other problems accentuated by its own weakness, insular nationalism in both large and small territories led to successful pressures for greater autonomy. These in turn grew by what they fed on. Each concession to the islands' desire for more local control strengthened particularism and weakened embryonic attachment to the centre. The economic gap among small and large units, already marked at the birth of the Federation, steadily widened.

Constitutional advances soon gave the two large islands more autonomy than the Federation possessed: a development which did nothing to smooth relations between them and the central government. Jamaica attained full internal self-government in 1959 under a constitution providing a Privy Council, a cabinet composed of the Premier and at least eleven other members, an enlarged nominated Legislative Council with no officials, and a forty-five-seat elected House of Representatives. Two or three members of the upper house were to be nominated by the Premier and the remainder appointed by the Governor after consultation with spokesmen for the diverse political points of view represented in the lower house. The Governor lost his executive and legislative reserve powers, while the Public, Judicial, and Police Service Commissions assumed certain executive responsibilities.

In the campaign preceding the Jamaican election of 23 July, 1959, three weeks after the new constitution took effect, Sir Alexander Bustamante, who had originally co-operated with the People's National Party in taking the island into Federation, made secession a plank of his platform. Mr Manley renewed his previous support of the union, but on condition that the national lower house should be strictly based on representation by population and the constitution amended to prohibit federal jurisdiction over industrial development, income taxes, and excise and consumption duties. 'Both parties in Jamaica,' commented a staff writer for *The Daily Gleaner*, 'are vieing with each other to disown Federation, but it is not a foundling. Both leaders supported it at one time or another and therefore cannot disown paternity now.'[34]

In the general election 68 per cent of the voters cast their ballots. The People's National Party, which in 1955 had won by only a small majority, now secured 54.9 per cent of the votes and twenty-nine of the forty-five seats in the House of Representatives. Sir Alexander's Jamaica Labour Party, with 44.3 per cent of the votes, captured the remaining sixteen.

In June 1957 and September 1958 the Trinidad and Tobago Legislative Council had passed two motions calling for more self-government. Discussions in London followed, and the Secretary of State for the Colonies agreed to recommend constitutional changes, including the introduction of cabinet government, which were effected by order-in-council in July 1959.

Hitherto Trinidad's Legislative Council had elected the ministers, including the Chief Minister. Thereafter the Governor appointed as Premier the leader of the majority party, who was empowered to choose and remove ministers and parliamentary secretaries. He normally presided, instead of the Governor, at meetings of the cabinet (enlarged from eight to nine members), the new name given the old Executive Council. The Colonial Secretary, now called Chief Secretary, and the Attorney General retained their seats in the cabinet and Legislative Council, but lost the right to vote in the cabinet. As long as the Premier retained majority support in the Legislative Council, the Governor was required to accept his advice on dissolution and prorogation. The Public and Police Service Commissions became independent executive bodies, and provision was made for a Judicial and Legal Service Commission with executive functions.

Dr Williams assumed the title of Premier, while continuing to serve as Minister of Finance, Planning, and Development. He hailed the new constitution as providing virtual independence. Two months later the former Chief Secretary, Sir Solomon Hochoy, a Trinidadian of Chinese origin, became the first West Indian Governor of Trinidad and Tobago. The Secretary of State for the Colonies later announced that future governors of Jamaica and Trinidad would be appointed after consultation with the premiers of these islands.

A select committee of Trinidad's Legislative Council, appointed in November 1958, presented in the following autumn proposals for further constitutional advance. These were discussed by the Colonial Office and re-examined when Iain Macleod, Secretary of State for the Colonies, visited Trinidad in June 1960. As a result Mr Macleod recommended full internal self-government for Trinidad and Tobago. The new constitution, effective after the general election of 4 December 1961, established a bicameral legislature, composed of a nominated Senate and a thirty-member House of Representatives elected by universal adult suffrage. Of the twenty-one senators twelve were appointed by the Governor on the advice of the Premier, two on the advice of the leader of the opposition, and seven at his own discretion to represent the major economic, religious, and social interests of the community. Presided over by a Speaker elected from its members, the second chamber might delay non-financial bills for a maximum of one year or two consecutive sessions.

The principal instrument of policy continued to be the cabinet, composed of the Premier and not more than eleven other members appointed on his advice. Thereafter the Attorney General, although still included in the cabinet, was no longer a public official, but a member of either legislative chamber, appointed after consultation with the Premier. The Governor lost his right, except on the advice of the Premier, to reserve or refuse assent to bills, unless he considered them inconsistent with the Queen's international commitments, prejudicial to the royal prerogative, or contrary to the constitution.

The smaller islands made more modest progress. From the inauguration of the Federation the Leewards and Windwards, supported by the larger territories, had maintained that in a union of equal partners each unit should be responsible for its own affairs. In March 1959 a conference of their representatives and the

federal government discussed further constitutional advance. Its recommendations were considered at London in June and formed the basis for changes
effective on 1 January 1960.[35]

Under the new dispensation the posts of Governor of the Leewards and
Governor of the Windwards were abolished and the Administrator of each unit
became the representative of the crown. The government leader in each territory
was styled Chief Minister. In every island except Montserrat the Executive
Council was formed by the Chief Minister and other ministers, one official
member (the Law Officer), and one nominated unofficial member. Montserrat's
Executive Council included the Chief Minister, two other ministers, one
nominated unofficial member, and two officials (the Financial Secretary and
the Law Officer). A Speaker presided over meetings of the Council, except in
Montserrat where the Administrator continued to do so.

The Legislative Councils were enlarged and their elected members increased
by two, except in Dominica, which obtained three additional seats, and St
Vincent, which obtained one. The nominated members of each Legislative
Council were reduced from three to two except in Montserrat, where they were
reduced from two to one. After the introduction of these new constitutions
general elections were held in the Windwards and Leewards in 1960 and 1961.

INTERGOVERNMENTAL CONFERENCE AND ITS AFTERMATH

Delegates from the Federation and its constituent territories, with two observers
from the Colonial Office, met in Port-of-Spain from 28 September to 9 October
1959 at an Intergovernmental Conference on constitutional revision. The lines of
battle had already clearly been drawn between Trinidad's desire for a strong
central government and Jamaica's insistence on one too weak to give important
leadership on any matter. Jamaica's attitude was partly explained by its distance
from the other islands and from the federal capital, although a common location
in Port-of-Spain scarcely developed cordial relations between the Trinidadian
and the national governments. Instead of lessening tensions this conference
sharply exacerbated them. The positions of both Jamaica and Trinidad were well
known in advance. Mr Manley showed no disposition to retreat from his
apparently immovable stand, although Dr Williams was prepared to discuss and
conciliate.

The Jamaican delegates advocated a revised national constitution prohibiting
the federal government from taxing incomes or profits or controlling industrial
development. They accepted the principle of customs union, but its
implementation only at some unspecified future date. Above all they wanted an
enlarged national lower house based more nearly on representation by

population. As Jamaicans made up 52 per cent of the Federation's population, they demanded thirty-two out of sixty-five members, or 49 per cent of the total. Of the remaining thirty-three seats they proposed that Trinidad and Tobago should have fifteen, Barbados five, and the Leewards and Windwards thirteen among them.

Simply to expedite union, they explained, their government had originally agreed to far fewer representatives than the island's population warranted. A perhaps more convincing explanation is that at Montego Bay and later pre-federal conferences Jamaica had been represented by Sir Alexander Bustamante. With little real interest in federation, he agreed to accept seventeen out of forty-five seats. While Sir Alexander was Chief Minister, Mr Manley did not object to this arrangement, which prevented the Jamaica Labour Party and its leader from exercising much power in federal politics.

When, however, Mr Manley became Premier of Jamaica, he viewed the matter differently, although he was first returned in 1955 and for the next four years made no complaint about Jamaica's representation. By 1959 Sir Alexander was pressing for more seats for the island. Mr Manley doubtless found it difficult to oppose this demand. At any rate, fresh from his second electoral victory, he then argued that his country had an unanswerable case for increased representation. However mathematically fair this contention, its acceptance would have meant that, with one supporting vote, Jamaica could determine every issue as it wished.

The Trinidadian delegates hastened to point out that on the basis of population their territory was also entitled to more seats. Yet for an effective federation they were prepared to make sacrifices — even to support freedom of movement and major taxing powers for the central government. Dr Williams, the leading advocate of a powerful national state, made a strong case for the proposals in his *Economics of Nationhood*.

These, however, were not even discussed, because the Jamaicans refused to consider any other matters until the issue of representation had been debated. Although Antigua proved to be Jamaica's only supporter, the delegates eventually agreed, despite strong protests, to concede the principle of representation by population, with no diminution in the number of seats currently held by each territory. They also decided to appoint two committees on constitutional and economic problems.[36] Here agreement ended, although all except the Jamaican delegates urged prompt attainment of dominion status by the Federation. Numerous other important issues were left undiscussed. After eight days of acrimonious debate many leading delegates were no longer speaking to each other, and the Jamaicans flew home, leaving various unsolved problems to be explored by committees.

Reporting back to the Jamaican House of Representatives on his return, Mr Manley stated that he thought the island could become an independent dominion, but that this would be too expensive and would not give it the status enjoyed by a united West Indies. He believed that Jamaica should remain within the union and try to make it work. He added, however, that 'any attempt to shape the Federation on the lines proposed by Trinidad would destroy Jamaica's economy. No Government of Jamaica would dare to continue in the Federation on those terms and this Government would not.'

Yet he reminded his countrymen that the Jamaican house had on eight occasions over nine years unanimously supported participation in a federal state, because its members realized that despite geographical separation West Indians were one people, with similar historical origins and problems. The trend throughout the world was towards aggregation, not separation, of territories. He still believed it immensely worthwhile for Jamaica to achieve nationhood within the framework of the Federation, if this were not at the expense of its economic development. The situation was different in the smaller islands of the Eastern Caribbean which, because they received grants-in-aid, could not have an independent economic policy. Jamaica had its own problems of overpopulation and poverty, and anything that retarded economic growth there or in Trinidad would injure the whole union. If the territories could not agree on the type of federation they wished to have, he believed no power would seek to force Jamaica to remain a member against its will.

D.C. Tavares, secretary of the Jamaica Labour Party, pressed for a referendum on whether the island should remain in the Federation. 'There are men who say,' Mr Manley replied, ' "go to the people – take a referendum ..." Maybe one day it will come to that. But not now ... It would be a betrayal of leadership and a betrayal of responsibility to do that now ... The people put us here on a stated policy to fight to achieve certain ends.' His own party was then sharply divided on the merits of federation. Within seven months he was to announce his decision to hold a referendum.

Sir Alexander, in response, said he wondered how Mr Manley could tell the Port-of-Spain conference that, if his government did not get the changes it wanted, Jamaica would secede, and then announce on his return home that this would be a tragedy. For his part, he was for federation, but not a slave to it. Jamaica should honour its contract to remain for five years, although it would be more autonomous if it achieved dominion status independently instead of having to 'drag those little islands along.' Yet 'if we cannot lead we must leave.' Jamaica, he declared, conveniently ignoring the repeated and unanimous votes of its legislature, had not been asked whether it wanted federation or not. He believed it ought eventually to secede, regardless of whether it secured all the changes it wished, but should remain for the next two or three years because it had agreed to do so.[37] At the conclusion of the debate the House of Representatives decided that Jamaica could not withdraw immediately and should take this step only if a federation on its terms could not be obtained. Sir Alexander, however, promptly demanded new elections on the question.

Dr Williams formally announced his government's policy at a mass meeting in Woodford Square on 10 January 1960. Jamaica's fear that federation would destroy its economy he considered unfounded since, like the other islands, it was represented in the national parliament. He agreed that there had been inadequate consultation with the constituent territories by the central government, a condition against which his People's National Movement had consistently protested. But to transfer control over industrial development from the federal to the unit governments, as Jamaica wished, would in his opinion mean replacing the existing union by 'some sort of Confederation the like of which exists nowhere in the world.' He thought Trinidad had a right and duty to defend its proposals for a revised constitution giving adequate powers to an independent federation. The secession of any unit would put the clock back to 1947. He urged on all the territories further examination of their mutual problems, not as supporters or opponents of Jamaica, but as members of the West Indian Federation.[38]

In December 1959 the Governor General forwarded to the Colonial Office a resolution by the national House of Representatives calling for cabinet government and independence as early as possible. On 12 January Mr Macleod cabled his agreement that the Federation should soon obtain full cabinet government subject to the concurrence of its territories, and explained that there was no difference of opinion about its becoming an independent member of the Commonwealth in the near future. He considered, however, that a date for independence should not be set before the Intergovernmental Conference reconvened to resolve the outstanding problems currently under consideration by its committees.

West Indians later criticized the United Kingdom as insufficiently interested in their young nation to intervene to preserve it at this and subsequent critical junctures. This view underestimated the difficulties of an imperial power in the second half of the twentieth century. The decision to federate was fundamentally an expression of British Caribbean anti-imperialist and nationalistic sentiment. Throughout the protracted pre-federal discussions British spokesmen reiterated that the United Kingdom would support Caribbean union only if the territories concerned clearly wanted it. As their enthusiasm dwindled and their internal disagreements multiplied, West Indians would almost certainly have resented any suggestion of pressure by the United Kingdom. When they found co-operation within a federal framework at first difficult and eventually impossible, no imperial government could have imposed unpopular decisions on them or forced them to dwell together in reluctant unity.

Doubtless there was justification for the criticism that, despite its lack of powers and funds, the Federation might have given a stronger lead on questions of economic development vitally important to the units by establishing an advisory body staffed by highly qualified experts. It might also have made more effective efforts to win the respect and confidence of its scattered citizens. Yet its position was singularly difficult, with leading members of the ruling national party increasingly antagonistic towards each other and towards the federal government. 'The real question,' as Sir Grantley pointed out, in 1959, was not 'whether the federal principle can work in the West Indies but whether the people of the West Indies want to make it work.'[39]

7

Mounting tensions, 1960-1

DOMINION STATUS FOR JAMAICA?

From the beginning of 1960 the future of the Federation grew increasingly precarious. In January Mr Manley and a delegation of Jamaicans discussed in London their island's position in relation to the national government. They emphasized the contrast between Trinidad's desire for a strong centre and their own view that Jamaica could not remain in a federation that could disrupt the island's development. If agreement on the character of an independent West Indies proved impossible, Jamaica would secede, leaving the other territories to a union of their own design.[1]

Mr Manley asked the Colonial Secretary to state the minimum requirements for dominion status and to indicate whether Jamaica might qualify, even if not in the Federation. He received a noncommittal reply, although it was later said and widely believed that he had been given a definite affirmative. The British government explained that a Commonwealth member must have adequate defence and diplomatic services and common tariff and immigration policies. Membership also implied a reasonable size, population, and financial resources. Jamaica alone would perhaps be in a marginal position. It would be impossible to anticipate the attitude of other members, but a Jamaican decision to leave the Federation would severely disappoint the United Kingdom and the rest of the Commonwealth. If its withdrawal broke up the federal union, this would undoubtedly affect consideration of any subsequent application for Commonwealth membership made by Jamaica.[2]

On his return home Mr Manley announced that he had told the Colonial Office that his government would not remain in a federation which, when independent, could control economic development throughout the British Caribbean. Unless his island's efforts to reach agreement with the other territories were soon successful, 'we will feel compelled and entitled to part company ... Jamaica will leave the Federation and will seek independence on her own ... I am satisfied that Jamaica is free to follow that course ... and ... that Britain will not attempt to force Jamaica to remain in the federation against her will.'[3]

Mr Manley was doubtless correct in assuming that the United Kingdom would not attempt to coerce an unwilling territory. He ignored, however, the fact that the federal constitution made no provision for secession by any unit and that major amendments, such as the withdrawal of a member, technically required legislation by the British parliament which had brought the Federation into being.

Mr Manley's interpretation of Mr Macleod's criteria for dominion status was both curious and partial. By no stretch of the imagination could the Colonial Secretary's stand be construed as giving unqualified advance approval of Jamaica's secession. Nor could any British government have been expected to give a forthright affirmative to a hypothetical question about the attitude it and other Commonwealth leaders would adopt on an issue of major importance, not only to Jamaica, but to all parts of The West Indies. Mr Manley's view that Jamaica was free to secede if it wished infuriated both the federal government and the other nine participating territories and played a significant part in destroying the Federation.

His journey to London was obviously designed to strengthen his hand in subsequent bargaining on the future of the Federation. When the Regional Council of Ministers met on 15 February, Jamaica's representatives sharply attacked the reduced Colonial Development and Welfare grants allocated to their island by the federal government for 1959-64. Dr Williams, in striking contrast, asked that the grant for Trinidad and Tobago be transferred to the University College of the West Indies.

For obvious reasons Mr Manley supported the federal government's proposals for equalization of freight rates among the various territories. Throughout the Eastern Caribbean, from Trinidad in the south to St Kitts in the north, uniform rates were levied, regulated by an intercolonial freight tariff committee: a voluntary organization of shipping interests of which the federal government was a member. A surcharge of BWI $7.50 a ton had hitherto been imposed on cargo from Jamaica to the Eastern Caribbean, to cover costs involved in the additional distance. Accepted in principle by all the other units, this proposal to equalize rates was strongly attacked by Trinidad and Tobago, on the ground that the small islands should not have to subsidize Jamaica. Trinidad and Jamaica were then the only major industrial producers within the Federation and the existing arrangement clearly favoured manufacturers in Trinidad.

THE JAMAICAN MINISTRY PAPER NO. 3

A working party of ministers and civil servants (on which Mr Manley and his Minister of Education, Mr Glasspole, represented Jamaica) recommended on 17 February 1960 that Jamaica should have thirty-one and Trinidad and Tobago seventeen members in a sixty-four-seat national House of Representatives. Mr Manley expressed satisfaction with this proposal which would give his island 48.5 per cent of the seats as opposed to the 37.7 per cent it then held.

Five days later he presented to the Jamaican House of Representatives a white paper (Ministry Paper No. 3) designed to counter Dr Williams's *Economics of Nationhood* and set forth his administration's proposals on the Federation. This paper argued that before independence the central government's relationship with the participating territories must be defined in a new constitution. It stressed the dichotomy at the Intergovernmental Conference between Trinidad's view that an autonomous federation should have full control over the economy of its units (which Jamaica rejected out of hand) and Jamaica's belief that the federal union should begin with the minimum powers necessary for recognition as an independent state and a flexible constitution with machinery for amendment. The inconclusive discussions in London had apparently satisfied Mr Manley that, if it proved impossible to agree on an independent federation acceptable to Jamaica, the island might secede without undue pressure or sanctions and eventually achieve independence alone.

The Ministry Paper proposed amending the national constitution to provide more accurate representation by population in the House of Representatives, more limited federal jurisdiction, a more powerful Regional Council of Ministers, delay in implementing customs union, restriction of national revenues to customs receipts, and removal of industrial development from the concurrent legislative list. It also again advocated amendment of the central constitution by majority vote. This would have enabled Jamaica, with the support of one other unit, to determine every issue. 'Within the framework of these proposals,' the paper concluded, 'Jamaica is prepared to accept to the full all her obligations as a partner in the venture of Federation.'[4]

The Jamaican press described this Ministry Paper as hard-headed and practical in recognizing that West Indian nationhood could not be imposed from above and that 'a highly organized and expensive central administration' would place 'an intolerable burden upon unit governments and the people of the West Indies.'[5] Non-Jamaicans considered its attitude towards the Federation remarkable in a man who had long championed British Caribbean union and still led the ruling Federal Labour Party. In 1951 Mr Manley had criticized the Rance *Report* for giving too little power, especially over taxation, to the central government.

Five years later he had declared that Jamaica had everything to gain from federation.[6] The exigencies of his political position at home helped to explain his apparent volte-face.

Many of his party stalwarts, including certain cabinet ministers, had publicly and repeatedly attacked Jamaica's participation in the national union. Until the spring of 1960, when it was too late, his government made little effort to win popular support for the Federation. By April of that year the political reporter of the able and influential *Gleaner* was arguing that the vast majority of Jamaicans wanted nothing to do with federalism and that the ruling People's National Party had become, for all practical purposes, anti-federationist.[7] Sweeping victories in the Jamaican local government elections of 1960 strengthened the party rather than its leader. Desire to conciliate his followers and to have the whip hand at the Intergovernmental Conference may have been largely responsible for Mr Manley's visit to England and for the views presented on his return home. Whatever his reasons, if his original decision not to become federal Prime Minister dealt a vital blow to The West Indies, his Ministry Paper demanding a central government even weaker than that established in 1958 gave it the *coup de grâce*.

TRINIDAD AND CHAGUARAMAS

Although Dr Williams of Trinidad had long been the chief advocate of a strong union, his attitude lent no more comfort to federal supporters. The national government had been given exclusive jurisdiction over external affairs, but Dr Williams wished to conduct independent negotiations with Venezuela about tariffs, with the Netherlands Antilles about retirement and repatriation of British West Indian workers in the oil refineries of Aruba and Curaçao, and above all with the United States about Chaguaramas.

The federal Prime Minister, Sir Grantley Adams, who sympathized with the desire to regain Chaguaramas but preferred to avoid antagonizing the Americans, announced on 11 December 1959 that The West Indies would confer with the United Kingdom and the United States on the 1941 agreement to lease bases in the British Caribbean. The federal delegation, he explained, would include representatives of the constituent territories, who would state the positions of their islands. On several occasions he requested the governments of the units concerned, Trinidad and Tobago, Jamaica, Antigua, and St Lucia, to express opinions on this matter.

When Dr Williams was invited to a preliminary meeting to consider the question, he countered by asking the federal government's view. Its unilateral decision to participate in such discussions he promptly attacked as treachery and a stab in Trinidad's back. He wanted the meeting to be a four-power conference with Trinidad a separate party, not merely a member of the federal delegation.

The long-standing breach between the governments of Trinidad and Tobago and the Federation was made public at a press conference held by Dr Williams on 5 March 1959. Here he attacked the United States and United Kingdom for unwarranted interference in West Indian affairs and announced that Trinidad and Tobago would not support a federal government which was 'the stooge of the Colonial Office.' Sir Grantley retorted that this statement was 'beneath contempt' and Dr Williams 'vituperative and untruthful.'[8]

Dr Williams responded by alleging that the central administration was hostile to the legitimate interests of Trinidad and the People's National Movement. His islands, he said, would secede unless the federal constitution were refashioned to meet their views, diametrically opposite to those of Jamaica. 'Let me state the alternatives bluntly,' Dr Williams told a cheering audience of some 10,000 people, 'either a strong independent Federation with all of us, or a weak Federation without Trinidad and Tobago.'[9] As the Jamaican *Gleaner* commented editorially, it seemed clear that Mr Manley's proposals in Ministry Paper No. 3 and Dr Williams's in the *Economics of Nationhood* could not be reconciled within the same Federation. There appeared no likelihood that either would give way.[10]

Irritated by Sir Grantley's acceptance in June 1958 of an American proposal to shelve the Chaguaramas issue for ten years, Dr Williams rejected in advance any arrangements on the matter made by the United States, the United Kingdom, and The West Indies. His attack on the national government was emphasized by Trinidad's refusal to contribute towards the expenses of a visit to Port-of-Spain by the Princess Royal. Similarly the local Trinidad and Tobago branch declined to assist with costs of a conference of the Commonwealth Parliamentary Association at Federal House. Trinidad government and opposition members both objected to the Federation allocating levies for these purposes without first consulting the constituent territories.

On 22 April 1960 thousands of People's National Movement supporters demonstrated in Woodford Square, demanding independence for Trinidad and Tobago and revision of the agreement for leasing bases to the United States. 'I will either break the Chaguaramas Agreement,' said Dr Williams, 'or the Chaguaramas Agreement will break me.' He publicly burned what he described as 'the seven sins of colonialism,' among them the constitutions of Trinidad and Tobago and The West Indies. The latter he considered 'colonialism and nothing but colonialism. We in Trinidad and Tobago ... demand either Independence or no Federation.' As he handed over each document for the fire, he declared, 'I consign it to the flames; to hell with it.' To the crowd, assembled in pouring rain, he announced, 'Now you are spiritually free.'[11]

The other five documents were the Mudie Report on the Federal Capital Site, the Telephone Ordinance, the United States Lend-Lease Agreement, the Trinidad *Guardian*, and a Democratic Labour Party statement on British Guiana. The American Consul-General in Port-of-Spain was presented with a memorial approved by acclamation of the assembled crowd. This demanded revision of the Leased Bases Agreement and the return of Chaguaramas and other bases 'ceded without consent and against the will of the people.' Six years later Dr Williams told a convention of the People's National Movement that the demonstration on 22 April 1960 was 'a march for Chaguaramas, a march for full internal self-government, and a march for an independent West Indies Federation and against the very West Indies Parliament and government which was resisting independence for that Federation.'[12]

The struggle for survival of The West Indies had become a battle of views and of wills among the leaders of Trinidad, Jamaica, and the Federation, with the smaller territories of the Eastern Caribbean unhappy spectators but ineffective participants. Amid a rising chorus of Jamaican and Trinidadian charges that the Federation harmed the interests of the units, the *West Indian Economist* was almost alone in contending that it had been an asset rather than a liability to the British Caribbean.[13]

PROPOSED CHANGES IN THE FEDERAL CONSTITUTION

The Political and Economic Committee appointed by the Intergovernmental Conference met in Port-of-Spain from 2 to 4 May 1960 to consider reports by subcommittees on revision of the federal constitution. Before it opened, Sir Alexander Bustamante wrote his colleague, Donald Sangster, an advocate of federation and a member of the Jamaican delegation to the talks in Trinidad, declaring that their island must secede. On 6 May the press published a letter from Sir Alexander to Mr Manley, expressing concern about Jamaica's future in 'this farcical Federation,' and urging that the Premier ought to take the island out of a union it should never have joined. 'What,' he asked rhetorically, 'does Federation mean to Jamaica? More direct taxes, ... interference with our industries, ... more hunger, ... and more tears.'[14]

Under these unpropitious circumstances the Political and Economic Committee told the representatives assembled in Port-of-Spain that it concurred with its subcommittee's recommendation that Jamaica's representation in the federal House of Representatives should be increased. Jamaica proposed gradual assimilation of tariffs over a ten-year period. On this suggestion Trinidad reserved its position, being determined that freedom of movement of goods and of persons should go together.

The discussions were again dominated by a bitter clash between Jamaica's and Trinidad's views on federation. All the delegates, however, agreed that customs union must come eventually. They also approved increasing Jamaica's seats in the lower house from seventeen out of forty-five to thirty-one out of sixty-four. The Working Party on the economic and financial implications of independence was directed to prepare two drafts of a revised national constitution, based respectively on the Jamaican and Trinidadian proposals.

Most of the Leewards and Windwards, perennially irritated by Trinidad's restrictions on immigration and frequent deportations, especially of Grenadians and Vincentians, reluctantly supported Jamaica's wish for a weaker central government. Their stand owed less to faith in the merits of this position than to belief that without Jamaica the union would disintegrate. Decision on the fundamental issue of whether the Federation should be strong or weak was postponed until autumn.

At the first session of the national House of Representatives in 1960 Sir Grantley Adams tabled a White Paper setting forth his administration's proposals on full cabinet government for the Federation. He read a despatch from the Secretary of State for the Colonies, noting that this had already been approved in principle by all the territories and that the Colonial Office was studying detailed recommendations and awaited West Indians' decision on a revised constitution. 'While independence implies an ability to stand on one's own feet financially as well as politically,' ran Mr Macleod's despatch, 'Her Majesty's Government recognises that the West Indies may not be able to assume at once the whole weight of the financial burdens which would normally fall to an independent member.' It was therefore ready to consider ways in which temporary help might be given.

Appreciating Caribbean concern lest independence be delayed by financial problems, Mr Macleod gave an assurance of help from the United Kingdom during the transitional period before the Federation achieved autonomy, and of its continued eligibility thereafter for aid from Commonwealth Assistance Loans on the same basis as other less developed independent members of the Commonwealth. The British government, he said, was solely concerned to ensure that the Federation should be able to exercise effective sovereignty and that the date proposed for independence was practicable.[15]

Among the changes in the national constitution advocated by Sir Grantley was replacement of the existing provision enabling the Governor General to act, under certain circumstances, without advice from the Council of State, by the requirement that he should always act on the advice of the cabinet. The latter (no longer called Council of State) should, in his view, direct the federal government and be collectively responsible to the legislature. No nominated members should attend meetings of the cabinet, whose numbers should be determined by the Prime Minister. The existing provision for electing the Prime Minister should be replaced by a requirement that the Governor General appoint to this office the member of the House of Representatives best able to command the confidence of the House.

The Secretary of State for the Colonies, Mr Macleod, visited the West Indies in June 1960 to discuss internal self-government with Trinidad and Tobago, cabinet government with the Federation, and other issues with Sir Grantley and the leaders of the constituent territories. He proved himself an able conciliator, managed to reduce tensions between West Indian statesmen, and persuaded Dr Williams temporarily to refrain from publicly attacking Jamaica's decision to hold a referendum. Independence for the federation, Mr Macleod emphasized, waited only on agreement among the islands as to what they wanted. In a farewell broadcast he renewed his promise of continued financial aid from Britain after independence and stressed that the United Kingdom considered federation the best solution for the islands and their peoples.[16]

ANNOUNCEMENT OF THE JAMAICAN REFERENDUM

The prospects of the Federation were then variously assessed. Dr Williams announced that the United States might as well make up its mind to deal directly with Trinidad on such issues as Chaguaramas, because The West Indies was unlikely to endure. Mr Manley, however, thought the situation was improving as the other islands came to appreciate the force of Jamaica's proposals.[17] Sir Alexander Bustamante urged withdrawal from the Federation and told a labour rally that he wanted to 'smash it up.'[18] Mr Manley described this stand as playing politics with the island's future.

Sir Alexander resigned on 30 May 1960 from the national Democratic Labour Party he had hitherto led, declared that the Jamaica Labour Party was now opposed to the Federation, and called for a referendum on whether the island should remain in it. This decision, apparently taken on his own initiative, without consultation with colleagues in Jamaica or elsewhere in the West Indies, was roundly condemned as despicable by the Democratic Labour Party of Trinidad and Tobago. Without federation, it contended, the British Caribbean territories would be insignificant.[19]

On the following day Mr Manley promptly accepted his cousin's challenge and told the Jamaican House of Representatives that a referendum on whether the island should or should not remain in the Federation would be held in 1961, when the shape of the revised national constitution had been determined. His decision, although unanimously confirmed by his party's annual conference in

November, was curious at the time and disastrous in its sequel. His People's National Party, which formally supported the Federation, less than a year before had been returned to power with a greatly increased majority. Less than seven months earlier Mr Manley had declared that a referendum would be a betrayal of leadership and of responsibility.

Although the national constitution made no provision for secession by any unit, he did not consult the Governor General, the British or federal governments, or the other islands before announcing the referendum. He did not mention the fact that, after more than a decade of discussion, the Jamaican legislature, by numerous votes in favour of federation, had committed the island to a contract which ought to be honoured. Nor did he suggest that, under a system of cabinet government, a general election was more appropriate than a plebiscite for determining a vital issue.

To Jamaicans their Premier explained his decision in a broadcast on 12 June and to West Indians as a whole in a press conference at Federal House five days later. As long as both Jamaican parties supported federation, he considered it reasonable to assume that they represented public opinion. When, however, the Jamaica Labour Party announced its opposition to continued participation in the union, he thought it right for the voters to decide the question in a referendum. With this decision, he said, federation had for the first time become a living issue in Jamaica. He believed it would be twice as expensive for the island to achieve independence alone as in company with the other units. No one had more faith in federation than he. To those who argued that men could not eat independence, he would reply: 'You can't eat your destiny, but you can betray it for a mess of pottage.'[20]

When the Jamaican House of Representatives debated the bill providing for a referendum, Mr Manley elaborated his views and insisted that the island could not remain in an independent federation while one of its two parties was threatening to secede.[21] Hence it was necessary to settle the matter once and for all. If the people voted to take Jamaica out of the union, his government would not consider itself defeated and resign, but would implement their wishes.[22] From that day it was clear, a Trinidadian journalist later commented, that Mr Manley was 'a better Jamaican than West Indian.'[23]

Robert Lightbourne, replying for the Jamaica Labour Party, contended that young and inexperienced West Indian politicians had been hoodwinked by the Colonial Office. In the hope of sloughing off territories no longer profitable, the United Kingdom had promised independence, tied to the string of federalism. There could be no conflicting loyalties in nationhood, he argued, and no type of federation that his party would advise his countrymen to support.

Jamaicans were clearly concerned as to what, except higher taxes, federalism offered an already heavily taxed island. The obvious answer, 'West Indian nationhood,' appeared obvious to very few. Mr Manley's announcement of the referendum increased his bargaining power at the forthcoming Intergovernmental Conference and posed a choice to the other territories: dissolving the Federation or continuing it on Jamaica's terms.

During August 1960 Mr Manley made a ten-day tour of the Eastern Caribbean islands, ostensibly to explain where the West Indian Federal Labour Party and Jamaica stood on federation. It was widely rumoured, however, that his visit was also a campaign to make himself known as a promising candidate for the national prime ministership.

Before his decision to hold a referendum was announced, he said at St Kitts, opinion in Jamaica was overwhelmingly against federation; it had since been swinging more and more in the opposite direction. In Barbados he told a large audience that although the referendum was a calculated risk he had to take, 'we would be shamed before history if, having declared for Federation and marching toward independence, we should break it up by the withdrawal of one unit from the nation.' At St Lucia he pledged himself to fight with all he had to keep Jamaica in the Federation, but refused to comment on the rumour that he himself was 'likely to go Federal.'

At a private meeting in Antigua on 7-8 August 1960 Mr Manley and Dr Williams apparently agreed to modify their more extreme views about a revised federal constitution. The latter seems to have been willing to concede most. The immediate result was temporarily decreased tension between Trinidad and Jamaica. Inevitably, however, their well-publicized meetings, whose conclusions remained secret, accentuated already acute irritation among the two largest islands and the federal Prime Minister and added to the suspicions of the Leewards and Windwards. Of his two rivals, Sir Grantley observed bitterly: 'They met like the Pope and the Emperor dividing the world between them.'

Dr Williams announced that he and the Jamaican Premier were agreed on the need for a strong central government. When people talked about secession, he wondered where West Indians were to go: 'into the Caribbean Sea, to Castro, the United States, the Rastafarians and back to Africa?'[24]

To the smaller islands Mr Manley emphasized that federation was essential to all the units, including Jamaica, that the transfer of powers to the national government must be gradual, not immediate, and that, at least for the present, responsibility for economic planning should remain with the constituent territories. On his return home he said he had everywhere found much interest in the Federation and great concern about the attitude of Jamaicans. He was convinced that they must not fail their brothers throughout the British Caribbean. The Trinidad press described Mr Manley's role as that of a missionary and his visit to the other units as a turning point in their relations with Jamaica. If Sir Alexander's views prevailed, it contended, The West Indies would become a laughing-stock of the world.[25]

Not until the decision to hold a referendum was announced did Mr Manley seriously try to develop informed opinion in Jamaica about what the Federation involved. On the issue of continued participation in it his own party remained sharply split. Even in educated circles there was surprisingly little recognition that The West Indies was an entity which Jamaicans had helped to create and which their legislature had several times approved. There seemed few qualms of conscience about the prospect of withdrawing from an agreement two or three years after its conclusion. The usual attitude was to ask, 'What does Jamaica stand to get out of Federation?', not 'What can Jamaica contribute to it?'

POLITICAL DEVELOPMENTS IN JAMAICA

By the autumn of 1960 living costs in Jamaica had risen, crimes of violence had increased, and signs of internal conflict had become obvious in both parties. Sir Alexander was then seventy-six and Mr Manley ten years younger. A behind-the-scenes struggle over succession to the leadership of both parties seemed inevitable. The latent anti-federalism of the Jamaica Labour Party was made overt by Sir Alexander's resignation as leader of the national Democratic Labour Party. This revealed fissures hitherto concealed and produced new ones in his Jamaican party which had been twice defeated in island elections. A Jamaican member of the Federal Democratic Labour Party, Winston Williams, who attacked Sir Alexander's opposition to federation, was suspended from the Jamaica Labour Party. Bustamante's domination and desire for highly centralized leadership in the latter body was still strong, as was his insistence on the right to choose his successor.

The Jamaica United Party, formerly known as the United West Indian party, under the presidency of George J. Edwards, announced early in 1961 that it would do everything in its power to oppose Jamaica's remaining in the Federation. About the same time a group formed by Mrs Rose Leon, previously chairman of the Jamaica Labour Party, split off to form a new organization, the Progressive Labour Movement, dedicated to rescuing the island from 'the unholy alliance of the Two Cousins' rule.'[26] It soon merged with the anti-federationist People's Political Party, originally founded in 1929 by Marcus Garvey and revived in April 1961 under the aegis of Millard Johnson, a barrister who advocated black racialism.[27] A year later this group was dissolved. None of these minor parties achieved any significant success, although at the time of the referendum the People's Political Party was credited with adding at least fifty thousand votes to the anti-federationist camp.

THE FEDERAL AND TRINIDADIAN OPPOSITION

Meanwhile in Port-of-Spain the national opposition laboured under the twin disabilities of internal dissensions and an anomalous existence as a federal party many of whose members were publicly attacking the Federation. During the budget debate in the Trinidad and Tobago Legislative Council in April 1960 members of the opposition Democratic Labour Party hurled insults at each other in a shouting match which drowned the Speaker's efforts to maintain order. The leader of the opposition, Simboonath Capildeo, was removed from this post and later expelled by his brother, the new leader, Dr Rudranath Capildeo.[28] Other members expelled from the party as 'mischief makers' were Mitra Sinanan, L. Romaldo Gomes, and the party secretary, F.E. Brassington.

On 17 May members of the Federal Democratic Labour Party walked out of the national House of Representatives in protest against a controversial bill on emergency powers. The following month Ashford Sinanan, who had succeeded Sir Alexander as leader of the party, launched a violent attack on Sir Grantley Adams. Robert Lightbourne, formerly first deputy leader of the Federal Democratic Labour Party, had resigned from parliament in July 1959 to contest a seat in the Jamaican elections. His post had been filled by another able Jamaican, Morris Cargill, who resigned from the federal House on 15 June, shortly after Sir Alexander.

Meantime signs of revolt in the Trinidad wing of the Federal Democratic Labour Party were brought to a head by Albert Gomes's public characterization of Ashford Sinanan and Dr Capildeo as dictators, his demand for a national party convention to discuss Sir Alexander's resignation, and his statement in the House of Representatives that he hoped the pro-federationists would win the Jamaican referendum. There were only two West Indian parties, he said: those for Federation and those against it. He stood with those who would fight to preserve the union and believed that if everything was to be subordinated to power politics, the nation was doomed. These remarks resulted in his expulsion from the party.[29]

While opposition members were busily engaged in attacking each other, Sir Grantley told the Antigua Labour Party that West Indians must unite or perish, and must show the world that they intended to make their Federation a success.[30] In a speech marking The West Indies' attainment of cabinet government on 16 August 1960 he expressed gratification that the country was no longer a 'glorified crown colony' and hope that in the task ahead he could count on the concerted efforts of all his countrymen.[31] An order-in-council, effective on that date and based on the proposals in Sir Grantley's White Paper, conferred internal self-government on the Federation. The United Kingdom retained responsibility only for defence and certain aspects of international affairs and the public service.

REPORTS OF THE INTERGOVERNMENTAL COMMITTEES

The two committees of the Intergovernmental Conference on revision of the federal constitution produced their reports in February 1960, and in May met with leaders and ministers of the national and unit governments. The opinions of Trinidad and Tobago had been re-emphasized the previous day in the Speech from the Throne at the opening of the new session of its Legislative Council. This announced that, while the goal of Dr Williams's government was a strong and workable federation, it would make every reasonable effort to meet varying views. The Jamaican press, by contrast, argued that if the other territories did not want the island on her own terms, they would force her to withdraw.[32]

The committee on customs union recommended a harmonization of tariff rates designed to afford reasonable protection to local industries and achieve full internal free trade by the end of an agreed transitional period. It suggested insular consumption duties as a means of mitigating consequent losses of revenue.

The committee on constitutional and political aspects of an independent West Indies federation reached agreement on certain points. It recommended that the national government have limited taxation powers; sole responsibility for defence, external affairs, university education, and other subjects on the exclusive list; and authority, in association with the unit governments, to intensify its efforts to secure external aid. All the constituent territories should have full internal self-government and retain their existing right to legislate on subjects on the exclusive list until federal measures had been enacted. Unit governments should retain sole responsibility for all matters not on any legislative list. There should be provision for common citizenship, freedom of movement within the Federation, and accession of new units.

The revised national constitution should contain, in addition to the concurrent and exclusive legislative lists, a new reserve list of matters which, although 'recognised as properly subjects of Federal interest, would remain for the time being within the legislative competence of Unit Governments but would be transferable by a constitutional procedure to be decided upon.'[33] Income tax and industrial development were to be placed on this reserve list: a device apparently invented, as a compromise, by Mr Manley and Dr Williams.

The committee also recommended that the revised constitution should provide for a consultative Regional Council of Ministers, composed of the Premiers and Chief Ministers of the islands under the chairmanship of the national Prime Minister. This body would be entitled to discuss any matter of general interest and specifically to examine in advance any proposal that the federal government should assume sole or partial responsibility for any subject on the concurrent list.

Trinidadian representatives strongly objected to unqualified freedom of movement from the inauguration of a new federal constitution, unless this provided a strong central government. They demanded immediate independence for the Federation, and full self-government, within five years, for all the units.

The committees of the Intergovernmental Conference had appointed two 'working parties,' called Alpha and Orion and respectively chaired by John Mordecai, the Federal Secretary, and Egerton Richardson, the Jamaican Financial Secretary. Orion was to examine problems involved in customs union and Alpha constitutional issues. The latter was specifically enjoined to consider possible economic and social disruption resulting from unrestricted freedom of migration within the Federation, procedures for constitutional amendment and transfer of subjects from the reserve list, and alternative proposals for national revenue based on the twin needs to secure flexibility and equitable contributions from all the units.

At meetings in October 1960 Working Party Alpha, in accordance with its instructions, gave detailed estimates on the costs of two alternative frameworks for federation: one weak and decentralized, the other strong and concentrated. It was within their competence, the national Minister of Finance, Robert Bradshaw, reminded members, to recommend a federation barely meeting minimal qualifications for nationhood, one capable of fulfilling West Indian expectations, or a combination of the two.

Dr Williams presented to the meeting a White Paper on economic development, asking the British government to contribute over £90 million to the Federation. Mr Manley reiterated Jamaica's determination that national revenues should be confined to customs duties, which his government considered adequate to finance a federation responsible only for defence, external affairs, and regional Caribbean services.

As the delegates finally agreed on the impracticality of an early customs union, it was not surprising that on returning to Jamaica Mr Manley jubilantly announced: 'We have managed to secure what we wanted, which is what we think is good and right not only for us but for the Federation as a whole.'[34] He had reason for satisfaction. The recommendations of the committees, if approved by the Intergovernmental Conference, meant that amendment of the national constitution by some undetermined procedure would be necessary to give the Federation the right to levy income taxes and control industrial development. The small islands were understandably less happy at the triumph of Jamaica's views. A St Lucian member of the federal parliament accused it and Trinidad of 'taking all and giving nothing in return,' and declared he would rather see his island a province of Canada than a member of a federation giving it opportunities inferior to those offered Jamaica and Trinidad.[35]

It was equally understandable that Mr Manley's enthusiasm was not shared by the federal government. Sir Grantley Adams believed that the Premiers of Jamaica and Trinidad were conspiring to oust him. In his budget speech on 21 November 1960 the Minister of Finance warned that, failing the provision of more adequate revenues, a sizeable deficit would be inevitable in 1962. National expenses would be considerably increased by implementing proposals of the Jackson Commission for larger salaries for public servants and unification and interchange of personnel among federal and unit civil services. Ten days later Mr Bradshaw announced his decision to leave the federal government and return to politics in St Kitts. While he did not elaborate his reasons, the frustrations of a national Minister of Finance with negligible funds at his disposal were sufficiently obvious.

A Federal Development Loan and Guarantee Fund with a capital of $8,200,000 (half supplied by the United States and one-quarter by the British Colonial Development and Welfare Fund) was established at the beginning of 1961. It provided loans for private investors in small- and medium-sized enterprises including the hotel industry. Within the limitations imposed by its budget this fund proved very useful. Other federal activities at the time were the provision of technical assistance to Montserrat to increase water supplies for its capital, Plymouth, and arrangements for the third meeting of the Natural Resources Council at the University College of the West Indies.

CHAGUARAMAS AGAIN

Dr Williams had argued in 1959 that it was impossible for any country which did not control all its own territory to enjoy full internal autonomy.[36] The Chaguaramas issue was again debated in June 1960 at meetings in Port-of-Spain attended by the Secretary of State for the Colonies. On the latter's suggestion it was agreed that at renewed discussions on revision of the 1941 Lend-Lease Agreement a national delegation including representatives from the territories concerned should give the British and American governments a detailed statement of West Indian views. At subsequent talks the special problems of the islands affected would be presented by their own representatives. Final discussions among the Federation, the United States, the United Kingdom, and legal advisers from the units would follow.

This proposal was accepted by the American government, and a conference on West Indian bases took place at London in November 1960. The federal delegation, which included representatives from Antigua, Jamaica, St Lucia, and Trinidad, expressed willingness to co-operate in strengthening mutual security and in continuing defence of the western hemisphere as part of the defence of the democratic world.

American representatives stated that they were prepared to release unconditionally the major part of the five areas they leased in the British West Indies and wished to retain only those essential to their responsibilities for defence. They undertook to withdraw from a deactivated section of Chaguaramas and, like the United Kingdom, promised economic aid to the Federation after it achieved independence. All parties accepted the view that an autonomous West Indies would have the right to form its own alliances and make such agreements as it wished about military bases on its territory. They also agreed to individual consultation with islands where there were American bases and to further talks on the matter later in the month.

The second stage of these discussions began on 30 November in Tobago. The American delegate, urging the need for realism, said the United States was willing to give up 80 per cent of its West Indian bases, but required one on the Gulf of Paria where Chaguaramas was situated, as otherwise this section of the Caribbean would be unprotected. He re-emphasized that his country was prepared to consider aiding social and economic development in the British Caribbean and to do what it could to advance the cause of West Indian nationhood. During the previous eighteen months the American International Co-Operation Administration had given technical assistance to the Leewards and Windwards, in addition to $5 million to the West Indies Federal Development Loan and Guaranty Fund.

The Tobago talks concluded on 8 December with an agreement (subject to review in 1969 and again in 1973) that by 1962 the United States would abandon some 21,000 acres of land leased under the 1941 agreement. These included all territory in Trinidad outside the northwest peninsula, as well as unused portions of the naval station at Chaguaramas. The rest of the peninsula could be utilized for the new federal capital. The United States would retain the balance of the Chaguaramas area for seventeen years, to enable its naval station there to fulfil important defence and electronic research missions. The situation would then be jointly reviewed. The Americans promised to give Trinidad and Tobago economic and technical assistance for such projects as improved port facilities at Port-of-Spain, road construction, railway renewal, and new buildings at the St Augustine branch of the University College of the West Indies. Although some of his lieutenants were opposed, Dr Williams hailed this agreement as Trinidad and Tobago's first diplomatic success in international affairs.[37]

The future of American bases in other islands was discussed during December in St Lucia, Antigua, and Jamaica. In St Lucia the United States consented to release immediately some 1700 acres of land, retaining approximately 1000 acres for research and development of space exploration. It also promised financial assistance for roads, hydroelectric power, and secondary education. As in the other territories, these new arrangements were to continue until 1977 unless it was agreed to extend the lease for a further period.

In Antigua the United States promised to release 900 acres, including the airport, while retaining 300 acres in connection with its space-exploration programme. It also undertook to assist such projects as an extended airfield runway and a deep-water harbour. In Jamaica the Americans contracted to release unconditionally 23,000 acres, keeping only 100 as a site for navigational aids. There also they guaranteed financial assistance for a variety of schemes, including low-income housing, extension of water supplies, and technical and university education.[38]

Finally, on 10 February 1961 at the third and last stage of the discussions, an agreement between the governments of the United States and The West Indies on American defence areas in the Federation was signed at Port-of-Spain. The British Caribbean press gave only grudging acknowledgment of the conspicuous generosity of the United States in promising to withdraw from four-fifths of the territory it had acquired on a ninety-nine-year lease in 1941 and at the same time to contribute, during the first six months of 1961, more than $2 million to the islands concerned. Sir Grantley Adams, however, at the closing session of the talks, paid tribute to the considerate and statesmanlike attitude of the United States and its readiness to recognize the Federation, on the eve of its independence, as an equal.[39]

The American Ambassador handed over to Trinidad and Tobago in August 1963 the beach areas between the old and new entrances to the United States naval station. Three years later, in accordance with its promise, the United States relinquished a major portion of its naval station at Chaguaramas, which it promised to close by 30 June 1967. It retained some 3300 acres of the original 6900, mainly as an air force test range and navigational station, until 1971 when the remaining portion of the peninsula was given back to Trinidad.[40]

PRIME MINISTER MACMILLAN'S VISIT TO THE WEST INDIES

At the invitation of the federal government the Prime Minister of the United Kingdom, Harold Macmillan, visited the British Caribbean in March 1961. In an address to its legislature he emphasized the strength of the parliamentary tradition in the islands, their long experience with free political institutions, and the potential influence of a united West Indies as opposed to that of any individual territory. He looked forward to welcoming the Federation as an independent member of the Commonwealth which would provide stability in the Caribbean, and promised that, within the limits of its resources, the United Kingdom would do all it could to help the new nation stand on its own feet. He concluded by urging his listeners to resolve their remaining difficulties about the future of a united West Indies which ought to take its proper place among the nations of the world.[41]

The ovation which greeted his speech owed less to unanimous faith in the Federation than to the fact that Mr Macmillan's visit came at a time when his own prestige and that of the United Kingdom were unusually high in the British Caribbean. Less than a fortnight earlier the Commonwealth Prime Ministers' Conference had been so outspokenly critical of apartheid that South Africa withdrew her request to remain a member of the Commonwealth after becoming a republic. West Indians had resented the fact that Sir Grantley Adams was not invited to this meeting, which they felt he was better entitled to attend than the Prime Minister of the Central African Federation. The conference's attitude towards South African racial policies, however, had dispelled much of their irritation.

Most of the remainder vanished with Mr Macmillan's declaration to their parliament that the Commonwealth's continuing significance depended on its multi-racial character and that, as a society where people of many different origins dwelt together in unity, The West Indies could make an important contribution to the outside world. If his listeners' views on federation were mixed and their unity tenuous, they were at least united in approving such sentiments.

THE PRE-REFERENDUM CAMPAIGN AND THE FEDERATION

Meantime in Jamaica Sir Alexander Bustamante launched a pre-referendum campaign urging his supporters to vote against federation. According to him and his colleagues, federation meant control of Jamaica by the smaller islands. It also meant increasing their countrymen's poverty, because of the need to help support the even poorer peoples of the Eastern Caribbean.[42] These emotional appeals steadily undermined the position of Mr Manley's government. They proved far more effective than his reasoned contention that the costs of Jamaica 'going it alone' would in fact be much higher than those of remaining in the union. 'I am 100 per cent − 1,000 per cent,' he stoutly declared, 'in favour of Federation.' To his mind a revised national union would be stable and mature, devoted to democracy and the rule of law.[43]

Dr Williams, without commenting directly on the struggle in Jamaica, told his islands' Legislative Council in April 1961 that, although the future of The West Indies overshadowed all local problems, Trinidad and Tobago could not reasonably be expected to assume responsibility for a federation without Jamaica.[44] This was a frank and ominous warning of his subsequent stand.

Sir Grantley visited the Leewards and Windwards in February and March of that year to try to muster support for the federal cause. On 11 April a White Paper setting forth his government's stand was introduced in the House of Representatives by Mr Bradshaw. This attacked the compromise proposals made by committee Alpha: a view supported by most of the small islands.

The recommendations on constitutional revision of the Intergovernmental Conference committees created a storm of protest in the Leewards, Windwards, and Barbados. If these were implemented, Senator J.J. Charles of Dominica declared, he would lead the fight to have his territory secede from the Federation. Senator J.B. Renwick of Grenada called them unprecedented, unfair to the smaller units, and based on complete misunderstanding of what federalism involved. Their acceptance would produce a milk-and-water constitution which would destroy the Federation.

The White Paper was also sharply criticized by other senators from Dominica, Grenada, and St Lucia. They particularly objected to placing income tax and industrial development on a reserve list under conditions which gave Jamaica a veto, to delaying not only customs union but freedom of movement (the major interest of the small islands), and to weakening the national government by giving great power to the Regional Council of Ministers. Everyone recognized, said Senator Renwick, how disastrous it would be if one of the large territories seceded, but to avoid this other members should not consent to total ruin of the national state.[45] These criticisms had much foundation.

To both friends and foes of the Federation it was becoming increasingly apparent that attainment of Mr Manley's demands would produce a union so weak as to be almost useless. This was cogently argued by Morris Cargill, a federal opposition member. 'It will be interesting to see,' he wrote as Thomas Wright in his *Daily Gleaner* column on 13 April 1961, 'to what extent Jamaica, in its own interests, can negative every Federal concept, ... while still being able to maintain the pretence that the new arrangement will, in fact, be a Federation at all. Should Jamaica's demands be agreed to in total, it will be difficult to word the question for the Referendum. For it will not be a choice between Federation and no Federation. It will be a choice between two names for Jamaican independence. Which, from our point of view, is just as well. Heads we win, tails they lose.' Similar opinions were voiced by Albert Gomes of Trinidad in a letter published by *The Daily Gleaner* on 27 April 1961.

In this discouraging atmosphere Sir Grantley marked the third anniversary of the federal parliament by a broadcast to the nation. During the past three years, he pointed out, while the whole basis of the Federation was being re-examined, his government had tried to build a house on shifting sand. Despite weakness and poverty, it had done its best and established fruitful relationships with the outside world. He urged his hearers to reflect that the forthcoming Inter-governmental Conference might well provide the last opportunity to consolidate all the work done since 1945 to create a West Indian nation able to take its place among other states. 'If we miss this train,' he cautioned, 'there may not be another in our time.' The United Kingdom, while prepared to give help and encouragement, recognized that the final decision lay with West Indians. If his countrymen did not wish to remain among the last British colonies, they should approach their problems with breadth of vision and willingness to compromise. 'All our history, our hopes, our struggles, our reputations, our future,' he concluded, 'hinge on our actions during the next three weeks.'[46]

SECOND MEETING OF THE INTERGOVERNMENTAL CONFERENCE

The Intergovernmental Conference of 1959 had settled only one major issue: representation in the national lower house. The cardinal problem of whether the Federation was to be strong or weak was still unresolved, save for the agreements between Dr Williams and Mr Manley at Antigua, where the latter's views apparently prevailed. When the conference resumed on 2 May 1961, Sir Grantley sharply attacked the secrecy of these agreements, the powers proposed for the Regional Council of Ministers, the need for a reserve list, the continued denial to the national government of the right to tax, and the postponement of freedom of movement within the Federation. On most points he was supported by Barbados, Dominica, St Kitts, and St Lucia, and on some by Grenada. Antigua, Montserrat, and St Vincent generally upheld Manley's insistence on a weak federal government because they believed that otherwise he would lose the referendum.

During two weeks of discussions, despite effective pleas from Sir Grantley for a strong federation, most outstanding issues were settled (subject to confirmation by the various legislatures) as Jamaica wished, except the procedure to amend the constitution by transferring subjects from the reserve list. On this there was no agreement. Mr Manley wanted such amendments to be approved by two-thirds of each federal house and by absolute majorities in a majority of the territorial legislatures representing at least two-thirds of the Federation's population. Most delegates objected to this proposal because, as Jamaicans formed over half the national population, it would give them an effective veto.

No similar veto was conceded to Trinidad and Tobago on freedom of movement within the area: an issue equally important to its government.

The Port-of-Spain conference agreed that freedom of movement should not be introduced for nine years, but split on Jamaica's objection to Dr Williams's insistence that this should be linked with a similarly phased introduction of customs union. Decision on the amending procedure was postponed until Mr Manley could discover whether any alternative was acceptable to Jamaicans. Before the London Conference in June he informed the Governor General and West Indian political leaders that he could not offer better terms, as his People's National Party cabinet, executive, and annual conference were all unanimously opposed to changing the formula.

The Intergovernmental Conference decided (over strong objections from the federal government, Barbados, St Kitts, and St Lucia) that central revenues should be obtained from import duties on specified items estimated to produce an annual revenue of BWI $28.3 million. It also agreed on exclusive and concurrent lists of jurisdiction and on a sixty-four seat federal House of Representatives, in which Jamaica would have thirty members, Trinidad and Tobago sixteen, Barbados five, Montserrat one, and the other islands two each. In ten years, as its population increased, Jamaica might anticipate returning more than half the members of the federal lower house.

Despite his well-known desire for a strong national government Dr Williams adopted a conciliatory position at the Port-of-Spain meetings, realizing that if Mr Manley lost the referendum the Federation was doomed. Trinidad and Tobago alone, he reiterated, could not assume responsibility for a union to which Jamaica did not belong. He stressed the need to understand the attitude of Jamaica, which provided 40 per cent of national revenues, although he believed its government underestimated the advantages of federalism and overestimated the liabilities of a British Caribbean customs union. He emphasized the need for a regional, in contrast to an insular, outlook, and the superiority of the international personality of a federated West Indies as opposed to any influence which could be exerted by small, even if independent, islands.

In the event, the threat of secession enabled Jamaica to win reluctant majority support for most of its demands.[47] The Port-of-Spain meetings clearly illustrated the strong divergences in opinions and the jockeying for position of individual politicians. It also illustrated, as one delegate observed, that the federal framework was being fashioned around personalities rather than principles.[48]

At the ensuing public moratorium the amiable façade erected by official press releases promptly crumbled. When reporters asked Sir Grantley what he thought of the conference, he replied: 'I have no comment to make, but if I said anything it would be an atom bomb.' *The Times* (London), however, published generally favourable reports of the discussions.[49]

While the Jamaican Premier expressed natural gratification at the outcome, a local journalist commented: 'For a man who believes in Federation, Mr Manley has been remarkably adroit in reducing it to a purely nominal formality ... Anxious for a Federation on the one hand, and rightly apprehensive of its effects on Jamaica on the other ... [he] has decided to eat his cake and have it too. The result is a "compromise" ... possible only at the expense of a total sacrifice of all true Federal concepts.'[50]

Mr Manley's stand at the conference was confirmed, on his return to Jamaica, by an emergency meeting of the People's National Party. Here he stated that he would make the referendum a party issue and fight it on party lines. 'My life, my work, my leadership,' he said, 'the party's life, leadership and future are at stake in this issue.' Yet one of his party stalwarts, Vivian Blake, was already warning that half the defeatism about federation came from the People's National Party.

The Jamaica Labour Party vainly reiterated a demand already voiced by Sir Alexander Bustamante, that the referendum be held before the London Constitutional Conference. While Mr Manley was in England, the Jamaica Labour Party staged an anti-federation march in Kingston, where Sir Alexander led the crowd in shouting: 'Freedom for Jamaica! Away with Federation!'[51]

In a radio broadcast to Trinidadians on 24 May 1961, a week before the Lancaster House Conference began, Dr Williams explained why he had consented to depart drastically from the strong national government eloquently advocated in his *Economics of Nationhood*. He had done so because he could see no other way of saving the union. To insist on his own conception would, he had become convinced, be to break up the Federation. He remained implacably opposed, however, to a permanent Jamaican veto over the reserve list and to freedom of movement before freedom of goods was attained.

On the eve of his departure for London Sir Grantley Adams declared that his government would be adamant, since no federation as weak as that proposed at the Intergovernmental Conference could be successful. In other words, he was not prepared to accept as final decisions made at this meeting. Indeed, at the Port-of-Spain discussions he had announced his intention of reopening all these at Lancaster House. Sir Grantley increasingly resented his own position as vice-president of the Federal Labour Party, which he considered incompatible with the general belief that the leader, Mr Manley, controlled it. To his mind this situation created constant misunderstanding and made parliamentary government impossible.

WEST INDIES CONSTITUTIONAL CONFERENCE, 1961

The West Indies Constitutional Conference at Lancaster House, London, from May to June 1961 was dominated by a fundamental clash between supporters of a strong and of a weak national union, springing from two conflicting concepts of what federalism involved. There were two outstanding issues: freedom of movement and the procedure for transferring subjects on the reserve list to federal control. Was a Jamaican veto to be supported? If not, Mr Manley had made it clear that his island would withdraw from the Federation. As in the past, Jamaica insisted that economic development should be controlled by the units. Trinidad and Tobago, which opposed this view, had given way at the Intergovernmental Conference on the purely practical ground that a federation without Jamaica would be useless.

Jamaica, Trinidad and Tobago, and Barbados normally balanced their budgets. Most other islands relied heavily on grants-in-aid from the United Kingdom which they feared might be reduced after independence. These allocations, totalling £8,750,000 between 1959 and 1963, ranged from almost 50 per cent of public revenues in Montserrat to some 14 per cent in St Lucia.

Although the British people and press had hitherto shown little understanding of the mounting problems confronted by The West Indies, the Constitutional Conference was given comprehensive coverage by such leading newspapers as *The Times* and *The Guardian*. 'Without federation,' the latter observed, 'the islands become a chain of question marks stretching for a thousand miles across the Caribbean, but where federation has been accepted it is too often only as an intellectual necessity, not an emotional conviction.'[52]

At the opening session the Secretary of State for the Colonies again explained the criteria necessary for independent nationhood, among which adequate financial resources were prominent. Although the United Kingdom recognized that difficulty in achieving these objectives might require advance 'at a deliberate speed and over a period of years,' it still considered no colonial territory more fitted for full independence than The West Indies.

To the British Caribbean, Sir Grantley declared in an impressive opening address, independence meant a status yearned for 'as long as the West Indian has a memory ... We have not been able to share an identical vision of the future of our Federation, but we are prepared to let history judge, in the light of our future actions and fortunes, where the palm should lie ... For us, this is the most important conference which has ever taken place because it will seal our fortunes, for good or ill, in the years that lie ahead.' The real significance of federation, to his mind, was that it would give The West Indies an international personality and an image to present to the outside world.[53]

Notwithstanding soft words from Britain, inter-island rivalries held the centre of the stage. Dr Williams, presenting Trinidad's views, cited the comment of the Royal Commission of 1897 that the United Kingdom had placed the labouring population of the area where it was and could not shed responsibility for the future of the British West Indies.[54] During discussions of migration from one territory to another he pointed out that there were over 38,000 unemployed and over 120,000 underemployed in Trinidad and Tobago, where in 1959 alone 6,000 immigrants from other islands had arrived. This influx of people seeking work threatened the schools, housing, and whole social system of Trinidad. Although he was acutely concerned about immigration, he considered the most important matter before the Conference was whether British Caribbean society would be totalitarian or democratic. He himself had few doubts. Castro's Cuba, he prophesied, would hold the West Indies together.[55]

The small islands contended that only a firm promise of British economic aid would persuade them to agree to a long delay in implementing freedom of movement. Like Barbados they viewed free migration throughout the area as vital. Without such a guarantee they considered that they were expected to sacrifice what to them seemed the chief asset of federalism. Their dilemma was caused by the fact that they also thought some form of union preferable to none. In the event the delegates finally agreed that for the first nine years after independence the national government should not legislate on freedom of movement without agreement by insular governments and that a common external tariff should be introduced gradually during the same period.

Over sharp objections from Sir Grantley, and with Barbados, St Kitts, and St Lucia dissenting, the meeting confirmed the decision of the Intergovernmental Conference that in the first years after independence the federal government should be financed by customs duties on a limited number of items. A long and acrimonious discussion about the two-thirds formula for amendment of entrenched provisions in the constitution, including all its most important sections, finally ended with acceptance of Mr Manley's insistence on giving Jamaica a veto. This was achieved only by his frank threat: 'What is decided by this conference this evening will decide whether Jamaica stays in the federation. If you decide against the stand I have taken, federation so far as Jamaica is concerned is at an end.'[56] Without this formula, he declared, his government had no hope of winning the referendum. Dr Williams had already made it clear that if Jamaica withdrew Trinidad and Tobago would follow suit, as it could not carry alone the financial costs involved.

Delegates discussed, but eventually rejected, a compromise proposed by Mr Macleod whereby the reserve list was eliminated, but any amendment empowering the federal government to legislate on industrial development or to levy an income tax must be approved by a two-thirds majority in both national Houses of Parliament and a simple majority in each unit legislature. This would have enabled every territory, including little Montserrat, to veto such a change.

Trinidad again failed to obtain a similar veto over freedom of movement. This increased the hostility of Dr Williams, who said he would not accept decisions made by the conference but would take the whole issue to the people of Trinidad and Tobago and let them decide. He later described the Lancaster House conference as 'Trinidad and Tobago versus the United Kingdom.'[57]

So many speakers, from the federal Prime Minister to the Chief Ministers of the Leewards and Windwards, emphasized the need for continued financial assistance from Britain after the Federation became independent, that one West Indian observer remarked cynically that the sessions resembled a chorus from the *Beggars' Opera*.[58] 'The small islands' one interest,' according to a Jamaican journalist, lay 'in knowing how, in future, they may be supported in a style to which they are not accustomed.'[59]

As usual, the United Kingdom got few thanks for its aid to the British Caribbean. 'May we remind our colonial benefactors,' remarked the Chief Minister of St Vincent, 'that had Colonial Development and Welfare to the territories of the West Indies come earlier, ... the basic means of assisting our development would now have been achieved.' The Chief Minister of St Lucia said his island's concept of federalism involved a strong centre with sufficient power and financial resources to shape the region's development. He urged the conference not to repeat the mistake of 1956 which placed the national government in a financial straitjacket, unable to contribute to the development of less fortunate units. His delegation did not want to go home 'singing of independence' when in fact all that had been accomplished was to transfer colonial rule from one country to another.[60]

Both the small islands and the federal government considered essential a definite promise of continued aid from the United Kingdom. They demanded discussion of this matter, but the Secretary of State for the Colonies insisted on confining the early sessions to constitutional problems. The result was a bitter attack by delegates from the Leewards and Windwards on Britain, whom they held responsible for all West Indian ills, from draining the islands of their wealth in past centuries to neglecting them in the twentieth. The Chief Ministers of Montserrat, St Kitts, and St Lucia argued that the United Kingdom had an enduring obligation to the British Caribbean and that without financial help independence was meaningless. They demanded an interim payment of BWI $28 million and a guarantee of large additional grants to the Federation in the decade following independence to offset hardships caused by the moratorium on freedom of movement.

Mr Macleod replied that an autonomous federation would receive whatever economic assistance was necessary and possible, and that this might well be larger than during the colonial period. The United Kingdom was prepared to consider sympathetically proposals for temporary grants, pending consideration of an overall programme of financial aid to the Federation during the first ten years after independence. He agreed to send an official mission to the West Indies to consider short-term projects of special importance to the smaller islands and, in January 1962, to convene another conference to examine financial, economic, defence, and international matters.[61]

Many delegates were dissatisfied with these comments and considered Mr Macleod's stand a breach of the undertaking given their parliament in May 1960. He had then promised that, if the federal government could not at once assume all the normal burdens of an independent member of the Commonwealth, the United Kingdom would be willing to consider assistance during a transitional period. West Indians had been heartened by his acknowledgment, in this statement, that the financial viability usually required for independence might at the outset be impossible for the Federation.[62] Delegates at Lancaster House consequently considered that they were offered less than they had previously been led to expect. Their resentment was lively.

After two weeks of heated discussion the conference concluded with its leading members practically at each other's throats. The spirit of compromise evident at the Intergovernmental Conference was notably absent. The earlier *rapprochement* between Mr Manley and Dr Williams had vanished. Jamaica and Antigua alone appeared glad to have fashioned so weak a federation. Despite Trinidad's continued efforts at conciliation, Jamaica made no concessions. To Dr Williams's disgust, the small islands, which in fact believed with Trinidad in a strong central government, reluctantly swung over to support Jamaica, because they realized that without her there would be no federation.

Sir Grantley and his ministers had long been bitterly at odds with both Mr Manley and Dr Williams, but to have these two leaders not on speaking terms was a new and correspondingly alarming situation. Each thought he had been betrayed by the other. Dr Williams believed, with reason, that he had departed a long way from what he really wanted to accommodate Mr Manley and that he had genuinely tried to consider and make allowances for Jamaica's position. He deeply resented the fact that Mr Manley had achieved a veto on customs union while Trinidad had secured no similar veto about freedom of movement. Yet in order not to embarrass the Jamaican Premier before the referendum Dr Williams made no public comment about the Lancaster House discussions until November: two months after Manley had lost the referendum. Other members of the conference were less reticent.

Despite these critical differences of opinion the delegates finally agreed on a new constitution for The West Indies, subject to acceptance by all legislatures concerned. Two days after the meetings ended, the Colonial Office announced that, if the new constitution were duly ratified, the Federation would become independent on 31 May 1962.

The report of this conference recommended what British Caribbean leaders had long advocated, that each constituent territory should enjoy equal status by the time the Federation achieved autonomy. Another conference to consider appropriate amendments to the constitutions of the Leeward and Windward Islands was accordingly held while their delegations were still in London. This proposed that the Queen's representative in the smaller islands should have the title of Governor, be appointed on the advice of the local Premier after consultation with the federal Prime Minister, should lose the power of disallowance, and should act, not on royal instructions, but on the advice of the cabinet or of a responsible minister. Single-chamber legislatures should be retained, with one nominated member in Montserrat and two elsewhere. The title of Chief Minister should be replaced by that of Premier and the executive be styled the cabinet. The Governor should appoint as Premier the member most likely to command the confidence of the majority, with other cabinet members appointed on the advice of the Premier. There should be no official representatives in the cabinet except in Montserrat, where the Financial Secretary would continue to be a member.[63] These proposals were designed to make the constitutional status of the smaller islands similar to that of Barbados, Jamaica, and Trinidad. They ignored, however, the question of viability and whether it was sensible for tiny territories to possess the full panoply of responsible government.

POST-MORTEM

On his return to Jamaica Mr Manley was greeted by thousands of vocal supporters and smaller numbers of opponents hurling sticks, stones, and bottles, whose demonstration was broken up by policemen armed with batons and tear-gas bombs. After a three-day debate the Jamaican House of Representatives passed a motion by Mr Manley to accept the decisions of the West Indies Independence Conference. It defeated an amendment by the Jamaica Labour Party that the island should promptly become an independent member of the Commonwealth.

Sir Grantley Adams told Barbadian journalists that he was thoroughly disappointed with the London Conference, because he saw no point in federalism without a strong central government. In the national House of Representatives he declared that he would leave the political scene rather than support a federation with no power to control taxation of incomes and freedom of movement. He congratulated the smaller islands on their determination to preserve the union. If it broke up, the major causes would be differences of opinion about freedom of movement and the federal government's power to tax. He did not see how West Indians could complain about restrictions on immigration to the United Kingdom when Trinidad was unwilling to admit people from neighbouring islands. Trinidadian representatives promptly attacked what they considered slanders against their island and declared that federation was impossible without some local control over immigration.[64]

Thus the stage was set for the struggle over the referendum in Jamaica, where the opposition was naturally strengthened by the national parliament's prompt attack on the Lancaster House proposals. As the Secretary of State for the Colonies cautiously commented, it was clearly too early for rejoicing.[65]

Real nationalist sentiment existed in the West Indies, but principally in the Eastern Caribbean. The university was a powerful unifying force, as was cricket. The British Caribbean labour movement and various professional organizations were all gaining strength, and the growing volume and quality of West Indian literature and art were sources of regional pride. The territories shared common political institutions and a common, if embryonic, sense of nationhood. Although economic competitors, they were jointly concerned to present an unified front on guaranteed markets and prices for major agricultural exports and on consequences for the British Caribbean of the United Kingdom's possible entry into the European Common Market. A regional approach to the problems of tourism, agricultural research, shipping, and air communications was gradually developing. Inter-island trade was steadily increasing. The federal Court of Appeal had proved outstandingly successful. It was the tragedy of the British Caribbean that in the last analysis these significant bonds proved too fragile to overcome bitter differences of opinion and personal rivalries.

8

The break-up of the Federation

THE JAMAICAN REFERENDUM

Norman Manley's successful insistence on a deflated national government ultimately defeated his own ends by enabling Sir Alexander Bustamante to argue forcibly that such an emasculated federation was a useless luxury which West Indians could not afford. From mid-June to mid-September 1961 the referendum campaign dominated all other issues in Jamaica. At a political meeting on 3 August Mr Manley announced that the referendum would be held on 19 September and that he himself would stand for the national House of Representatives at the next federal election.

During the previous three years the island had been a leading member of the Federation. Yet only in these last three months of meetings, speeches, and letters to the press had many Jamaicans their first serious opportunity to learn what federalism really meant. The widespread ignorance and inertia about fundamental facts of political life were a comment on the ruling People's National Party which, during its six years in office, had officially supported the Federation but failed to cultivate an informed public opinion on what it involved. This failure, mainly caused by anti-federal sentiment within the party, was a major reason for the eventual defeat. From the outset Premier Manley fought an uphill struggle, almost single-handed, whereas Sir Alexander enjoyed active help from his principal colleagues. 'It is a fight against odds,' wrote *The Gleaner*'s political reporter, 'against apathy, against a determined opposition and against the natural insularity of Jamaicans, grown proud in their own concept of nationhood.'[1]

Mr Manley's campaign received little aid from his political cohorts in Jamaica and none from the rest of the West Indies. It was, however, supported by the powerful National Workers' Union and by an unlikely recruit, Kenneth Hill, formerly Acting First Deputy Leader and Whip of the Federal Democratic Labour Party. Late in July Mr Hill announced his resignation, both from the national parliament and the Jamaica Labour Party, because he believed Jamaicans had 'no honourable or practical alternative' to remaining in the Federation and that their character and reputation were at stake. He later rejoined the People's National Party. If the vote went against federation, he declared, 'no country would ever trust Jamaica, its Government or its people, for generations to come.'[2]

Mr Manley himself argued that a vote against federation would be a breach of faith deserving worldwide contempt. More than a year earlier he had publicly recognized that if Jamaica seceded, the national union would come to an end. On his return from the London Conference he contended that the 43 per cent of the federal budget paid by Jamaica was less than one per cent of the island's local budget, and that to 'go it alone' would cost more than twice as much as remaining in the Federation. His main financial argument was that most national expenses were for common services such as the university and the two federal ships, for which Jamaica would have to pay her share whether in the union or not.[3]

The Jamaica Labour Party attacked these figures as 'a masterpiece of deception,' argued that federation meant dominance of Jamaica by the small islands, and appealed to voters to save their beloved country from this peril. 'Who,' Sir Alexander demanded, 'ever heard of federating poverty?' The rich, he maintained, were arguing for a federation for which the poor had to pay. On a slogan of 'Jamaica – Yes – Federation – No' his party conducted an effective and ultimately victorious campaign based on an appeal to class and insular divisions.[4]

Although the Jamaican legislature ratified the constitution designed at Lancaster House, thus defeating Sir Alexander's amendment demanding immediate independence for the island, its people eventually chose to leave the Federation. The referendum result was 256,261 or 54.1 per cent against remaining in the Federation, as opposed to 217,319 or 45.9 per cent in favour. Of the 60.8 per cent of registered voters sufficiently interested to cast their ballots, a majority of 8.2 per cent or 49,000 supported secession. Thus less than 10 per cent of those who voted in one of ten constituent territories destroyed The West Indies. Jamaica's capital city of Kingston voted four to one for federation, but the day was carried by country constituencies which outnumbered urban by thirty-five to ten.

In all probability few Jamaicans realized the full implications of their decision or seriously considered the economic and political problems of independent nationhood. The referendum aroused far less popular interest than the Jamaican general election of 1962, in which almost 73 per cent of the electorate went to the polls. 'It is something to be deeply regretted,' said the *West Indian Economist*, 'that the long and often weary negotiations, the detailed studies, the hard-won concessions, the reluctant sacrifices, and the volume of sheer hard, grinding work involved in building the Federation should be negated in one day by one vital popular vote.'[5]

The issue was decided, not on the merits or demerits of federalism, about which ordinary Jamaicans knew little, but by the prejudices of up-country peasant farmers who, like rural peoples elsewhere, were suspicious of the unfamiliar. Repelled by the chilly logic of an austere intellectual like Norman Manley and by his idealistic challenge to support a wide concept of West Indian nationhood, they were attracted by the superb and humorous demagoguery of his cousin. They responded to Sir Alexander's appeal to isolationism and self-interest, to his contention that Jamaica's choice was between independence and subservience, that the referendum involved a vote for or against the Manley government's whole record, that the issue was in reality between the rich and the poor, and that the new brown ruling class favoured an expensive federal system which would further impoverish their unfortunate black countrymen, who would have to support impecunious little islands in the Eastern Caribbean. Edward Seaga (later leader of the Jamaica Labour Party) voiced an often reiterated argument when he maintained that there was too much need and want in Jamaica to think of using its resources to help others.[6]

The People's National Party had come to the fore on slogans of freedom and independence for the island. This made it difficult for its members to attack the Jamaica Labour Party's appeal to insular nationalism. Many voters were fearful of increased taxation and saw a conflict between continuance in the Federation and the long-sought goals of Jamaican self-government and nationhood. The question was not put to them as a choice between two alternative routes to independence, of which one lay through West Indian unity. Support for the Federation was among the most unpopular planks in Mr Manley's platform and opposition to it perhaps the only popular one in Sir Alexander's. For the People's National Party to appeal to the electorate on this single issue was a calamitous mistake.

Despite more than one public statement that he staked his political career on the outcome, Mr Manley did not throw the whole weight of his party behind the campaign. When he first announced the referendum, he stressed that his government would loyally support whatever decision the electorate made. This stand, widely condemned outside Jamaica as a sacrifice of principle to expediency, added nothing to his stature and precipitated his political downfall. Had he chosen to call a general election, or to gamble his future on the plebiscite by indicating in advance that he would resign if federation were rejected, his great personal popularity might have turned the scale. Instead, however, he explained that the referendum was a national issue on which voting would be free.

A majority of his followers rightly believed that he would not consider failure in it sufficient reason to resign. Many accordingly either abstained or cast their ballots against federation, in the comforting conviction that defeat would not mean the fall of his government. Had all of his professed supporters voted in favour, he would have won the plebiscite. His campaign was not helped by Sir Grantley Adams's concurrent attack on the Lancaster House proposals.

Mr Manley's political opponents did not allow these circumstances to go unregarded, but stressed his pre-referendum statement that he had pledged his political future to the Federation and would stand or fall by it. 'Well,' remarked 'Thomas Wright' of The Daily Gleaner, 'Federation has fallen and Mr Manley has decided to stand rather than fall.'[7]

It has seldom been possible to restrict a plebiscite to a single issue, detached from party considerations. The device is particularly unsuitable for a country with cabinet government. Where, as in Jamaica, the majority of unsophisticated voters were ill-qualified to determine a complicated political question, the decision to hold a referendum was singularly ill-advised. As a commentator in Jamaica pointed out, it was a means of 'playing political dice with destiny.'[8] Many Jamaicans probably believed that they were voting against change and for the status quo, as have most electorates in most countries, notably Australia, when asked to make a decision by a plebiscite.

The Jamaica Labour Party treated the matter as a straight party fight and, in the absence of other clear policies, was doubtless fortunate in being presented with a highly emotional issue. Since Jamaican, like most West Indian parties, were distinguished more by the personalities of their leaders than by political tenets, this lack of ideas was not surprising. Yet, as the West Indian Economist observed, people who shrink from discussing principles can scarcely believe strongly in federalism, which is designed to give effect to certain ideas.[9]

Mr Manley attributed the result of the referendum mainly to Jamaica's intense spirit of nationalism, fostered by geographical and psychological remoteness from the other British Caribbean islands. The internal autonomy won in 1959 undoubtedly exaggerated its already lively local patriotism. Mr Manley admitted his own deep disappointment at the outcome, which blocked what he considered the best and only safe road for Jamaica. To the rest of the British Caribbean he expressed his 'profound sorrow and regret.' Tens of thousands of West Indians, he said, 'will grieve at this defeat of all their hopes for the future and I share their sorrow.' At the moment of defeat Mr Manley probably realized better than anyone else the disastrous nature of his decision to hold a plebiscite: a last desperate gamble, with the stakes not simply his own political future but that of his island and of the concept of a united West Indies. His bitter disappointment at the outcome was unquestionable.

Six years later, however, he was contesting with Sir Alexander Bustamante which of them deserved more credit for enabling Jamaica to leave the Federation although, as Mr Manley frankly acknowledged, the referendum was a breach of the national constitution and of legislation by the British Parliament which brought The West Indies into being. 'I relied,' he said candidly, 'on the fact that no one would have dared to attempt to apply force to Jamaica.'[10]

To Sir Alexander the result clearly indicated that Jamaica was determined not to be ruled by Barbados, Trinidad, or any other territory. He called on the Premier to resign, but Mr Manley refused, on the curious ground that the referendum showed no clear lack of confidence in his administration, because a substantial number of his party followers had obviously voted for secession. Neither he nor his supporters, he argued, had been defeated on a party issue. He promised, however, to hold an election to decide which party should have the honour of leading Jamaica out of the Federation.[11] Within a week after the referendum he resigned as leader of the West Indies Federal Labour Party and severed his party's affiliation with it.

AFTERMATH OF THE REFERENDUM

The unexpected result of the referendum naturally shocked the federal government and the other territories. It also provoked much critical comment from outside as well as within the British Caribbean. Sir Grantley Adams described Jamaica's decision as a tragedy, but denied that this must break up the federal union. He urged his countrymen to profit from past mistakes and start afresh. 'If we want to make it succeed,' he declared, 'it can succeed and I am optimistic that The West Indies can become a stronger Federation.'[12]

Jamaica, wrote a Grenadian journalist, 'has sounded the death knell of the West Indian Federation.' The hard-pressed backwoods Jamaican, said a St Lucian, 'poor, ragged, barefoot, ... has spoken and utter confusion and chaos reigns among the leaders of the remaining islands.' In the Jamaica Labour Party, a *Gleaner* editorial commented, 'much of the cohesion and thrust which were thrown into the anti-Federal drive derived not only from Sir Alexander's consistent distrust of Federation, but also from the passion of some of his close and more dynamic colleagues to get to power quickly and to see, each outdoing the other, who shall succeed.'[13]

Jamaica's decision raised the immediate problem of whether the union could survive. As far back as 1912 a perceptive advocate of federation, Sir Algernon

Aspinall, had remarked that 'the West Indies without Jamaica would be like Hamlet without the Prince of Denmark.' Before the referendum Sir Grantley had said that without Jamaica the Federation's future would be bleak. After it he called an emergency cabinet meeting but declined to comment on the outcome. The Governor General interrupted a holiday in Scotland to confer with the Secretary of State for the Colonies, while Sir Grantley led a delegation to London to discuss the crisis. These September meetings were private and the official communiqué issued at their conclusion was noncommital, although it indicated that the federal government would continue for the time being to operate under the existing constitution.[14]

Mr Manley, for his part, immediately after the referendum, cabled the Secretary of State for the Colonies, requesting prompt discussion of Jamaica's secession and of a date for its independence. Before the federal ministers had departed from London, a Jamaican delegation arrived. Sir Grantley was much irritated when, without consulting him, the Colonial Office announced on 5 October 1961 that the British government accepted the result of the plebiscite as a firm indication of Jamaica's views and would introduce legislation providing for the island's withdrawal from the Federation and for its independence in 1962.

Mr Manley told a press conference that he thought the question of Jamaica rejoining a West Indian federation unlikely to be revived during his lifetime. To any surviving common services, however, his island would be willing to contribute its share.[15] On his return from England to Jamaica he received a tumultuous reception from enthusiastic supporters shouting 'power.' An opposition motion calling on his government to resign was defeated. A Select Committee of the legislature, composed of representatives from both major parties, was promptly appointed to draft a new constitution for independence.

THE POSITION OF TRINIDAD AND TOBAGO

When the rest of the West Indies recovered from the initial shock of the Jamaican referendum and began to examine the situation, there seemed some reason to suppose that the Federation was not necessarily doomed and might even be strengthened. An Eastern Caribbean union of the remaining territories, although only half the size of the original state, would form a more natural geographic entity. Many West Indians, especially in the Leewards and Windwards, hoped it might be possible to agree on a revised federal constitution giving greater power to the centre and less to the units. The feasibility of this view clearly hinged on the attitude of Trinidad and Tobago, whose 850,000 people would provide half the population and over half the wealth in such a truncated federation.

Its Premier, as has been seen, had more than once declared that, if Jamaica withdrew, his territory would follow suit. A few days after the Jamaican referendum the annual convention of the People's National Movement adopted a resolution that there should be no discussion of the national crisis until an election had been held in Trinidad. Dr Williams explained that he could not interfere with his islands' domestic needs by talking about federation, because Trinidad and Tobago came first. As the national constitution made no provision for secession, he argued that Jamaica's withdrawal was illegal, the Federation had consequently ceased to exist, and all that was left was a caretaker government. One from ten left nothing, not nine.[16]

Despite his official silence Dr Williams's views were indicated, not only by his jocular arithmetic, but by his public description of the Lancaster House agreements as a 'violation of every federal concept' and a 'total sell-out to Jamaica,' at the expense of antagonizing Trinidad and Tobago. To his mind their implementation would make the West Indies 'the laughing stock of the entire world.' The Jamaican referendum had set back for a generation the whole Caribbean region. He had refrained from stating his opinions at the London Conference of June 1961 only because the Colonial Secretary had persuaded him to hold his hand.[17]

The fact that the Trinidad opposition, led and dominated by East Indians, continued after the referendum to urge adherence to the Federation probably increased Dr Williams's antagonism to it. He reiterated his determination to reject Dr Capildeo's demand that Trinidad's position on the matter should be a major election issue.

If Trinidadians supported the proposed new federal constitution, Dr Williams warned, he himself would retire from public life rather than become a party to bastardizing the Federation. In his view Trinidad had participated long enough in this 'tom-foolery.'[18] Unlike Mr Manley, he was genuinely prepared to stake his political future on the issue. The Jamaican press argued that these statements clearly confirmed the wisdom of Jamaica's secession, since Dr Williams would in any event have refused to support the Lancaster House agreements.[19]

As the Premier of Trinidad declined to attend any conference called by the Prime Minister of The West Indies, it was impossible during the crucial last three months of 1961 for the federal government to initiate discussions with the leaders of the remaining territories. Moreover Trinidad's official silence was paralleled by that of the United Kingdom. Presumably in the belief that the first necessity was for West Indians to set their own house in order, it neither suggested further constitutional meetings nor convened the promised conference on additional economic assistance for the Leewards and Windwards. Indeed when the Secretary of State for the Colonies was asked in the British House of

Commons on 19 December 1961 what steps were being taken to give more financial aid to the Caribbean, his reply was discouraging. He regretted that, owing to Britain's own economic problems and adverse balance of trade, he saw no present prospects of increasing the £5 million a year already given the West Indian territories through the Colonial Development and Welfare fund, plus £2 million additional for grants-in-aid.

Under these gloomy circumstances Sir Grantley Adams threw himself wholeheartedly into a struggle which required all his native optimism. 'I feel in my bones,' he declared shortly after his return from London, 'that the Federation of the West Indies will survive.' It would remain in existence, he emphasized, until the Parliament of the United Kingdom modified the British Caribbean Federation Act of 1956. Its future depended on whether enough people believed in West Indian nationhood to preserve it.[20]

His views were supported by Dr Philip Sherlock, later Principal of the University of the West Indies, in a moving broadcast on the crushing blow dealt British Caribbean unity by Jamaica's decision. 'The work of fourteen years of discussion and negotiation,' he said, 'has been brought to nothing in a day, the expenditure of many hundreds of thousands of pounds turned to waste, a solemn compact between governments and peoples broken, the forces of separatism and faction strengthened, our stature as a nation diminished, ... by a decision springing out of a heritage of colonial parochialism.' In this desolate moment he asked whether the sense of West Indian nationhood was a deception, whether the peoples of the region were doomed to remain fragmented and set apart from each other, not by the sea, but by decisions of their own making. Himself a distinguished West Indian, Dr Sherlock concluded that there was indeed a recognizable British Caribbean community, if only because the islanders shared a common heritage of history, language, and laws.[21]

These sentiments were echoed by the Governor General, Lord Hailes, who stressed that the need for unity was never greater and the reasons for federating no less cogent than fifteen years earlier. In a radio address he appealed to West Indians to fight the parochialism and selfishness which were the enemies of all progress.[22]

ATTITUDE OF THE EASTERN CARIBBEAN

The small islands, for their part, refrained from embarrassing Dr Williams before the Trinidadian election by asking him to state his intentions, although it was difficult for them to make plans without knowing the attitude of Trinidad and Tobago. They themselves were divided as to their future, about which various views were propounded. Opposition members in Antigua demanded that it also should withdraw from the Federation. The Chief Minister of Dominica, E.O. LeBlanc, showed more grasp of reality in arguing that the Leewards and Windwards should espouse a strong central government and reduced local legislatures and ministerial establishments.

These views were supported by John Compton and J.D. Bousquet of the ruling St Lucia Labour Party. The former contended that ministerial systems were too expensive in the smaller territories where money could be used more advantageously to improve their economies. He advocated a revamped national constitution with power concentrated in a strong federal government. Although anxious to see the union survive, Mr Bousquet called on all the small islands to redouble their efforts to achieve full internal self-government. Hunter François, president of the Opposition People's Progressive Party in St Lucia, announced, however, that he would rather see the island remain a colony than 'be tied to Trinidad's apron strings as a pauper.'[23]

By November 1961 Principal Arthur (later Sir Arthur) Lewis of the University College of the West Indies, who had visited the Eastern Caribbean islands after the referendum as a special adviser to Sir Grantley, reported that Barbados and the Leewards and Windwards all wished to continue to be federated with each other and with Trinidad and Tobago. Should Trinidad, like Jamaica, opt for independence alone, the remaining eight territories wanted to remain federated under the leadership of Barbados. They unanimously rejected the idea of a unitary state. He found widespread agreement that Jamaica's secession had made possible a much stronger and more practicable union, and that the small islanders were united by the common sympathy essential for any successful federation but never felt by Jamaica for the Eastern Caribbean.

Most thoughtful West Indians in the area, he believed, considered that its fragmentation into independent countries whose people regarded each other as foreigners, would be a tragedy for which its authors would have to answer at the bar of history. He proposed an Eastern Caribbean Federation with a strong central government and a marked decrease in the administrative structures of the constituent islands, but acknowledged that the latter suggestion would be strongly resisted by certain Chief Ministers.[24]

TRINIDAD AND TOBAGO ELECTION, 1961

As the Trinidad and Tobago election campaign progressed, Dr Williams's attacks on the Federation multiplied. He was soon describing it as 'the biggest scandal in the West Indies,' conceived for the purpose of intriguing against Trinidad. The region, in his view, would have been 'in a bigger mess' if Jamaica had decided to remain in an union so weak as to be worthless. There had already been one referendum too many, and he did not propose to have another in Trinidad. If, however, one were held, he was convinced that 90 per cent of the electorate would vote 'to go it alone.' When Jamaica withdrew, 'everything mash up.'[25]

Trinidad's opposition Democratic Labour Party continued strongly to support the Federation and vainly to demand that its future be an issue in the election. Dr Williams steadily continued to refuse this and even declined to allow the legislature to debate what stand the island should take. He promised, however, after the election, to hold a series of public meetings to educate the public on issues involved in Federation.[26]

If some Trinidadians were alarmed by his attitude, they found little comfort in the exhortations of his rival, Dr Capildeo, to Democratic Labour Party supporters to arm themselves to break up meetings of the People's National Movement, march on Government House, and take over the country.[27] Dr Williams reacted with a threat to deal with profiteers who helped finance the opposition. Ten days before the election the tense political situation in Trinidad exploded into violence, when gangs armed with stones and cutlasses smashed cars, chased political opponents through the streets, and broke into homes.

There, as in Jamaica, short-lived minor parties proliferated. The Trinidad East Indian Congress, standing for equal rights for Indians, appeared on the scene in August 1961. In the following month Victor Bryan, a federal member of parliament, launched the United Labour Party, a working-class body dedicated to the ideals of Captain Cipriani. The left-wing West Indies Independence Party, chaired by Lennox Pierre, a solicitor, and founded in 1952 but quiescent since 1956, briefly re-emerged but did not contest the election. Uriah Butler, leader of the Home Rule Party, returned to the political scene, and the African National Congress appeared on it. In October the West Indian National Party for American Federation was formed by Jeeboda Ramtahal two days after he had conceived the brilliant notion of federal union between Trinidad and the United States.

In a series of articles in the *Sunday Guardian* Albert Gomes, maverick member of the federal opposition, conducted a lively one-man campaign to preserve the Federation. He attacked as completely undemocratic the Trinidadian ruling party's refusal to state its stand on the one really vital issue: the future of the Federation. He condemned its acquisition of the British West Indian Airlines as 'a potentially dangerous anomaly' involving operation by one island of a 'patently national amenity.' He criticized Dr Williams's recent appointment of a High Commissioner to London as implying independence for Trinidad, although the electorate had not been consulted. Why, he asked, should the man who had long advocated a Caribbean union including the French and Dutch territories, wish to break up the existing British West Indian Federation, the logical precursor to wider regional co-operation? Further fragmentation, he argued, would be disastrous.[28]

In the Trinidadian election of 4 December 1961, the first held under its new constitution, Dr Williams was supported by two powerful factors in the community: the National Trades Union Congress and the Roman Catholic Church. In a record poll of over 88 per cent of the electorate his party won a resounding victory and increased its majority, securing twenty of the thirty seats in the House of Representatives and 57.7 per cent of the vote, as opposed to ten seats and 40.8 per cent of the vote won by Dr Capildeo. The People's National Movement captured all four seats in Port-of-Spain, both seats in San Fernando, Trinidad's second major town, and the two seats in Tobago. Other parties failed to elect any members. This outcome owed much to Dr Williams's own conspicuous ability and to the success of his Five Year Development Programme, his scheme for free secondary education, his policy of spreading wealth, his effective party organization, and — a novelty in Trinidad — his administration's honest and stable government.

The rival Democratic Labour Party suffered from internal dissension, lack of any specific programme apart from support for the Federation and dislike of the People's National Movement, as well as from the fact that it was almost exclusively based on a racial appeal to East Indians. It retained three seats in the Caroni sugar belt and others in southern constituencies, but failed to win any in the suburbs or in Port-of-Spain, where election forecasts had favoured Dr Capildeo. At a party meeting to celebrate his victory Dr Williams described the Federation as a 'disgraceful episode,' wherein Britain and the United States had brought constant pressure to bear on Trinidad and Tobago to support a union which Jamaica then proceeded to smash and Barbados to repudiate.[29]

BARBADOS ELECTION, 1961

On the same day as Trinidadians, Barbadians also went to the polls, where only 60 per cent of their electorate voted. In the twenty-four-member House of Assembly the representation of the Barbados Labour Party, long presided over by Sir Grantley Adams and in power for the past fifteen years, dropped from fifteen seats to five. The seventy-year-old premier, Dr H.G. Cummins, who had succeeded Sir Grantley, lost his seat, as did all but one of his ministerial colleagues.

An impressive victory of fourteen seats was won by the able Errol Barrow's Democratic Labour Party, which had originated in 1955 as a splinter group composed of Sir Grantley's erstwhile followers who had become dissatisfied with his personal domination. Mr Barrow, however, gained only 36.3 per cent of the votes, as opposed to 36.8 per cent for the Barbados Labour Party. Four seats and 22 per cent of the votes were secured by the Barbados National Party led by Ernest Mottley, perennial Mayor of Bridgetown, while the remaining seat went to an Independent. The defeat of the Barbados Labour Party doubtless sprang in part from its very long term of office and in part from the absence in Port-of-Spain of its leading personality, Sir Grantley. While his prestige had helped to hold his followers together, his sometimes autocratic stand had often created irritation.

TRINIDAD'S DECISION

The new Secretary of State for the Colonies, Reginald Maudling, who had succeeded Mr Macleod in October, visited the West Indies from 13 to 28 January 1962. After a brief initial interview with him Dr Williams refused to discuss the question of federation, on the ground that he could not commit Trinidad and Tobago until his party convention reached a decision. Less than twenty-four hours later the General Council of the People's National Movement approved a resolution to reject unequivocally participation in any Eastern Caribbean federation and to 'proceed forthwith to national independence.'[30] The unitary state of Trinidad and Tobago would, it said, nevertheless be willing to contemplate incorporating any territory in the area whose people so desired. All the small islands except Grenada viewed this tactlessly worded proposal as a calculated insult, designed to parade their poverty. They promptly reacted by announcing their desire for a new federation without Trinidad and Tobago.

The resolution was, however, accepted both by the party as a whole and by Dr Williams's government. An alternative motion by Andrew Rose, Federal Minister of Communications and later High Commissioner for Trinidad and Tobago in Canada and in the United Kingdom, was withdrawn when it became clear that this had no chance of success. Mr Rose had advocated participation by Trinidad in a strong and centralized Eastern Caribbean federation.

The extremely lengthy resolution of the General Council of the People's National Movement set forth a detailed catalogue of Trinidad's grievances against Jamaica, the Leewards and Windwards, the United Kingdom, and the United States. Prominent among these was the complaint that Britain had not indicated how much aid it would in future provide for the small islands, to compensate for 'centuries of maladministration and underdevelopment.' The Federation, according to the resolution, had wasted time and money, frustrated the basic interests of the Caribbean peoples, and encouraged 'foreign intrigues in West Indian affairs, on such issues as Chaguaramas and Venezuela, thereby aggravating the basic conflict between the Government of Trinidad and Tobago and the Federal

Government.' Trinidad was willing to associate itself with all West Indian peoples in a Caribbean Economic Community, but would not participate in an Eastern Caribbean union involving it in major expenditures for the seven grant-aided islands which could not pay their own way. The Federation, the Premier told the House of Representatives, had 'died at Lancaster House and was buried in Jamaica in September, 1961.'[31]

In all this it was hard to recognize the party which in 1956 had promised support for a 'strong and vibrant Federation,' or the leader who in 1960 in *The Economics of Nationhood* had stressed the need for harmonious co-operation between national and unitary governments and described the Federation as an opportunity to help bridge the gap between the richer and poorer territories. Clearly Dr Williams considered the Leewards and Windwards a financial burden too great for Trinidad to assume, without Jamaica, and Barbados a questionable asset. His bitterness against other West Indian leaders may also have affected his decision.

Since the federal issue had been purposely excluded from the election campaign, it was impossible to tell how far the people of Trinidad and Tobago supported their government's policy of secession, strongly attacked by the East Indian opposition and by various voluntary groups in the two islands. It was consequently difficult to see on what grounds Port-of-Spain's leading newspaper contended that Trinidadians unanimously desired to advance towards full autonomy without hesitation or discussion of alternative solutions such as participation in an Eastern Caribbean union.[32]

The bitterness occasioned in Trinidad by different views about secession was illustrated by a letter to the local press. 'We were told to vote for Federation,' it said, 'and we did so willingly. But no one explained clearly to the masses what Federation is and the benefits to be derived from it ... Now the cry is independence. What really is independence? The masses do not know ... One of these bright brains who led us blindly into Federation is leading the people into independence without an explanation, and again without giving us a chance to choose. What are we heading for and what are we to expect? The majority do not know.'[33] The South Trinidad Chamber of Commerce protested against dissolution of the Federation without proper recourse to the people or their representatives and without any serious attempt by Dr Williams's administration to preserve West Indian unity.[34]

His government's intention to withdraw from the Federation was announced five weeks after Trinidad's election and the promised public meetings on the issue were not held. Many letters in the local press expressed 'profound disappointment' at the stand of the General Council and executive of the People's National Movement, while columnists variously described the decision to secede as 'a crime against West Indian history,' and as 'unrealistic, untimely, and self-centred.[35] West Indians abroad, including the London branch of the People's National Movement, were equally critical about Trinidad seeking independence alone. With similar forthrightness Jamaican students in Britain and Canada had condemned their island's referendum and called for a strenuous campaign to reverse it.[36]

AN EASTERN CARIBBEAN FEDERATION?

The Leewards and Windwards reacted to the Trinidad government's decision to seek unilateral independence by holding a conference which agreed to continue the Federation without Jamaica or Trinidad but, if possible, with Barbados. To an invitation to attend this meeting Dr Williams vouchsafed no reply. All government leaders in the Eastern Caribbean territories, except Mr Bird of Antigua and Mr Barrow of Barbados, who declined to attend, met with Sir Grantley, Sir Arthur Lewis, and Mr Maudling to discuss the matter.

At subsequent meetings Mr Maudling examined the future of the smaller islands with the Premier of Barbados and the Chief Ministers of the Leewards and Windwards. From these conversations they insisted on excluding Sir Grantley and any other representatives of the national government. Their attitude was partially explained by the fact that the new Chief Minister of Barbados, the thirty-nine year old lawyer and economist, Mr Barrow, was Sir Grantley's chief political rival in the island. The political leaders of the remaining units, promptly dubbed the 'Little Eight,' told the Colonial Secretary that they wanted to form a new federation, with a capital in Barbados, to become independent in January 1963.[37]

Continuance of gradually declining grants-in-aid from the United Kingdom they considered essential to the success of this enterprise. They recalled Britain's promise, at the 1961 Constitutional Conference, to discuss financial assistance to the Leewards and Windwards. The Premier of Barbados stated that his island did not support Dr Williams's suggestion about establishing a Caribbean Community and, indeed, wished in future to have no economic dealings with Trinidad.

The Secretary of State for the Colonies, while at first unenthusiastic, eventually described the proposal for an Eastern Caribbean federation as 'a very promising and encouraging idea,' and said that Britain realized the dangers of fragmentation in the West Indies. He warned, however, that any new union would require careful consideration, especially as to its constitution, distribution of powers, and economic and financial viability, and should not have local administrations too expensive for its members to support.[38]

His caution was understandable. Alleged financial irregularities in four of the eight territories were then being investigated by the Colonial Office. Barbados's revenues from income tax were almost seven times those of St Kitts, the next most prosperous Eastern Caribbean island. The imbalance in population and wealth among the different units, which caused many of the old Federation's problems, would obviously be repeated and accentuated in the new. Most small islands showed little concern to reduce the cost of insular administrations or to establish a strong centre. Although supporting a modified version of Sir Arthur Lewis' recommendations, most wanted a far weaker national government than he had advocated.

Moreover there were obviously important differences of opinion in the Eastern Caribbean. In Dominica E.B. Henry, leader of the opposition United People's Party, cabled Mr Maudling protesting against the proposed new federation, because its peoples had no assurance that they would benefit from it. To seek independence before economic stability had been achieved struck him as ludicrous.

A St Lucian member of parliament thought that, while a federation of the Little Eight would be ideal, it should be based in St Lucia, although Barbados would naturally command 'great deference.' The People's Progressive Party, one of St Lucia's two opposition groups, also objected to an Eastern Caribbean federation as economically unviable, since seven of the eight territories, unable to balance their budgets, were financially dependent on British taxpayers. It preferred to see the individual islands go their own way. What, it demanded, had the Leewards and Windwards to gain from a new union which would once more saddle them with 'a ludicrous circus of Governors, Chief Ministers, Senators, etc., requiring an initial $4 million to establish?'

John Compton, however, leader of St Lucia's National Labour Movement, like Eric Gairy, Chief Minister of Grenada, urged careful study of Trinidad's offer of unitary statehood and accused the federal government of intrigue and sabotage.[39] George Charles, Chief Minister of St Lucia, while supporting a new union of the Eastern Caribbean islands, emphasized their strong spirit of nationalism and insisted that they would never become wards either of any federation or of Trinidad and Tobago.[40] An editorial in the island's leading paper, the *Voice of St Lucia*, said that, while there had always been much to recommend a unitary state or strong federation of the British territories, recent events demonstrated that West Indians were not ready for either. The thinly veiled contempt of Dr Williams's party for the small islands was scarcely ingratiating.[41]

The Times (London) is an able leading article argued that it would be less wise for the small islands to embark on a 'Lilliputian Federation,' with all the costs of independence, than to consider joining the united state of Greater Trinidad.[42] *The Daily Gleaner*, conveniently ignoring Jamaica's conspicuous contribution to West Indian disruption, observed ungraciously: 'It may be that Mr. Maudling is hoping that Trinidad will pull Britain's chestnuts out of the fire ... In any event, opportunism and cynicism are not the answers to the problems of the "Little Eight." '[43] The *West Indian Economist* criticized the Secretary of State for encouraging the small islands to view federalism as a means of preserving the privileges and powers of local politicians, and argued strongly for unitary government under Barbados.[44]

JAMAICAN INDEPENDENCE CONFERENCE AND 1962 ELECTION

Within a week of the Colonial Secretary's return to London the Jamaican Independence Conference of 1-9 February 1962 opened in the same hall at Lancaster House where, eight months earlier, Mr Manley and his colleagues had helped to fashion a revised constitution for the West Indies Federation. If the Jamaican Premier detected any irony in the situation, it was not apparent in his reference to his island's 'experimental trial marriage' with the other territories, whose peaceful termination, he said, set 'an example to the world of democracy in action.' Mr Manley and his colleagues (equally divided between government and opposition representatives) preferred laying ghosts to resurrecting them.

It was not a politician, but a distinguished West Indian journalist, Theodore Sealy, editor of the Jamaican *Gleaner*, who recalled that the last time he had sat in that hall, 'we all thought we were making history; we were starting a new nation, the Federation of the West Indies. How wrong we were!'[45] An opposition representative with an odd sense of history, Donald Sangster (later Prime Minister of Jamaica), observed that Jamaica had started on the road to independence and merely 'paused on the way to help the Federation.'[46]

In his opening address to the conference the Secretary of State for the Colonies said many people had hoped that Jamaica would exhibit the political maturity it had shown at home on a wider federal stage, in conjunction with its Eastern Caribbean neighbours. Many regretted that the referendum had ended this possibility, but the British government felt bound to accept and implement the Jamaican electorate's decision. In an apposite reference to Donne's famous passage, he reminded the delegates that in the modern world no country could be 'an island entire of itself.'[47]

The conference eventually approved a new constitution for Jamaica drafted by a bipartisan Joint Select Committee of its legislature. The United Kingdom agreed that on 6 August 1962 the island should become independent: an event likely to be greeted, observed a British writer, with 'muffled cheers.'[48] It also undertook to support Jamaica's desire, on achieving independence, to be accepted as a member of the Commonwealth.

The Jamaican election of 10 April 1962 determined that the presiding genius at these celebrations would be the seventy-eight-year-old Sir Alexander Bustamante, who defeated his cousin by a margin of under one per cent or less than three thousand votes. Mr Manley campaigned under the slogan of 'The Man with the Plan,' the opposition as 'The Party with a Programme,' with Sir Alexander described as 'The Father of Freedom.' The People's Political Party, appealing as the spokesman of the poor black majority, adopted Marcus Garvey's motto: 'Forward Ever, Backward Never.' The campaign was tempestuous. Riot squads of policemen were unable to prevent clashes at political meetings enlivened by stone-throwing and the use of pistols.

In a record poll of 71.6 per cent of the electorate the Jamaica Labour Party, with 49.7 per cent of the votes, won twenty-six seats in the House of Representatives, while the People's National Party, with 48.9 per cent of the votes, won the remaining nineteen. Millard Johnson's People's Political Party contested sixteen seats and Independent candidates eight, but all failed to return any members. In the referendum less than 62 per cent of the electorate had voted. Clearly far more Jamaicans were interested in insular politics than in the future of the Federation. In view of the referendum results, those of the election were not unexpected. A majority of the voters evidently preferred Sir Alexander's warm-hearted understanding of ordinary people to Mr Manley's hard-headed, efficient, and somewhat academic approach to the country's problems.

LAST DAYS OF THE FEDERATION

Before leaving Port-of-Spain the Secretary of State for the Colonies had told Sir Grantley's cabinet that he intended to recommend dissolution of the Federation. On 6 February 1962 he explained the situation in the West Indies to the British House of Commons. The Jamaican electorate, Mr Maudling pointed out, had indicated its desire to withdraw from the Federation, as had the government of Trinidad and Tobago, which had also decided not to join any Eastern Caribbean union. The Premier of Barbados and the Chief Ministers of the Leewards and Windwards, while favouring a new federal union among their territories, agreed that the present one should be dissolved. Under these circumstances the government of the United Kingdom regretfully concluded that it had no alternative but to arrange for dissolution of the existing Federation and to set up an interim organization, under a commissioner appointed by Britain, to administer certain common enterprises (such as the university and national shipping and meteorological services) until some permanent arrangements could be made.[49]

The West Indies Bill to dissolve the Federation on 31 May 1962 was introduced in the House of Lords on 1 March and passed the Commons on 2 April. It provided for secession by participating units and enabled the United

Kingdom to establish a new federation or any other form of government for the British Caribbean territories except Jamaica and Trinidad.

This was not a bill, said Mr Maudling, that any Secretary of State could propose with pleasure. Marking the end of an experiment on which many people had placed high hopes, it was necessitated by divisions of principles and personalities. The long series of West Indian constitutional conferences had been bedevilled by economic and financial considerations. The British government, as it had told Sir Grantley Adams, had no power to object to the decision of a self-governing country like Jamaica to hold a referendum or like Trinidad to withdraw.

When during the debate in the House of Lords Britain's Conservative government was criticized for allowing Jamaica to hold a referendum, a Labour peer, Lord Ogmore, dissented. What, he asked, could Her Majesty's government have done to prevent this? 'Can anyone imagine, even if we had any battalions to spare, which we have not, that we could contemplate British troops shooting down Jamaicans because they wanted a referendum and we objected to it?' Your Lordships must remember, added the Earl of Perth, 'that these are free adult peoples, and, in the last analysis, they must do what they choose.'[50]

The United Kingdom, Mr Maudling believed, should proceed with caution on the proposed new union of the eight Eastern Caribbean islands, to be sure that this would be securely founded and financially viable, with an adequate central organization and reasonable machinery of government. Their total land area was smaller than that of Shropshire or Wiltshire and their combined population less than that of Herefordshire. Under these circumstances, eight chief ministers, cabinets, and legislatures seemed an unnecessarily substantial and expensive governmental structure.

The Labour opposition regretted the need for the bill but agreed that there was no alternative, although various members pointed out that until recently Britain had refused the right of secession to members of the Central African Federation. One Labour member, however, Denis Healey, who supported Mr Maudling's tribute to Sir Grantley Adams, complained that, although there was no part of the Commonwealth to which it owed a greater obligation, the United Kingdom had given many people in the British Caribbean 'an impression of bored indifference to their opinion' by its conduct over the Commonwealth Immigrants Bill. Despite the fact that most of their forefathers had gone there as slaves or indentured labourers, West Indians had always been distinguished by exceptional loyalty and all considered themselves British. It was time, he argued, for the United Kingdom to begin thinking about the region as part of the whole Caribbean and Central America. In this area of major concern to the United States it was possible that Canada, rather than Britain, would eventually be the most influential member of the Commonwealth. Like other speakers he urged consideration of a joint Commonwealth contribution to the British West Indies.[51]

Representatives of the Little Eight, meeting at Barbados from 26 February to 3 March 1962, could not agree to ratify the memorandum on a new union which they had presented to the Secretary of State for the Colonies. They forwarded a resolution to him declaring that the 'Save the Federation' mission then in London had no authority to speak for the Eastern Caribbean and requesting a meeting of the Little Eight before dissolution of the existing Federation. Despite diverse views about their future, they announced that, while they wanted a new union, they wished no further part in the old one.

The last days of The West Indies were undignified. The Premier of Barbados and the Chief Ministers of the Leewards and Windwards refused, as had Dr Williams, to discuss future plans with Sir Grantley and his cabinet. After the Jamaican referendum, the announcement that Trinidad also would withdraw, and the defeat of Sir Grantley's party in Barbados, many members from these three territories ceased to attend sessions of the federal legislature. Thus the Prime Minister and the rump of his parliament were more and more isolated and increasingly powerless to influence the course of events. They made, however, determined efforts to do what they could.

Sir Grantley announced his conviction that posterity would condemn Jamaica and Trinidad and history prove them wrong. Never before, he said, had there been unilateral repudiation of a federation whose constitution made no provision for secession.[52] During the last sessions of the national House of Representatives debate degenerated into an unedifying post mortem on apportioning blame for destroying the union. The decision of Jamaica and Trinidad to secede was bitterly attacked, as was the Colonial Office for permitting them to do so and failing to give more financial assistance or to consult adequately with the federal government. Certain members, however, acknowledged the part played by West Indians' 'fatal tendency to quarrel with each other' and to put their own interests before those of the nation.[53]

Outside the national parliament there was severe criticism of its members' decision to vote themselves, from dwindling federal funds, BWI $352,000 or some $18,000 apiece as disengagement compensation, although a pension for the Prime Minister was generally approved. The sharpest criticism was provoked by the belated inclusion of a token sum of $10 to compensate federal civil servants. The West Indies' parliament concluded its final sitting without making any further provision for its public officials. On 2 May 1962 it was notified by the Secretary of State for the Colonies that the United Kingdom had approved a compensation scheme based on recommendations of a working party composed of officials of the British Colonial Office and the federal and unit governments.

Debate on a motion by an Independent member of the West Indian parliament to oppose attempts to destroy the Federation ended with an unanimous vote of approval and a standing ovation for Sir Grantley. In a speech condemning Dr Williams's constant attacks on the national government, the Prime Minister blamed the Federation's failure primarily on Colonial Office intrigues in West Indian affairs. The United Kingdom, he complained, had neither informed nor consulted his government about the timing of the bill to dissolve the Federation.[54] A bipartisan delegation including members of both federal houses was appointed to request discussions with the British government.

The so-called 'Save the Federation' mission, led by Sir Grantley, spent five days in London before obtaining an audience with the Secretary of State for the Colonies on 13 March. By that time the bill to dissolve the union had passed its second reading in the House of Lords. Mr Maudling then informed the West Indian delegation that he would neither withdraw his promise to allow Jamaica to secede nor force Trinidad to hold a referendum before doing likewise. In a letter to him Sir Grantley described the dissolution bill as retrograde, arbitrary, and hurried.

From Sir Grantley's point of view insult was added to injury by a British order-in-council of 14 March 1962, about which he first learned from the London newspapers. This empowered the Governor General of The West Indies to act against the advice of his ministers and to refuse assent to measures passed by its parliament. The reason for its passage was to block payments by the national government of compensation and repatriation expenses to ministers and members of parliament when the Federation was dissolved. While the United Kingdom agreed that there might be a case for grants to parliamentarians, it considered the sum voted excessive in view of The West Indies' slender remaining resources and its failure to propose any adequate compensation for federal civil servants. Among the last acts of the national cabinet was a protest against a decision by the Secretary of State for the Colonies that the federal Prime Minister, Speaker, and ministers would receive terminal payments equivalent to three months' salary but that no such compensation would be given senators or members of the House of Representatives.

On his return to Port-of-Spain Sir Grantley attacked this British order-in-council as 'shabby treatment,' designed to strip his cabinet of power. The United Kingdom's actions, he added, although legal, were highly immoral. The British order-in-council also provoked a telegram of protest to the Secretary of State for the Colonies from the Premier of Barbados, no friend of Sir Grantley, who pointed out that for over three hundred years the United Kingdom had not legislated in this manner for his island.[55]

The last session of the federal parliament, from 9 to 11 April 1962, was largely devoted to recriminations by the one-third of its members who attended.

The legislature reiterated its previous condemnation of the United Kingdom, the Governor General, Mr Manley, and Dr Williams. It passed a unanimous motion deploring the fact that successive Secretaries of State for the Colonies had made no effort to preserve the Federation. Reporting to parliament on his mission to London, the Prime Minister stated that he had never been so humiliated as by Mr Maudling, who had for five days refused to see him and eventually talked with him for only fifteen minutes. In a farewell message on his final departure from Port-of-Spain Sir Grantley described the Federation's collapse as 'a shattering blow, ... fatal to the idea of West Indian unity.' Yet he voiced hope that time would heal present wounds and that from the ashes of the old union one Caribbean nation would eventually arise.[56]

His eloquence could not conceal the triumph of what Mr Manley at Montego Bay had called 'the vested interest of ambition in power.' In the acid words of a St Lucian, 'the power-spree that was the first West Indian Federation' had ended.[57] At midnight on 31 May 1962 the Federation was formally dissolved. The national flag was lowered, while buglers sounded the last post. This concluded the aspirations and hard work of many able West Indians and successive British Colonial Secretaries.

TRINIDAD AND TOBAGO INDEPENDENCE CONFERENCE

Three days earlier the Trinidad and Tobago Independence Conference had opened at Marlborough House in London.[58] The opposition Democratic Labour Party had bitterly attacked the decision by Dr Williams's administration to withdraw from the Federation without holding an election on the issue and without serious consideration of joining a new Eastern Caribbean union. Hence it was understandable that Trinidad's proposed constitution, unlike Jamaica's, was not based on agreement between the island's two major parties. This could scarcely have been obtained, since Dr Capildeo accused the Trinidadian government of autocracy and of drafting the new constitution prematurely, and had made a fruitless visit to London to lobby members of the British House of Commons in the interests of what he described as preserving democracy in Trinidad and Tobago.[59]

The draft independence constitution published on 20 February by Dr Williams's government had been widely distributed. The general public and private organizations were both invited to submit written comments by 31 March, a deadline the government refused to extend. The proposed new constitution ironically aroused far less general interest than preparations for Trinidad's famous carnival. Yet within the brief period allowed, over one hundred and sixty submissions requested constitutional changes, especially as to guarantees for civil and political liberties, which many considered inadequate.

Among the groups submitting comments were the Civil Service Association, the Indian Association of Trinidad and Tobago, and the African National Congress. Wherever a right or freedom was guaranteed, the Civil Service Association protested, it was nullified by qualifications. The Indian Association complained that the new constitution struck 'at the very root of the independence of the judiciary' and of individual liberties, while completely ignoring such important safeguards in the British constitution as an informed public opinion. The African National Congress contended that the proposed constitution established a legalized dictatorship and recommended that it be scrapped.[60]

From 25 to 27 April the Trinidadian government discussed numerous proposed changes at a conference of some two hundred people. Although the press was excluded and opposition members walked out of the meetings, Dr Williams described them as a landmark and their conclusions as the closest approximation to national unity yet achieved. Certain amendments arising out of these consultations were accepted by his cabinet and examined by a twenty-one member Joint Select Committee of both houses of the legislature, which included members of the opposition. The Democratic Labour Party nevertheless complained that, after several days' deliberation, its essential differences with the government remained. A revised version of the draft constitution, approved on 11 May by a majority of sixteen to nine on a straight party vote in the House of Representatives, formed the basis for discussion at the Trinidad and Tobago Independence Conference at Marlborough House. These meetings, from 28 May to 8 June 1962, convened in accordance with the Secretary of State's agreement that the territory should become independent as soon as possible, were attended by two official delegations from Trinidad and Tobago, one from the ruling People's National Movement and the other from the Opposition Democratic Labour Party.

Voluntary organizations also sent unofficial teams of varying sizes which presented diverse proposals, ranging from protests against the way in which the constitution had been drafted to suggestions for partition, proportional representation, or incorporation of Trinidad and Tobago into the United Kingdom. Among these bodies were two Indian organizations, the Samatan Dharma Mahasabha and the Indian Association. East Indians, who then formed over one-third of the population, were particularly fearful about their position in an independent Trinidad ruled by a predominantly black government. Local journalists promptly recognized that Trinidad's reputation was unlikely to be enhanced by all these rival delegations. To one *Sunday Guardian* commentator the spectacle suggested 'a degree of immaturity unsurpassed in the smallest or weakest West Indian island.'[61]

A threatened deadlock at the conference was finally resolved, largely owing to tactful compromises proposed by the Secretary of State for the Colonies.

Careful entrenchment of safeguards on important issues met the opposition's major demands. The last session culminated in wide agreement among government, opposition, and independent observers. At the delegates' unanimous wish, the United Kingdom willingly undertook to support Trinidad and Tobago's application to become an autonomous member of the Commonwealth. While Trinidadians were relieved by the outcome of the conference, many regretted that the independence inaugurated on 31 August 1962 was for their islands alone, not for the whole British Caribbean.

WHY DID THE FEDERATION FAIL?

The rapid decline and fall of The West Indies, reminiscent of the inexorability of a Greek tragedy, provoked much discussion about 'the Federation betrayed' or 'Who killed Cock Robin?' Why did the principal protagonists act as they did? Was the union, as Premier Barrow of Barbados maintained, an essentially 'unfederatable federation'? Could anything have been done to avoid the death of a state whose birth only four years earlier had been so enthusastically acclaimed? These questions were widely asked throughout the West Indies, where in many quarters there was a marked tendency to shift responsibility for the débacle to other shoulders.

The favourite but not invariable scapegoat was the United Kingdom. Jamaicans also blamed Trinidad and the federal government. Trinidadians blamed Sir Grantley, Jamaica, and the Colonial Office. The small islands blamed all three, but especially the two largest territories. The federal government blamed Britain, Jamaica, and Trinidad. Before the Federation's collapse its opponents criticized the United Kingdom for encouraging union in the first place. When Jamaica and Trinidad opted for withdrawal, its supporters attacked Britain for allowing them to secede.

During the years between the Montego Bay Conference of 1947 and the break-up of the Federation in 1962 two myths gained wide currency in the Caribbean. Federalism, it was said, had been forced on reluctant West Indians by a negligent imperial power indecently eager, after lucrative centuries of slavery and subjection, to slough off unwanted because no longer profitable dependencies. It was also alleged that the United Kingdom improperly withheld independence from the Federation. There is little evidence to support either of these views.

All British parties realized that it was impracticable, in the mid-twentieth century, to compel colonies eager for autonomy to remain dependent and none desired to do so. As far back as 1828 Wellington had declared in the House of Lords: 'We have not the power of governing ... colonies by force any more than we have the power of governing this country by force.'[62] A decade later Macaulay said of India that the result of exporting free political institutions would be elimination of the British.

The United Kingdom's reduced economic position after 1945 rendered it unable to defray the obligations of empire and to provide monetary assistance on the scale which the Caribbean islands considered their due. Without help most smaller territories could not balance their budgets. Few West Indians sympathized with Britain's financial difficulties, produced by its major role in the Second World War. Many found it simpler to accuse the United Kingdom both of attempting to 'divide and rule' and of urging them to unite. Yet at least since the late 1940s their political problems stemmed far more from themselves than from the Colonial Office.

Acute economic distress during the 1930s fostered the rise of Caribbean trade unions and political parties which demanded first self-government and then independence. British and West Indians alike originally believed that the only way in which the Caribbean territories could fulfil this aspiration was through some form of union. For this reason successive Labour and Conservative governments in the United Kingdom supported the federation long debated and many times approved by all West Indian legislatures. Delay in its establishment was occasioned solely by Britain's insistence that the peoples concerned must be sure that they wanted to unite and agreed on the form which union should take. In response to the colonies' urgent demands, federation was fostered, never forced, by the United Kingdom. Final decisions were wisely left to West Indians.

The *Report* of the Standing Closer Association Committee, as its Grenadian member, J.B. Renwick, pointed out, was prepared by West Indians. No outside source determined its decisions, which resulted from 'West Indian imagination or lack of imagination.'[63] Grantley Adams had told the Barbados legislature in 1948 that the British officials on this committee emphasized that it was for West Indians to determine the type of constitution they wanted; 'all we are going to do is ... our utmost to help you to go along the path that you are choosing for yourselves.' Eight years later he declared that nothing had been 'pushed down the throat of the West Indies by the Colonial Office; they have emphasized that they have left it to the West Indies to create their own constitution.'[64]

Norman Manley said in the Jamaican House of Representatives in 1955 that it was not 'the British Government which is keeping the Federal Parliament in a lower status. It is the inability so far of the people of the territories to agree to accept a large measure of responsibility.' When asked in 1958 why the Federation was not independent, he answered: 'Perhaps the timidity of West Indians ... The British Government is not withholding self-government from the people of the West Indies; we can have full self-government whenever we ask for it, and we West Indians alone will decide when to ask for it.'[65]

Three years later, at the opening session of the West Indies Constitutional Conference, Sir Grantley Adams also referred to the United Kingdom's readiness to grant independence as soon as the British Caribbean peoples could resolve their difficulties. 'It is one of the very good features of our post-war relationship with Britain,' he said, 'that the popular will in The West Indies and the policy of the metropolitan power have been directed at an identical dénouement of the historical drama in which we have been involved for more than three hundred years.'[66]

The facts of the matter did not deter the Jamaican press from asserting, both before and after dissolution, that the 'ill-starred Federation was the creation of the Colonial Office.'[67] The above comments by Caribbean leaders provide ample evidence, however, that, whatever its shortcomings, the Federation was made in the West Indies by West Indians and could have achieved autonomy when it wished.

As Harold Macmillan frankly told the federal parliament in March 1961, no matter how intoxicating the prospect of self-rule, its attainment would not abolish the difficulties the islands faced, but simply placed the onus for their solution more squarely on themselves. However poor a territory, he said, independence should be linked with determination to achieve the greatest measure of financial autonomy feasible. This in itself would stimulate economic effort but required a change of outlook in a region with few natural resources and long accustomed to financial aid from Britain. Some responsible West Indians agreed with him. Mr Bradshaw, the Federal Minister of Finance, pointedly reminded his countrymen that they could not call themselves independent but 'keep going cap in hand ... begging for technical assistance and everything else.'[68] Nevertheless a firm offer by the United Kingdom of additional financial aid for a given period might have helped to woo the Jamaicans and Trinidadians who anticipated from federation heavy financial liabilities and few economic advantages, and considered hopelessly inadequate the assistance given to the Caribbean by British grants-in-aid and the Colonial Development and Welfare Fund.

When the Federation's difficulties multiplied, it was impossible for the United Kingdom to force increasingly divided territories to work together. Yet in the critical period between the referendum and Mr Maudling's visit, Britain might possibly have helped by promptly convening a conference to discuss plans with federal and insular governments and by promising greater long-term financial assistance. Ultimately, however, the United Kingdom could not decently bribe unwilling peoples to co-operate.

Most West Indians believed that the Colonial Office had led them to suppose in 1960 that sizeable additional funds for the small islands would be forthcoming. Dr Williams considered this extremely important because greater economic development, especially in the Windwards, might have reduced unemployment and consequently pressures on Trinidad to admit immigrants from neighbouring islands. At the Lancaster House Conference in 1961, however, the British government insisted that the agenda should be confined to constitutional problems, although it agreed that later in the year another meeting should consider economic aid to the Leewards and Windwards. Because of disputes about the national constitution, these promised discussions were never held.

The veto for each unit on extending the federal government's financial and economic powers, secured at Mr Manley's insistence, meant that Jamaica or any other one territory could prevent both customs union and central control over development. Dr Williams bitterly resented the fact that Trinidad and Tobago was given no similar power to block immigration. His strong objection to allowing free entry to other West Indians increased his existing hostility to the Federation. This, coupled with his longstanding belief in a strong national government and conviction that, without Jamaica, Trinidad could not bear the major costs of union probably explained his refusal, between the referendum of 19 September and the Trinidad election of 4 December 1961, to indicate his attitude towards the Federation or to discuss plans for its future.

Two major British policy decisions in 1961-2 created much bitterness in the Caribbean. The first was the Commonwealth Immigrants' Act of 1962, which severely restricted entry to the United Kingdom. Confronted by the acute problem of trying to support too many people in too little space, West Indians believed that this measure was dictated by pure colour prejudice. Dr Williams was especially critical, because he thought British limitations on immigration likely to increase neighbouring islanders' demands for admission to Trinidad.

Many people in the United Kingdom sympathized with such West Indian views, even if they thought Dr Williams illogical in attacking Britain for imposing restrictions he considered reasonable when imposed by Trinidad. 'More than anywhere else in the old colonial empire,' wrote Sir Jock Campbell of Bookers (later Lord Campbell of Eskan) in a perceptive letter to *The Times*, 'the West Indies are what we made them. Consciences cannot be cleared by a judicious and tidy withdrawal from sovereignty. We brought the Negro slave and the indentured Indian to the West Indies, and it was we who started the West Indies on their present course. Already, to the great majority of West Indians, the Commonwealth Immigrants Act has seemed like a repudiation of the consequences of our own actions.'[69]

The other policy with no less serious implications for the British Caribbean was the United Kingdom's decision to seek admission to the European Common

Market. The Treaty of Rome, signed in March 1954, took effect at the beginning of the next year. In August 1957 the Regional Economic Committee in Barbados appointed an economist to study the consequences for the area of the proposed free trade area within the European Economic Community. West Indians watched the subsequent negotiations with anxiety.

This matter was discussed at the Lancaster House Conference in June 1961, when the Government of Trinidad and Tobago circulated a paper on European union. In the following month the Earl of Perth, Minister of State for Colonial Affairs, visited the British Caribbean and discussed with federal and territorial governments the implications for the region if the United Kingdom decided to apply for entry to the European Common Market. He promised that in this event Britain would consult closely at all stages with West Indian and other Commonwealth governments and do its best to safeguard their interests. After his departure the federal House of Representatives passed a unanimous motion that, failing adequate safeguards, Britain's entry would be detrimental to The West Indies and was accordingly opposed by its parliament, which requested representation at every stage of the negotiations.[70]

The islands' economies were then still predominantly agricultural, and their sugar, bananas, and citrus not competitive without traditional imperial preferences. Sales of bauxite and alumina, vitally important to Jamaica and British Guiana, might also be seriously affected if the United Kingdom joined the European Common Market, as almost half of Canada's aluminum and its by-products were exported to Britain and a sizeable additional fraction to Norway and Sweden, who might follow the United Kingdom into the Common Market.

British Guiana's Dutch neighbour, Surinam, a major rival producer of bauxite and alumina, already participated in the European Economic Community as part of the Tripartite Kingdom of the Netherlands. The French West Indies, because Departments of France, were also entitled to free entry for their products, as was oil from French wells in the Sahara. Other members of the European Common Market, including Italy and Greece, produced a variety of citrus fruits, as did North Africa and Israel, which might at some future date apply for membership. While sugar was partially protected by the International Sugar Agreement, similar provisions for citrus and bananas seemed unlikely.

The West Indies Federation, as a British dependency, qualified for the status of an associated overseas territory, and its products might be exported without duty to the European Economic Community, if reciprocal exemptions were extended to member countries, including the United Kingdom. It would, however, face competition from the associated territories of France, Italy, and Belgium, as well as from Surinam.

Although no colony, once granted associated overseas status, would lose this on achieving autonomy, approval of an application from an independent West Indies for membership in the European Common Market would involve gradual abolition of the customs duties from which the islands obtained an important portion of their revenue. Membership might also lead to political involvement in European affairs. If Britain joined the European Economic Community, West Indians were afraid that this would accentuate the Caribbean's existing problem of concentration on a few crops produced at high costs. Without special terms of entry for their primary products, they feared that they might face economic disaster.

It was not surprising that few people in the islands were concerned about the plight of a United Kingdom outside the European Common Market. Yet at the Commonwealth Prime Ministers' Conference of 1962 Dr Williams said that Trinidad, almost all of whose trade was with Britain and Europe, favoured both associate status for itself and the United Kingdom's membership in the Common Market. 'A weak Britain,' he declared, 'is of no use to us at all.'[71] When early in 1963 the United Kingdom's negotiations for entry were vetoed by France, Mr Manley expressed regret.[72] Such views, however, were not widely held in the West Indies. Hence, during the last two years of the Federation Caribbean relations with Britain were seriously strained on several grounds.

Most West Indians never really looked on the Federation as their own government. To many it seemed as remote and sometimes almost as unpopular as the British Colonial Office. The difficulty of forming a united community from widely scattered islands separated by geography and history and confronted by acute economic problems, was recognized from the outset. Yet some realistic West Indians acknowledged that their divisions sprang less from the estranging sea than from an estrangement of minds.[73]

The federal government never overcame the suspicion of the unknown which lay at the root of the British Caribbean's passionate insularity. West Indians' lack of familiarity with each other fostered a climate of misunderstanding, contempt, and suspicion uncongenial to the tolerance and co-operation essential for any successful democracy and above all for effective federalism. Brotherhood in race proved a frail bond among peoples who commonly viewed even adjacent islanders more as rivals than neighbours. The specious façade of unity, already crumbling when the Federation was established in 1958, turned out to be criss-crossed by divisions. Inter-island feuds challenged the concept of West Indianism, while hypothetical good will gave way to bickering.

Even the most patient and experienced statesmen have found federalism difficult. It was no fault of West Indians that they had had little practice in operating their own governments. Jamaica, for example, attained universal suffrage only in 1944 and did not gain full responsible government until 1959, a year after the Federation was launched.

Yet, despite all these considerations, failure of local leadership was beyond dispute. During the lifetime of the Federation British Caribbean politicians were noted neither for patience nor for willingness to compromise. A distinguished West Indian, Sir Arthur Lewis, believed it was primarily this failure, rather than internal problems, that destroyed the national union.

Sir Grantley Adams, Mr Norman Manley, and Dr Eric Williams, the three major figures in the ruling federal party (although only the Prime Minister had a seat in the national parliament), were all cultivated men of unquestioned ability and integrity. Their calibre would have made them outstanding in any country. So would that of the Federation's galaxy of dedicated senior public servants. Nevertheless acute personal antagonisms among these political leaders steadily exacerbated already difficult circumstances. For the most part they concentrated more on differences than on common goals. On controversial issues they had usually adopted well-publicized positions before arriving at federal conferences, where there was consequently little room for manoeuvre or conciliation. West Indian national parties did not, as in most federations, exert a unifying influence, because they never rose above their origins as loose aggregates of local groupings.

'Our sins, such as they are,' a member of the federal parliament wrote in 1961, 'are not of our Territories, but of leaders, whose political ambitions, despite their protestations, are still rooted in insular rather than regional achievements ... The reason why our Federation threatens to fall apart has nothing whatever to do with economic difficulties or physical distances but everything to do with the psychological malady with which West Indian leaders are afflicted. It is the personal power factor that has been threatening the Federation all along the way.'[74] The peoples of the British Caribbean deserved better from able West Indians who preferred ruling their little island kingdoms to fashioning a new state.

'Devoid of programme and consideration for the people,' C.L.R. James, secretary of the West Indies Federal Labour Party, said of local politicians, 'they saw federation and met among themselves only to arrange what their governments would get and what they would lose. That is always an important part of any political discussion. But if you are discussing nothing else, then the result is always the violent quarrels, in fact the unseemly squabbles for that is what they were, by which these gentlemen broke up the Federation and disgraced the West Indian people.'[75]

The largest and most prosperous territories naturally proved fittest in the struggle, as the independence, in rapid succession, of Jamaica, Trinidad, Guyana, and Barbados subsequently indicated. The economic interests of the more powerful islands triumphed over the ideal of West Indian unity. The Leewards and Windwards, divided among themselves as to their future, had long had their inferior position firmly emphasized by the other territories, as was illustrated by the well-known calypso: 'Small island, go back where you come from.' The two largest and wealthiest units took for granted their natural superiority to the smaller, poorer, and less constitutionally advanced. After the federal election of 1958 they found themselves paying the major costs of a national union less autonomous than Jamaica and with a cabinet dominated by the little islands to which they had long condescended.

Jamaica and Trinidad, accustomed to considering themselves the twin giants of the British Caribbean, found such a position from the outset galling and soon intolerable. The fact that their own governments were largely responsible for this situation made it the more humiliating. A federal state in which Jamaica and Trinidad were subordinate partners never had any chance of survival. As time went on, this became increasingly evident.

The Federation sprang primarily from anti-colonial sentiment and a wish for independence, rather than from a positive desire for unity. Its failure resulted from a variety of causes: inadequate finances, uneven economic and political development in the constituent units, the clashing personalities of its chief architects, and above all from a lack of any positive fellow-feeling among its scattered peoples.

'Nothing,' declared Dr Williams early in 1962, 'least of all a disintegrated Federation of the West Indies,' must block the path of Trinidad and Tobago to nationhood.[76] 'It was not that we loved others less,' said Donald Sangster of the Jamaica Independence Conference, 'but that we loved Jamaica more.'[77] Mr Manley echoed his political rival's sentiments.

If the leaders of Trinidad and Jamaica were clearly governed more by insular than national considerations, their people's views were less patent. The Federation collapsed because of the decision of one-third of the electors in one of ten constituent territories. Citizens of Trinidad and Tobago were given no opportunity to indicate whether they wanted to withdraw from the Federation or, when their government announced its intention of doing so, whether they preferred independence alone or as the leading partner in an Eastern Caribbean federation. What they thought about these crucial questions no one knew.

Ordinary people in Trinidad and Jamaica, catapulted into independence through a variety of circumstances largely beyond their control, viewed the prospect with a mixture of elation, curiosity, indifference, and natural misgivings. It was obviously difficult for even the most fluent orator to state precisely what independence meant or ought to mean. The less sophisticated were apathetic or puzzled because federalism did not solve their major problems, commonly attributed by Caribbean leaders to the evils of colonialism rather than to their islands' scanty natural resources, small size, and high birth rates. To the ill-educated and underprivileged majority of West Indians a national state unable to provide much needed concrete benefits made little appeal.

The federal government lacked money, power, and prestige. It could neither cure nor conceal the continued unemployment, illiteracy, poor health, and bad housing under which its peoples laboured. Nor could it be expected promptly to substitute wealth for poverty, although it might ultimately have stimulated trade and industry, encouraged improved methods of agriculture, and provided a more intelligent attack on regional problems. It was not surprising that such an union never succeeded in capturing the imagination or loyalty of citizens unable even to move freely from one part of The West Indies to another.

After the Federation was launched, the United Kingdom deferred to the islands' unanimous insistence on full self-government for each unit, with an attendant proliferation of cabinets and local pride. If this was a cardinal error, it was of the British Caribbean's own making. Effective federalism necessarily involves diminution of territorial powers. Such abortive West Indianism as existed was steadily eroded by rising demands for more local sovereignty. Under such conditions no federation could flourish.

Colonial aspects of the national constitution antagonised regional politicians hot for independence and resentful because the British Parliament retained power to legislate for all the units. Yet the United Kingdom could not reasonably be blamed because the Federation was not independent from the outset. At varying stages of constitutional development in 1958, most participating territories depended on aid from Britain, and in some local administration of finances left much to be desired. When the Canadian and Australian federations were formed, their provinces and states were also colonies, and decades elapsed before these older nations achieved full sovereignty.

Jamaica was partly responsible for the fact that The West Indies Federation never attained complete autonomy. The national parliament passed a motion in December 1959 requesting the British government to set an early date for full independence. Jamaica objected on the ground that the revised national constitution, then bitterly debated, should be settled first. With this view the Secretary of State for the Colonies agreed.[78]

It is easy to point to flaws in the federal constitution. All constitutions reflect, with varying degrees of accuracy, their citizens' temperaments and aspirations, strengths and weaknesses. They also reflect the geographic, historical, and economic circumstances which help to shape their people's outlook. West Indian history and traditions developed from isolationism, not co-operation. Whatever the formal provisions for amendment, constitutional inadequacies or mistakes, when recognized, can be changed when there is a will to do so. But to transform attitudes of mind, to put aside ancient animosities, to transcend familiar hurdles imposed by geography and long-established economic practices requires statesmanship of a very high order.

West Indians could have made their federal constitution work, whatever its shortcomings, had they been sufficiently eager for union and convinced that its assets outweighed its liabilities. In the British Caribbean such eagerness and convictions were conspicuously absent. This might perhaps have been altered by an early and intelligent attempt to develop among ordinary West Indians an informed public opinion on federalism and on the consequences of failure.

It can be argued that, for its own sake and that of the other territories, Jamaica should never have joined a union of far-away islands, many smaller than a Jamaican parish, about whose people it knew little and cared less. As Michael Manley observed in 1970, however central the idea of federation was in the rest of the Caribbean, 'it was always an afterthought in the dialogue of Jamaican politics.'[79]

Jamaica's secession gave Dr Williams an opportunity to fashion an Eastern Caribbean union to his own specifications, with the obviously desirable strong central government he had consistently supported. His unwillingness to assume financial responsibility for economically unviable islands was understandable. Yet it was sad that, at a critical juncture, the cause of West Indian nationhood was rejected by the regional leader who best comprehended what federalism involved and who had long advocated Caribbean unity.

Administrative costs in the Leewards and Windwards, although high enough to discourage Jamaica and Trinidad from assuming them, were in fact relatively small. The most serious objection to the inflated trappings of insular cabinet governments, much prized as status symbols, was that by fostering the little islands' sense of importance and pseudo-statehood they made united action on anything extraordinarily difficult.

These diminutive territories, unable to contribute much to the federal union, were most insistent in their demands on it and least willing to contribute what they could. Eager to get as much from and sacrifice as little as possible to the national government, some proclaimed their refusal to exchange rule by Britain for control by a strong West Indies federation. Their suspicion that the larger islands were likely to be less sympathetic to their needs and less generous than the Colonial Office was well founded. Yet their intense desire for self-government hampered achievement of any effective national union and thwarted development of any genuine sense of community.

Every territory, primarily concerned with its own pressing problems, distrusted the others. The insularity of each diminished the prospects of all. Trinidad and Jamaica were alarmed at the prospect of having to support the small islands, which in turn feared domination by those larger and wealthier. All were internally divided by cleavages of race, class, and colour, as well as by the yawning gulf between the rich and the poor. Under such circumstances it was difficult to develop a real sense of community even within a single island and much more difficult throughout the whole region. The Federation of The West Indies, as Sir Hugh Wooding wisely observed, 'was conceived in fear, lived throughout its brief existence with fear, and finally perished through fear.'[80]

In a revealing comment at the Montego Bay Conference Sir Alexander Bustamante remarked, 'To me Jamaica and Jamaica's interests come first. It must be so.' Federations, added Mr Manley, are born of social, economic, and moral necessity.[81] Once it became clear that the larger islands could achieve autonomy alone, their leaders saw no need for union, dreaded its financial obligations, and conveniently forgot what Mr Manley had described in 1957 as their 'tremendous responsibility' to assist the development of the whole British West Indies.[82]

In the British Caribbean fear of outside aggression did not, as in most federations, provide an argument for co-operative action. No external threat required pooling West Indian resources. Only the smaller islands could confidently expect from union clear economic advantages. The striking imbalances among the territories in size, wealth, and population, and consequently in power, were other major reasons for the Federation's failure.

National leadership was never strong enough to impose solutions acceptable to the large islands. Sir Grantley Adams and his cabinet received more criticism than appreciation of their singularly thankless task. Although the federal House of Representatives, like legislatures elsewhere, on occasion resembled a bear-garden, it is worth preserving a tribute to it by Morris Cargill of Jamaica. While acknowledging that he had spent many hours of excruciating boredom in the national parliament, he yet recalled that the debates were sometimes 'of a very high standard. Ashford Sinanan, Florence Daysh, and one or two other federal members of parliament were debaters of the highest skill: witty, penetrating and civilised; far in advance of anyone we've ever had in our Jamaica House with the exception of Mr Manley when he puts his mind to it. The Speaker, Erskine Ward, was an outstanding man as well as ... remarkably good at his job ... fair, well-informed and courageous.'[83]

A stronger, more efficient, and more tactful Prime Minister might have made a greater impact but probably could not have held together the Federation unless he had been a Jamaican or Trinidadian and thus able to attract from these two islands the support always essential but never forthcoming. Although the Premier of Jamaica led the West Indies Federal Labour Party of which the Premier of Trinidad was an outstanding member, the two men were soon at odds and rapidly became the Federation's major opponents. The national government's profoundly difficult position was made even more difficult by local journalists who, like their colleagues elsewhere, found disputes and recrimination better copy than patient efforts to secure agreement. Discussions on the most contentious issues were almost always conducted in a blaze of publicity.

The Federation won many friends abroad, but failed in the arts of conciliation and co-operation at home. It neither managed to reconcile the two largest islands nor to achieve their prestige. It was never successfully popularized among its own citizens and no one seemed to consider it his business to try to achieve this. 'The root cause of failure,' declared the Trinidadian Minister for External Affairs four years after the Federation's collapse, 'was lack of adequate preparation designed to get the people of the Caribbean to know and understand each other.'[84] Neither before The West Indies came into being nor during its brief life was any serious effort made by anyone to explain its rationale to its scattered citizens or to solicit their loyalty to the new nation.

On various matters rifts always apparent among the islands widened instead of narrowed during the life of the Federation. As a Conservative member of the British Commons remarked during the debate at Westminster on the West Indies Bill: 'there were always local island patriotisms, but there was never, unfortunately, a wider West Indian patriotism ... There was, to be perfectly honest, a sad failure of human relationships.'[85] This assessment should, however, be qualified by recognition of the intense West Indianism of many distinguished civil servants and professional people, who devoted years of hard work to building a nation, only to find it brought down about their heads. Most British Caribbean students at universities in the United Kingdom, Canada, and the United States were also convinced West Indians. Hence the saying that the Federation and West Indian nationhood were conceived in London and Toronto rather than in the Caribbean.[85]

Regional nationalism was always liveliest, not in attitudes towards federation, wherein insular sentiment usually dominated, but in a common enthusiasm for calypsos and cricket, ready pride in the work of Caribbean writers, and practical concern for territories afflicted by such natural disasters as hurricanes and tidal waves. A warm-hearted response to neighbours in need can invariably be relied on from even the poorest West Indian island. This generous sympathy in the face of others' misfortunes unfortunately did not carry over into the political sphere.

Ultimately the Federation failed because insular triumphed over national loyalties. This outcome seems in retrospect almost inevitable in an atmosphere where attacks on an effective federal Government became synonymous with local patriotism, and each constitutional conference, from 1948 to 1961, allocated less power and less revenue to the centre. For centuries the British Caribbean islands had been isolated, with their main lines of communication to the United Kingdom, not to each other. The development of air transport, which finally made union feasible, did little to break down the parochialism of the average West Indian who could not afford air fares, even to the next island.

The small white communities which for generations had formed the ruling élites had far more opportunities for education and travel than the vast majority of their darker compatriots. They might have been expected to exhibit more vision. Most, however, were primarily concerned with their own declining status and with maintaining their preferred economic position. Few chose to associate themselves whole-heartedly, or at all, with goals represented by the Federation. Very few were willing to work as partners and fellow West Indians with their black and brown countrymen to build a new state. Had they tried to do so they might have been rebuffed. On the other hand, their support and influence might have been significant.

An able Trinidadian commented that no one would have been 'more impressed and pleased than the black masses at a powerful, independent entry of the white people into the federation discussion. A politically sophisticated leadership, confident of itself and thinking of the nation, would have gone out of its way to encourage such a manifestation, however faintly it first appeared.'[87] The position of the whites was difficult and their attachment to the old colonial order understandable. Yet if posterity is likely to condemn the part played by leading West Indians in destroying their Federation, the sins of omission of the privileged white enclaves throughout the islands must be included.

The very receptiveness of the Colonial Office towards aspirations for a united West Indies also detracted from the liveliness of British Caribbean nationhood. 'In this rarefied atmosphere of benevolent co-operation,' it was aptly remarked, 'the flame ... was bound to flicker and burn low ... There was no cause left to keep West Indian nationalism fresh, and it quietly withered.'[88] As a Trinidadian observed, 'it is our loyalty to the parish pump that has brought us to the present sorry pass.'[89] Although some West Indians realized that the Federation provided their best hope of preserving civil liberties and democratic government, after four troubled years the islands abandoned what Mr Manley had once described as 'the greatest adventure of our people in all time.'[90]

Since the mid-twentieth century to abolish colonialism and achieve independence has proved relatively easy. To create and sustain a new nation firmly based on informed public opinion is singularly difficult. Without a sense of community they labour in vain who build a federal state.

The union was no sooner disbanded than its peoples demonstrated a lively desire to preserve some regional co-operation. 'The case for a West Indian federation,' Sir Arthur Lewis maintained in 1967, 'is as strong as ever.'[91] This view he based on the common cultural and political heritage of the British Caribbean peoples and on their need jointly to tackle common economic problems, to ensure competent administration, and to preserve political and civil freedoms.

Norman Manley once described federation as 'a dream and a hope and a promise of salvation.'[92] Belief in a comprehensive West Indianism was always an act of faith: the substance of things hoped for by men of vision. It may again quicken the peoples of the Commonwealth Caribbean. In Sir Arthur's words, another generation of West Indians 'may once more face their destiny, which is to come together as a nation.'[93]

9

Epilogue

To study the West Indian scene is to become aware of its long-standing and intractable problems. Some arise from slavery and neglect during the colonial period, others from insularity and personal rivalries among Caribbean politicians during the twentieth century. The most crucial, however, are caused by poverty, overpopulation, and limited natural resources in small territories geared to selling primary products on sharply fluctuating world markets.

The first six decades of this century were years of gradual constitutional advance, coupled with economic distress and social unrest. The period of independence and quasi-autonomy since 1962 has seen great strides in economic life, steady improvements in education, health, and welfare, and a marked growth in West Indians' sense of identity. This is not to suggest that all British Caribbean problems have been solved.

The birth and death of The West Indies Federation resulted from a combination of geographical, historical, economic, and political circumstances, as well as from the conflicting ideas and personalities of public men. The federal collapse was quickly followed by independence for Jamaica and Trinidad and Tobago in 1962, for Guyana and Barbados in 1966, for Grenada in 1974, and by associated statehood for all the Leewards and Windwards, except Montserrat, from 1966 to 1969.

To many people in the Commonwealth Caribbean autonomy at first seemed to promise a new era. It has undoubtedly brought marked economic advance, pride of nationhood, and conspicuous social improvements. It has enabled the five independent West Indian states to become members of the United Nations and to participate in related bodies. Yet it has also brought heavy additional expenses, especially for embassies abroad and representation at international conferences. Commonwealth Caribbean diplomats, despite their often remarkable calibre, have sometimes been frustrated by the restricted bargaining power of small countries.

As thoughtful West Indians realize, independence of itself provides no panacea for social and economic ills. Today, as in the past, their territories remain poor and still struggle to support too many people on too little land. Unemployment and underemployment continue to be endemic. Despite much progress in the past fifteen years, some children receive no education because there are not enough primary or secondary schools. The magnitude of these problems might well daunt the most able and experienced statesmen. Yet the peoples of the Commonwealth Caribbean are at least fortunate in confronting critical economic issues at a time when financial and technical aid from overseas is available on a scale hitherto unknown.

The real and alleged sins of imperial Britain long provided West Indians with a convenient whipping boy. They might have been expected to lose this asset when they became independent. With considerable adroitness, however, a vaguely defined 'neocolonialism' has been substituted as a modern scapegoat. Yet former colonies, now independent, can no longer reasonably blame a defunct imperialism for difficulties mainly caused by their small size, remoteness from large markets, high birth rates, and scanty natural resources. Colonial governments were clearly autocratic. Their strong rule nevertheless helped to mitigate tensions of race and colour. Under autonomy such restraints have largely vanished.

A sense of nationhood based on a real feeling of community has proved very difficult to foster within the Commonwealth Caribbean, especially in the racially divided territories of Guyana and Trinidad. Britain's withdrawal from the area has ironically quickened West Indians' appreciation of ideas and institutions for centuries nurtured by the United Kingdom. Independence has lent a new perspective to possible assets of the British heritage long obscured by lively local memories of slavery and domination.

Although colonialism obviously hampered development of democratic institutions, it at least ensured honest government, politically neutral civil services, and important civil liberties. With the advent of autonomy such assurances became tenuous. Many perceptive people in the Commonwealth Caribbean considered federalism the best safeguard for the continuance of these freedoms in a region where independent states were notoriously unstable, where Castro's Cuba was Jamaica's closest neighbour, and where in nearby Latin American states one revolutionary coup succeeded another with alarming regularity. Their apprehensions increased during the 1960s and 1970s when autonomous West Indian governments denied passports to radicals, limited movement from one territory to another, restricted liberty of speech and the press, and censored books.

With or without federalism liberal institutions avail little unless based on a spirit of compromise and fair play. Despite guarantees for political and civil rights in the constitutions of most newly independent nations, the temper of their peoples and politicians is everywhere the only effective safeguard for individual liberties. The problem of the modern Commonwealth Caribbean, as the Prime Minister of Trinidad and Tobago once observed, is no longer the transfer of power, but the manner of its use by local political leaders.

Most West Indian states still espouse a highly personal brand of politics centred on union-based parties. Political and insular jealousies have not vanished, nor has absorption with local as opposed to regional problems, despite steadily growing interest in the latter. Universal suffrage, in the Commonwealth Caribbean less than a generation old when autonomy was finally achieved, has in no country guaranteed a wise and informed electorate. 'Nothing in the long study of human history,' a liberal South African once wrote, 'bears out the thesis that majorities are always right or even tolerable, that every majority decision is the considered will of the people, or that every election puts into effect the national will ... An uninstructed people, voting on emotional grounds for a "leader," does not constitute a democracy.'[1] Responsibility for political decisions affecting them rested with West Indian governments for only a decade or so before independence. The best tribute to their leaders is the political maturity displayed after such brief experience of democratic practice.

Even when, as in the Commonwealth Caribbean, the path to autonomy has been smoothed by departing imperial rulers, the aura surrounding statesmen in power at the time of independence may conceal thinly veiled threats to democracy. In the first flush of freedom national leaders can do little wrong in the eyes of their followers. The natural temptation for politicians to feel themselves above criticism is increased when their education and tastes set them apart from the majority of their people. Where a new government is with difficulty distinguished from a new state there is a further temptation to consider opposition disloyal and to appeal to personalities rather than principles. In various African countries, as an able West Indian pointed out, parties in office when independence was achieved, were commonly resentful of an opposition and often decided to absorb or suppress it.[2] Such experiences offer a warning to the Commonwealth Caribbean.

Major assets of autonomy are quickened pride in the present and lively hopes for the future. Yet in the West Indies independence and quasi-autonomy have as yet given ordinary people few grounds to anticipate a future more kindly than the past. More than thirty-five years ago the Moyne Commission considered the demand for better living conditions by a rapidly expanding population as the most serious problem in the British Caribbean. Marked improvements during the past three decades have mainly benefited the middle and upper classes. Regional governments have spent large sums on building schools, houses, and hospitals and have tried to provide more employment by cultivating unused lands, diversifying agriculture, and encouraging industrial development. Yet in poor communities, where almost half the population is under fifteen years of age, it remains extraordinarily difficult to secure enough teachers, doctors, dentists, nurses, or social workers, not to mention skilled workmen. It is even more difficult to provide enough work, although Sir Arthur Lewis contended in 1972 that full employment might be achieved within a decade.[3] In a race against time the pressure of sheer numbers has continued to thwart the concerted endeavours of Commonwealth Caribbean governments.

West Indians are understandably concerned. For the vast majority of their countrymen, hard-pressed by rising costs of living, new politician may well seem but old planter writ large. However eloquently preached, the virtue of patience is more easily practised by the rich than by the poor. In some territories political leaders have reacted to mounting discontent and violence by proclaiming states of emergency and restricting civil liberties. Yet at heart they know that the real answer is not repression but more employment, better housing, improved education and welfare services, and greater opportunities for ordinary people. Governments do what they can, but usually too little and too late. The disadvantaged are not consoled by good intentions.

While in the Commonwealth Caribbean independence and quasi-autonomy naturally encouraged the insular sentiments from which they sprang, they also produced an opposite result. Perhaps nothing but achievement of their long-sought goal of self-government would have impressed on West Indians their fundamental interdependence. As colonies they had been suspicious of what many considered the United Kingdom's Machiavellian argument that the potential of an united British Caribbean would far surpass that of a baker's dozen of small and poor, if technically autonomous, territories. Under independence the cold light of economic realities has forced reluctant recognition that improved standards of living for all are attainable only through regional co-operation.

The economic basis of the five independent Commonwealth Caribbean territories is still precarious. In the associated states of the Leewards and Windwards it is infinitely more uncertain. These small islands of necessity continue to look to Britain, Canada, the United States, and the United Nations for financial assistance, and indeed to any quarter for capital investment and expanded markets. Material pressures have impressed on West Indian politicians the need for increased co-operation. Three of the Windwards — Grenada, St Lucia, and St Vincent — agreed in the summer of 1972 to introduce freedom of movement among their islands.

About the same time, at a private meeting in Tobago, a call for a new Eastern Caribbean union was issued by fourteen distinguished West Indians, including such stalwart supporters of the original Federation as Sir Arthur Lewis of St Lucia, Sir Fred Phillips of St Vincent, and Sir Hugh Wooding of Trinidad. All believed that the door should be left open for later accession by Jamaica and other Caribbean territories.

These signatories of a document urging a new regional political rapprochement contended that there was at least ground for a meeting of minds. They had grown up in an atmosphere which made them conscious of themselves as West Indians and of common British Caribbean ways of life, literature, and culture. They nevertheless recognized and were proud of their islands' diversity, which they saw as a source of strength rather than weakness. In their opinion the break-up of the Federation left all its peoples emotionally poorer and the younger generation without a sense of belonging. The time had come, they thought, to 'return to our task of creating a West Indian nation.'

Hence they stressed the need for a common external policy, greater regional co-operation, an expert pan-Caribbean public service, and, above all, a new sense of nationhood. They emphasized how fragile civil liberties were in small societies, the protection for them that a federal constitution and courts could provide, and the desirability of a central army, navy, and air force as opposed to separate insular services. On practical questions they were at once realistic and cautious. Thus they proposed that in a new federation residual powers ought to remain with the units, which should control their own agricultural and economic development, education, and social services. They considered it not yet politically feasible to introduce freedom of movement nor to finance a federal government from income taxes. They consequently urged that national funds should, as in the first union, come from customs duties. They nevertheless stressed their faith in a strong new federation and their conviction that, as in other such states, central powers would inevitably expand in relation to those of the constituent territories.[4]

These were proposals by a small group of West Indians, not by any Caribbean government. The Trinidad *Sunday Guardian* commended their initiative. The Jamaican *Gleaner* reported their suggestions without comment. The Barbadian Minister of External Affairs said his administration stood by views expressed a year earlier by the Prime Minister, Errol Barrow. He had then emphasized his lack of interest in a revived West Indian union. The most important priority, in his view, was to secure as much regional economic integration as possible.[5] The public opinion essential for another federation clearly remained to be formed. Yet it was significant that even a few West Indians, whose calibre made their views impossible to ignore, were again advocating a new union.

The Federation of 1958-62 failed chiefly because its leading politicians could not agree to co-operate. Nevertheless, as a Trinidadian journalist observed in

1964, 'West Indians who could not dwell together in unity, though stable concubinage is a hallmark of our societies, will have to learn to work together.'[6]

The Federation had, in fact, no sooner collapsed than its peoples showed marked enthusiasm for continued joint action. The islands promptly undertook to maintain the University of the West Indies, although Guyana decided to establish its own institute of higher education. The territories also agreed to continue regional shipping services, the seismological research station, and arrangements for the quarantine of plants. Sir Arthur Lewis of St Lucia, the distinguished former principal of the University of the West Indies, was soon appointed president of the new Caribbean Development Bank in Barbados.

By 1963 the heads of Commonwealth Caribbean governments had launched the first of a series of recurrent meetings. Three years later Guyana joined with Barbados and Antigua to form the Caribbean Free Trade Area (CARIFTA), which other former members of The West Indies Federation quickly joined. With qualified success this body tried to foster regional economic co-operation.

Under the Treaty of Chaguaramas in 1973 the Caribbean Free Trade Area was expanded into the Caribbean Community and Common Market (known as CARICOM), in which twelve former British West Indian territories participated. Primarily designed to further economic development and integration, the Community has managed to encourage greater trade within the area and more frequent meetings among West Indian politicians and public servants. It has also supported common external tariffs and tax incentives. While it presented a joint Commonwealth Caribbean point of view in negotiations with the European Common Market, this was an unusual example of successful harmonization of West Indian foreign policies. Even the Caribbean Investment Corporation, centred in St Lucia, has as yet been relatively ineffective.

Regional economic and political co-operation still remains more an ideal than a reality, although many West Indian politicians, notably Prime Minister Forbes Burnham of Guyana, officially support this goal. Among those who do not is Prime Minister Barrow of Barbados, who in 1973 said he hoped that 'we never get any political integration in which we will have some of the bandits that I now see masquerading as leaders presiding over the destiny of the unfortunate West Indian people.'[7]

All independent Commonwealth Caribbean countries except Grenada have in the 1970s achieved major economic advances. CARIFTA and CARICOM have, however, brought few if any gains to the little Leewards and Windwards, where there is hardly any industrialization.

What, if anything, it may be asked, might make another federation more acceptable than the old? First and foremost, a genuine sense of West Indian nationality, in the past conspicuously lacking. Second, a conviction that economic and political advantage can be gained from greater regional co-operation. A new and successful union would have to give its national parliament far greater constitutional and financial powers than The West Indies Federation of 1958-62 possessed.

Although most Commonwealth Caribbean states now seem agreed on the need for some joint economic activities, there has been no comparable consensus on common political action, although Prime Minister Burnham of Guyana has steadily advocated a new federation. Some form of political union between his country and those of the Eastern Caribbean is conceivable, yet only convinced optimists are likely to expect participation by Jamaica or Belize.

Is another West Indies federation practicable? The answer depends partly on whether viability means that a nation must be able to pay its own bills. Most large and prosperous industrial states now take for granted a huge balance of payments deficit. If this is feasible for them, what about tiny self-governing territories like Grenada? Very few such small countries have achieved independent statehood. Scarcely any modern nations are economically autonomous, in the sense of being able to produce everything they need.

Among the major arguments for almost all federal unions has been the prospect of economic advantage for their constituent parts. The West Indies Federation collapsed partly because it seemed likely to produce more economic liabilities than gains for the largest and wealthiest territories. It is difficult to see how in the future this situation can change, given the small size and limited natural resources of the Leewards and Windwards. A decision to form another federal union whose most prosperous members would have to anticipate more economic sacrifices than advantages would demand a rare degree of disinterested statesmanship and of regional identity.

The most serious obstacle to a new federation is the fact that from 1962 to 1974 five Commonwealth Caribbean territories became autonomous. No self-governing state can be expected easily to sacrifice any measure of recently achieved independence. At least until the older generation of West Indian politicians has passed from the scene, federation is unlikely again to become a practical issue.

The future of the Commonwealth Caribbean poses critical questions. Will autonomy create new problems without solving old ones? Will it forge closer links with Latin America, Canada, or the United States, when those with Britain have weakened? Will West Indians continue to uphold the democratic ideas and institutions conspicuous by their absence both in neighbouring independent republics and in Central and South America? One prophecy may be hazarded. If the prospects for a new political union remain at best problematical and at worst slight, increased economic co-operation appears certain.

Slowly but surely the peoples of the Commonwealth Caribbean are ceasing to concentrate on the centuries of enslavement and dependency and are turning towards an identity of their own making. If the colonial past was thrust upon them, the future is theirs to shape. Confronted by multitudinous intractable problems, they look to other nations for sympathetic understanding and practical assistance. Their foremost claim, however, is on their own countrymen's initiative and capacity for hard work and co-operation. The striking progress made since the abolition of slavery and especially in the past quarter-century give grounds for belief that this claim will be honoured.

'We have gone a long way,' Norman Manley once said, 'and we are, I doubt not, on the right road ... of confidence and pride in ourselves and our history and our past. The right road is the road of equality of opportunity for all our people ... [it] aims to abolish poverty and to provide work for all. The right road will have us all walk together — black, white, and brown — in peace and harmony, united because we are citizens of one land.'[8] Although he was speaking to and thinking of Jamaicans, his ideas have a wider applicability. It is for the peoples of the Commonwealth Caribbean to determine whether the vision of unity by which West Indians were once fired remains an aspiration or becomes a reality.

Notes

NOTES TO CHAPTER 1

1 Lambros Comitas, 'Metropolitan Influence in the Caribbean,' *Annals of the New York Academy of Sciences*, LXXXIII (1960), 809-15

2 Sir William Des Voeux, *My Colonial Service* (London, 1903), I, 116. See also Judith Ann Weller, *The East Indian Indenture in Trinidad*, Caribbean Monograph Series No. 4, Institute of Caribbean Studies, University of Puerto Rico (San Juan, 1968); and Dwarka Nath, *A History of East Indians in British Guiana* (London, 1950).

3 William Grant Sewell, *The Ordeal of Free Labour in the British West Indies* (New York, 1861), pp 82, 92; Joseph Sturge and Thomas Harvey, *The West Indies in 1837* (London, 1838); Edward Bean Underhill, *The West Indies: Their Social and Religious Conditions* (London, 1862)

4 Hume Wrong, *Government of the West Indies* (Oxford, 1923), p 48

5 Anthony Trollope, *The West Indies and The Spanish Main* (New York, 1860), pp 94-6, 103-7, 222

6 John Augustine Waller, *A Voyage in the West Indies* (London, 1820), pp 19, 21, 90-1

7 Henry Nelson Coleridge, *Six Months in the West Indies in 1825,* 2nd ed (London, 1826), p 294

8 Charles Kingsley, *At Last: A Christmas in the West Indies* (London, 1890), p 2

9 J.W. Fortescue, *A History of the British Army* (London, 1899-1912), III, 3-4

10 Trollope, pp 124-5, 156, 168

11 Des Voeux, I, 115. Sir William Des Voeux served successively as a senior magistrate in British Guiana, Administrator and Colonial Secretary of St Lucia, and Governor of Trinidad.

12 Sir Lionel Smith, Governor of Jamaica from 1836 to 1839

13 William Morris, Receiver General of the Province of Canada, *The West Indian Diary of William Morris* (unpublished), Queen's University Library, Kingston, Ontario

14 Cited in Eric Williams, *Capitalism and Slavery* (Chapel Hill, 1944), p 180

15 This issue is ably discussed by D.J. Murray, *The West Indies and the Development of Colonial Government* (Oxford, 1965), chap. 12.

16 Sir Henry Taylor, *Autobiography* (London, 1885), I, 248-57. Best known as the author of *The Statesman*, Sir Henry Taylor was then Assistant Under-Secretary in charge of West Indian affairs at the Colonial Office.

17 Theodore Walrond, (ed), *Letters and Journals of James, Eighth Earl of Elgin* (London, 1873), p 27

18 Herman Merivale, *Lectures on Colonization and Colonies* (London, 1928), appendix, pp 657-8. These lectures were originally published in 1841.

19 H.A. Will, *Constitutional Change in the British West Indies, 1880-1903* (Oxford, 1970), p 39

20 Letter to Mrs Hertz, 28 Feb. 1867, *Goldwin Smith Papers*, Cornell University Library, Cornell University, Ithaca, New York. The Morant Bay rebellion forms the setting of the novel, *New Day*, by the well-known Jamaican writer, Victor Reid.

21 An able survey of the principles of crown colony government is given in Great Britain, Colonial Office, *Report* by the Hon. E.F.L. Wood, M.P., on his Visit to the West Indies and British Guiana, Cmd. 1679 (London, 1922). See also Lord Olivier, *Jamaica, The Blessed Island* (London, 1936), chap 33.

22 Coleridge Harris, 'Constitutional History of the Windwards,' *Caribbean Quarterly*, VI (May 1960), 163-4; G.E. Cumper, 'The Differentiation of Economic Groups in the West Indies,' *Social and Economic Studies*, XI (Dec. 1962), 325

23 An interesting account of what was accomplished by a devoted Governor of St Lucia from 1869-76 is given by John Brown, 'William Des Voeux: A Portrait of a Crown Colony Governor,' *Chronicle of the West India Committee*, LXXXIX (Jan. 1964), 23-6.

24 Cited in Will, pp 26-7

25 Thomas Henry MacDermot (Tom Redcam), cited in W. Adolphe Roberts, *Six Great Jamaicans* (Kingston, 1952)

26 Great Britain, *Report of the West India Royal Commission*, Cmd. 8655, 8657, 8667, 8669 (London, 1897)

27 Great Britain, House of Commons, *Parliamentary Debates*, 4th series, vol 63 (2 Aug. 1898), col 873

NOTES TO CHAPTER 2

1 Great Britain, *West India Royal Commission Report, 1938-39*, Cmd. 6607 (London, 1945), p 57

2 *The Caribbean Confederation: A Plan for the Union of the Fifteen British West Indian Colonies* (London, 1888), p 106. This Cobden Club publication includes an effective indictment of J.A. Froude's biased but influential book, *The English in the West Indies* (London, 1887), which is an ill-concealed apologia for slavery.

3 *Port-of-Spain Gazette*, 7 Jan. 1890

4 Great Britain, *Report* by the Hon. E.F.L. Wood, M.P., on his visit to the West Indies and British Guiana, Cmd. 1679 (London, 1922), p 31

5 Ibid, pp 80, 106-7, 118-22, 134, 146-9, 153-8, 164, 168-9. A more detailed description of West Indian governments is given in Morley Ayearst's excellent study, *The British West Indies* (London, 1960).

6 Great Britain, *Report* of the West India Royal Commission, Cmd. 8655, 8657, 8667, 8669 (London, 1897), passim; B.C. Roberts, *Labour in the Tropical Territories of the Commonwealth* (Durham, North Carolina, 1964), pp 9-10

7 Eric Williams, *History of the People of Trinidad and Tobago* (Port-of-Spain, 1962), pp 171-9

8 Great Britain, *Report of the Commission of Enquiry into the Recent Disturbances at Port-of-Spain, Trinidad*, Cmd. 1662 (London, 1903), pp 12, 25, 31-2

9 Cecil A. Kelsick, 'Constitutional History of the Leewards,' *Caribbean Quarterly*, VI (May 1960), 196

10 *Report* by the Hon. E.F.L. Wood, pp 5-30, 43-55, 60

11 Candidates had to possess real property worth $12,000, or producing an annual income of $960, or have an income from any source of over $1,920 yearly. An informative account of the Legislative Council from 1831 to 1950 is given by Hewan Craig, *The Legislative Council of*

Trinidad and Tobago, vol. VI in Margery Perham, ed, *Studies in Colonial Legislatures* (London, 1952).

12 C.L.R. James, *The Life of Captain Cipriani, The Case for West Indian Self-Government* (London, 1932), pp 20-6, 40-9, 68-84, 103-7

13 John Wickham, 'Clennell Wickham: A Man For All Time,' *New World*, III (Barbados Independence Issue, 1966), 12; *The Herald* (Bridgetown, Barbados), 1924-8; F.A. Hoyos, *The Rise of West Indian Democracy: The Life and Times of Grantley Adams* (Bridgetown, 1963), pp 24-28

14 Grantley Adams, 'Blunders, Struggles and Regrets,' *Weekly Gleaner* (Kingston), 27 Jan. 1971; Hoyos, pp 53-5

15 The background of these changes is given in Great Britain, British Guiana Commission *Report*, Cmd. 2841 (London, 1927); and the *Memorandum prepared by the Elected Members of the Combined Court of British Guiana in reply to the Report of the British Guiana Commission*, Cmd. 3047 (London, 1928).

16 W.M. Macmillan, *Warning from the West Indies* (London, 1936), pp 54-6

17 Great Britain, *Report of the West Indian Sugar Commission*, Cmd. 3517 (London, 1930), pp 5, 13, 123

18 Great Britain, Colonial Office, F.W. Dalley, *Report on Trade Union Organisation and Industrial Relations, 1947* (London, 1947)

19 These comments were made by Norman Manley at the Montego Bay Conference. Great Britain, Colonial Office, *Report of Conference on the Closer Association of the British West Indian Colonies*, part II, Col. No. 218 (London, 1948), p 139

20 W. Arthur Lewis, *Labour in the West Indies: The Birth of a Workers' Movement*, Fabian Society Research Series No. 44 (London, 1939), pp 8-19; George T. Daniel, 'Labour and Nationalism in the British Caribbean,' *Annals of the American Academy of Political and Social Science, CCCX* (March 1957), 168

21 Great Britain, Colonial Office, *Annual Report on the Social and Economic Progress of the People of British Guiana, 1938*, Col. No. 1926 (London, 1940), pp 30-1

22 Great Britain, Colonial Office, *Report of the Barbados Disturbances Commission, 1937* (London, 1937), passim

23 In 1967, after years of distinguished service with the University of the West Indies, Dr Springer became the assistant and right-hand man of Arnold Smith at the newly established Commonwealth Secretariat. Union membership figures cited in the text are taken from an article by Sir Grantley Adams, 'Early Trade Unionism in Barbados,' *The Bajan*, No. 159 (Nov. 1966), pp 21-2.

24 Sir Grantley Adams, 'Blunders, Struggles and Regrets,' *Sunday Advocate-News* (Bridgetown, Barbados), 14 Feb. 1971

25 Mitchie Hewitt, 'Union was born during state of gloom,' *Sunday Advocate*, 20 Nov. 1966

26 'Butler, as almost everyone in Trinidad now knows,' a local journalist wrote in 1966, 'is an amalgam of impulsiveness, passion, and good intentions. Not even marriage has tamed him.' *Sunday Guardian Magazine* (Port-of-Spain, Trinidad), 26 June 1966

27 Great Britain, *Report of Commission on Trinidad and Tobago Disturbances, 1937*, Cmd. 5641 (London, 1938), pp 57-67, 76-89, 115-18

28 Lewis, 24-5

29 *West India Royal Commission Report*, Cmd. 6607, p 198

30 George Eaton, 'Trade Unions Big Boost to Modern Industry,' *Gleaner Independence Supplement*, 21 July 1962

31 *Daily Gleaner*, 24 May 1938

32 Cited by Colin Rickards, *Caribbean Power* (London, 1963), p 25

33 Government of Jamaica, *Report (with appendices) of the Commission appointed to enquire into the disturbances which occurred in Jamaica between the 23rd May and the 8th June, 1938* (Kingston, 1938), pp 3, 12

34 An informative account of Mr Bustamante's colourful career is given by O.W.
Phelps, 'Rise of the Labour Movement in
Jamaica,' *Social and Economic Studies*,
IX (Dec. 1960), 417-68, on which the
above synopsis of events in 1937-8 is
based.
35 *Daily Gleaner*, 31 Aug. 1938
36 *Weekly Gleaner*, 16 Feb. 1966, 17
Sept. 1969
37 Peter Newman, *British Guiana, Problems
of Cohesion in an Immigrant Society*,
issued under the auspices of the Institute
of Race Relations (London, 1964), p 77
38 Great Britain, House of Commons,
Parliamentary Debates, vol 332 (1938),
col 797
39 Arthur Creech-Jones, preface to Lewis
40 Great Britain, *Report by Major C. St. J.
Orde Browne on Labour Conditions in
the West Indies*, Cmd. 6070 (London,
1939), pp 12-17; Great Britain, Colonial
Office, *Labour Supervision in the
Colonial Empire, 1937-1943*, Col. No.
185 (London, 1943)
41 Macmillan, pp 37, 196-202
42 Orde Browne *Report*, pp 23-31, 39-50
43 *West India Royal Commission Report,
1938-9*, p 8
44 Ibid, pp 32-3, 60, 194, 202, 210, 422-52
45 Jamaica, House of Representatives, *Proceedings* (Aug. 1951), p 317
46 The recommendations were published as
a separate command paper, Great
Britain, Colonial Office, *Recommendations of the West India Royal Commission*, Cmd. 6174 (London, 1940). The
usual explanation for delay in publishing
the full report is that the conditions it revealed might have been used as enemy
propaganda.
47 Great Britain, *Statement of Policy on
Colonial Development and Welfare*, Cmd.
6175 (London, 1940), pp 1-8
48 Great Britain, House of Commons,
Parliamentary Debates, vol 361, (21 May
1940), cols 4-45. The debate on this measure may be consulted in cols 41-126 of
this volume. See also E.R. Wicker, 'Colonial

Development and Welfare, 1929-1957:
The Evolution of a Policy,' *Social and
Economic Studies*, VII (Dec. 1958).
49 Frank A. Norman, *Whitehall to West
Indies* (London, 1952), p 205. See also
Great Britain, Colonial Office, *Labour
Supervision in the Colonial Empire:
1937-43*, Col. No. 185 (London, 1943).
50 Great Britain, Colonial Office, *Development and Welfare in the West Indies,
1943-44*, Report by Sir Frank Stockdale, Col. No. 189 (London, 1945), pp
1-6, 27-31, 50-3
51 Great Britain, Colonial Office, *Development and Welfare in the West Indies,
1940-42*, Report by Sir Frank Stockdale, Col. No. 184 (London, 1943), 8-
14, 27-33, 59-67
52 T.S. Simey, *Welfare and Planning in the
West Indies* (Oxford, 1946), p 11
53 Great Britain, Colonial Office, *Development and Welfare in the West Indies,
1945-46*, Report by Sir John Macpherson, Col. No. 212 (London, 1947),
passim. This report lists schemes completed by the end of March 1946.
54 This attitude was signalled by the appointment from 1941 to 1946 as
Governor of Puerto Rico of Rexford
Tugwell, long an associate of President
Franklin Roosevelt and a conspicuous
liberal. An interesting account of his
career, with some comments on differences between American and British
colonial policy, is given in his *The
Stricken Land: The Story of Puerto
Rico* (New York, 1947).
55 Bernard L. Poole, *The Caribbean Commission: Background of Co-operation in
the West Indies* (Columbia, South
Carolina, 1951), pp 180-242. This
study gives an able outline of the commission's origins and accomplishments
during its first eight years. More detailed
information may be obtained from the
commission's publications: the *Caribbean Commission Monthly Bulletins*
and the *Caribbean Economic Review*.
See also Paul Blanshard, *Democracy and*

Empire in the Caribbean (New York, 1947).

NOTES TO CHAPTER 3

1 Cedric O.J. Matthews, *Labour Policies in the West Indies* (Geneva, 1952), p 71
2 Great Britain, House of Commons, *Sessional Paper No. 169* (London, 1939)
3 Sir Arthur Richards, cited in the *Daily Gleaner* (Kingston), 30 Sept. 1942
4 *Weekly Gleaner*, 5 March 1969; leading editorial on 'Jamaica and Federation: The Valley of Decision,' *West Indian Economist*, III (July 1960), 5-6
5 James G. Allen, *Editorial Opinion in the Contemporary British Commonwealth and Empire*, University of Colorado Studies, Series C, Studies in the Social Sciences I (Boulder, 1946), p 581
6 Alex Zeidenfelt, 'Political and Constitutional Development in Jamaica,' *Journal of Politics*, XIV (Aug. 1952), 530-1
7 Cited by Sir Harry Luke, 'The West Indies since the Moyne Report,' *Geographical Magazine*, XXII (May 1949-April 1950), 172; *Daily Gleaner*, 3 Jan. 1945
8 *Daily Gleaner*, 16 Feb. 1945; 6 March 1967
9 Jamaica, Central Bureau of Statistics, *Trade Unionism in Jamaica: 1918-1946* (Kingston, 1946), p 3
10 O.W. Phelps, 'Rise of the Labour Movement in Jamaica,' *Social and Economic Studies*, IX (Dec. 1960), 461-3; Morley Ayearst, *The British West Indies: The Search for Self-Government* (London, 1960), p 75
11 'Labour and Management in the West Indies,' *West Indian Economist*, II (April 1960), 18
12 Eric Williams, *The Negro in the Caribbean* (Washington, 1942), p 94
13 F.W. Dalley, *General Industrial Conditions and Labour Relations in Trinidad* (Port-of-Spain, 1954), pp 32-3

14 *Sunday Guardian* (Port-of-Spain), 7 July 1946
15 Trinidad and Tobago, *Trinidad Constitutional Reform Committee*, Minority Report (Port-of-Spain, 1948), p 15
16 Ayearst, pp 88-94
17 Colin Rickards, *Caribbean Power* (London, 1963), pp 107-8. This account of leading political figures in the British West Indies contains detailed information not easily obtainable elsewhere. See also Coleridge Harris, 'Constitutional History of the Windwards,' and Cecil A. Kelsick, 'Constitutional History of the Leewards,' *Caribbean Quarterly*, VI (May 1960), 160-209.
18 The early history of this protracted controversy is given by R.A. Humphreys, *The Diplomatic History of British Honduras, 1638-1901* (London, 1961).
19 Great Britain, Colonial Office, *British Honduras, Report of an Inquiry held by Sir Reginald Sharpe, Q.C., into Allegations of Contacts between the People's United Party and Guatemala*, Cmd. 9139 (London, 1954), pp 6-30. Excerpts from the *Billboard* articles of 24 Sept. and 7 Oct. 1951, are published as appendix II of this report. See also D.A.G. Waddell, *British Honduras* (London, 1961), pp 54-6, 109-13; British Honduras, *Report of the Commission of Inquiry on Constitutional Reform* (Belize, 1951).
20 Great Britain, Colonial Office, *An Economic Survey of the Colonial Territories, 1951*, vol. IV (London, 1953), 61; A.A. Thompson, 'University Education on Labour-Management Relations,' *Caribbean Quarterly*, III (1954), 57-8
21 Great Britain, Colonial Office, *British Guiana, Report of the Constitutional Commission, 1950-51*, Col. No. 280 (London, 1951). Among the members of this commission, chaired by E.J. Waddington, were Professor Vincent Harlow, noted historian of the Commonwealth, and Dr Rita Hinden of the Fabian Society.

22 *Sunday Advocate-News* (Bridgetown, Barbados), 25 July 1971; W. Arthur Lewis, *Labour in the West Indies* (London, 1939), p 42

23 Great Britain, Colonial Office, *Report of the Commission of Enquiry into the Sugar Industry of British Guiana, 1949,* Col. No. 249 (London, 1949), para 157

24 Great Britain, Colonial Office, *Development and Welfare in the West Indies,* Col. No. 212 (London, 1947), p 22

25 'Labour and Management in the West Indies,' *West Indian Economist*, II (April 1960), 15

26 This point is emphasized in a thoughtful article by George Eaton, 'Trade Unions Big Boost to Modern Industry,' *Gleaner Independence Supplement,* 21 July 1962.

27 This view is elaborated by T.M. Forrest, Education Officer of the Bustamante Industrial Trade Union, *Weekly Gleaner*, 22 April 1964.

28 Editorial, *West Indian Economist*, II (May-June 1960), 14

29 *Daily Gleaner*, 15 July 1961. See also B.G. Roberts, *Labour in the Tropical Territories of the Commonwealth* (Durham, North Carolina, 1964).

30 Maurice Salles-Miquelle, President of the Caribbean Employers' Confederation, *Sunday Guardian*, 24 April 1966

31 *West Indian Economist*, III (Feb. 1961), p 5

32 C.L.R. James, *Party Politics in the West Indies* (San Juan, Trinidad, 1962), pp 124-5

33 W. Arthur Lewis, *Politics in West Africa*, The Whidden Lectures for 1965 (Toronto, 1965), p 16

NOTES TO CHAPTER 4

1 This incident is cited by Hugh Springer, *Reflections on the Failure of the First West Indian Federation*, Occasional Papers in International Affairs No. 4 (Cambridge, Mass: Harvard Centre for International Affairs, 1962), p 9.

2 Other Leeward Islands are Anguilla, the bare rock of Sombrero, and Barbuda and Redonda, dependencies of Antigua since 1859 and 1872 respectively. The Virgin Islands, annexed in 1672 to the Leewards, obtained their own Council and Assembly in 1773.

3 Cecil A. Kelsick, 'Constitutional History of the Leewards,' *Caribbean Quarterly*, VI (May 1960), 179-89; C.S.S. Higham, 'The General Assembly of the Leeward Islands,' *English Historical Review*, XLI (April and July 1926), 190-209 and 366-8

4 Great Britain, *Report of the Royal Commission Appointed in December, 1882 to enquire into the public revenue, debts and liabilities of the islands of Jamaica, Grenada, St. Vincent, Tobago and St. Lucia and the Leeward Islands*, Cmd. 3840 (London, 1884)

5 C.S. Salmon, *The Caribbean Confederation* (London, 1889), pp 78, 131-8, 168

6 V. Schoelcher, *Les Colonies Françaises* (Paris, 1852), cited by Daniel Guérin, *The West Indies and their Future* (London, 1961), p 174

7 'Economic Problems of the Smaller West Indian Islands,' *Social and Economic Studies*, XI (1962), 47-51; David Lowenthal, 'Levels of West Indian Governments,' *Social and Economic Studies*, XI (Dec. 1962), 384-88

8 Memorandum of 22 Feb. 1876, cited in F.R. Augier and Shirley C. Gordon, *Sources of West Indian History* (London, 1962), pp 275-6. An account of this controversy is given by Bruce Hamilton, *Barbados and the Confederation Question* (London, 1956).

9 Great Britain, House of Commons, *Parliamentary Debates*, 3rd series, vol 355 (1891), col 1785

10 Great Britain, *Report of the Royal Commission to inquire into the condition and affairs of the Island of Dominica, 1894*, Cmd. 7477 (London, 1894), pp xxxvi-xxxvii

11 Great Britain, *Report of the West India*

Royal Commission, 1897, cmd. 8655 (London, 1898)

12 Great Britain, House of Commons *Parliamentary Debates*, vol 63 (1898), cols. 652-3; Norman Lamont, *Problems of the Antilles: A Collection of Speeches and Writings on West Indian Questions* (Glasgow, 1912), p 42

13 G.B. Mason, 'The Needs of the West Indies,' *Empire Review*, V (July 1903), 636-41

14 Great Britain, House of Commons, *Parliamentary Debates*, 4th series, vol 146 (17 May 1905), cols 696, 701, 713, 715, 722; *Report of the Royal Commission on the Sugar Industry* (London, 1896); Jesse Harris Proctor, Jr, 'The Functional Approach to Political Union: Lessons from the Effort to Federate the British Caribbean Territories,' *International Organization*, X (1956), 36; Algernon E. Aspinall, 'West Indian Federation: Its Historical Aspects,' *United Empire* (Royal Colonial Institute Journal, X n.s. (Feb. 1919), 58-63

15 'Imperialist,' 'The Problem of the West Indies,' *Fortnightly Review*, LXXV (July 1907); *The Times* (London), 24 Aug. 1907; Norman Lamont, 'The West Indian Problem: a Reply to "Imperialist," ' *Contemporary Review*, XCII (July-Dec. 1907), 672-8

16 'The West Indian Recovery,' *Contemporary Review*, CI (Feb. 1912), 232-41

17 Louis S. Meikle, *Confederation of the British West Indies versus Annexation to the United States of America – A Political Discourse on the West Indies* (London, 1912), pp 20, 21, 39, 59, 114, 133

18 C. Gideon Murray, *A Scheme for the Federation of Certain of the West Indian Colonies* (London, 1911) and *A United West Indies* (London, 1912). Mr Murray became chairman of the West India Committee and a member of the House of Commons before his elevation to the Lords as Viscount Elibank.

19 Jesse H. Proctor, Jr, 'The Development of the Idea of Federation of the British Caribbean Territories,' *Caribbean Quarterly*, V (June 1957), 13

20 'The Crown Colony Problem,' *Nineteenth Century*, LXXXIX (April 1921), 611. On various occasions Sir Samuel urged the same views in the British House of Commons: Great Britain, House of Commons, *Parliamentary Debates*, 5th series, vol 142 (7 June 1921), cols 1669-70; vol 143 (14 June 1921), cols 215-16; vol 144 (12 July 1921), col 1078.

21 Letter to *The Times* (London), 18 Dec. 1923

22 Sydney Olivier, 'Mr. Wood on the West Indies,' *Contemporary Review*, CXXII (July-Dec. 1922), 157; Great Britain, *Report* by the Hon. E.F.L. Wood, M.P. on his Visit to the West Indies and British Guiana, December 1921-February 1922, Cmd. 1679 (London, 1922), pp 29-32

23 *Proceedings* of the West Indian Conference, convened by the Dominica Taxpayers' Association (Roseau, 1932), p 102; Great Britain, Parliamentary Papers, *Report of the Closer Union Commission* (Leeward Islands, Windward Islands, Trinidad and Tobago), Cmd. 4383 (London, 1933), appendix A, p 5

24 *Report of the Closer Union Commission*, appendix A, pp 3-10; appendix B, pp 35-40

25 Great Britain, *West India Royal Commission Report, 1938-39*, Cmd. 6607 (London, 1945), pp 324-9, 424-5; F.A. Hoyos, *The Rise of West Indian Democracy: The Life and Times of Sir Grantley Adams* (Bridgetown, 1963), pp 83-99

26 Great Britain, House of Lords, *Parliamentary Debates*, 5th series, vol 125 (27 Jan. 1943) cols. 777, 784, 789, (9 Feb. 1943), cols 961, 972-3; House of Commons, 5th series, vol 387 (17 March 1942), cols 123-6, vol 388 (15 April 1943), cols. 1437, 1482

27 Eric Williams, *The Negro in the Caribbean* (Washington, 1942), pp 103-5

28 S.S. Ramphal, 'Federal Constitution in the West Indies,' *International and Comparative Law Quarterly*, II (April 1953), 199

29 Great Britain, House of Commons, *Parliamentary Debates*, 5th series, vol 402 (20 July 1944), col 410.

30 This despatch was published as appendix I to Great Britain, *Report on Closer Association of the British West Indian Colonies*, Cmd. 7120 (London, 1947), p 16

31 Sir John Mordecai, 'Federation and After,' *New World* (Barbados Independence Issue), III, (1966), 88; Caribbean Labour Congress, *Official Report:* Conference held at Barbados from 17th to 27th December, 1945 (Bridgetown, 1946)

32 *Minutes of a Conference on Closer Union of the Windward and Leeward Islands held at St. Kitts, 1st February, 1947,* Leeward Islands *Gazette*, Supplement, 3 Feb. 1947

33 *Report on Closer Association of the British West Indian Colonies*, p 709 .

34 Great Britain, Colonial Office, *Resolution, Statement and Draft Bill by the Caribbean Labour Congress, Col. No. 218, Proceedings of the Conference on Closer Association of the British West Indian Colonies, Montego Bay, 11-19th Sept. 1947*, part II (London, 1948), pp 121-31

35 Ibid, pp 4, 8-9, 20-7, 57-62

36 Ibid, pp 31-4, 43, 47, 51-4

37 Great Britain, *Report of Conference on the Closer Association of the British West Indian Colonies, Montego Bay, 11-19th Sept. 1947*, Cmd. 7291 (London, 1947), pp 3, 5, 7, 15

38 Great Britain, Colonial Office, *Report of the British Caribbean Standing Closer Association Committee, 1948-49*, Col. No. 255 (London, 1950)

39 Great Britain, Colonial Office, *Report of the Commission on the Unification of the Public Services in the British Caribbean Area, 1948-49*, Col. No. 254 (London, 1949), commonly known as the Holmes *Report*; Great Britain, Colonial Office, *Report of the Commission on the Establishment of a Customs Union in the British Caribbean Area, 1948-50*, Col. No. 268 (London, 1951), commonly known as the McLagan *Report*.

40 Great Britain, Parliamentary Papers, *British Dependencies in the Caribbean and North Atlantic, 1939-52* (London, 1952), p 22

41 A brief summary of the debates on these reports in various British West Indian legislatures is given by the Earl of Listowel, et al., *Challenge to the British Caribbean*, Fabian Colonial Bureau Pamphlet, Fabian Research Series No. 152 (London, 1952), pp 27-33.

42 In 1952 the Executive Secretary of the Regional Economic Committee was Mr (later Sir) John Mordecai, who in 1956 became Secretary of the Pre-Federal Organisation. In January 1958 he was appointed Federal Secretary in the new Federation, and in 1960 Deputy Governor General of The West Indies. The most distinguished public official in the British Caribbean, in all these capacities he played a leading role in bringing West Indians closer together and fostering a spirit of common nationhood. The best study of the Federation is his book *The West Indies: The Federal Negotiations* (London, 1968).

43 This memorandum was published by the Government of Jamaica, *Despatch with Enclosures from the Comptroller for Development and Welfare on Financial Aspects of Federation of the British West Indian Territories* (Kingston, 1953).

NOTES TO CHAPTER 5

1 Great Britain, *The Plan for a British Caribbean Federation agreed by the Conference on West Indian Federation held in London in April 1953*, Cmd. 8895 (London, 1953). Detailed

analyses of the changes in the constitution made at this conference are given in two articles: Jesse H. Proctor, Jr, 'The Framing of the West Indian Federal Constitution: an Adventure in National Self-Determination,' *Revista de Historia de América,* LVII-LVIII (Dec. 1964), 80-9; and Gordon K. Lewis, 'West Indian Federation: The Constitutional Aspects,' *Social and Economic Studies,* VI (June 1957), 215-46.

2 Barbados House of Assembly, *Debates,* 19 Jan. 1956, p 1957

3 Great Britain, Colonial Office, *Report of the Conference on Movement of Persons within a British Caribbean Federation, held in Port-of-Spain, 14-17 March, 1955,* Col. No. 315 (London, 1955), pp 1-6

4 Speech in New York, 13 June 1954, at the Abyssinian Baptist Church, cited in the *Daily Gleaner* (Kingston), 26 June 1954; speech in the Jamaican House of Representatives, 22 July 1954, cited in the *Sunday Gleaner,* 16 March 1958

5 Charles H. Archibald, 'A West Indian Party,' *Daily Gleaner,* 7 Oct. 1955

6 Great Britain, *The Plan for a British Caribbean Federation: Report of the Fiscal Commissioner,* Cmd. 9618 (London, 1955), pp 24-70

7 Great Britain, *The Plan for a British Caribbean Federation: Report of the Civil Service Commissioner,* Cmd. 9619 (London, 1955), pp 15-19, 23, 43

8 Great Britain, *The Plan for a British Caribbean Federation: Report of the Judicial Commissioner,* Cmd. 9620 (London, 1955), pp 1-13

9 Great Britain, *Report by the Conference on British Caribbean Federation, held in London in February, 1956,* Cmd. 9733 (London, 1956), pp 3-15

10 Speech at Woodford Square, 5 Jan. 1956, published in *Federation, Two Public Lectures* (Port-of-Spain, 1956), pp 11-12

11 Great Britain, Colonial Office, *British Caribbean Federal Capital Commission Report,* Col. No. 328 (London, 1956), p 20

12 Ibid, p 21. See also David Lowenthal, 'The West Indies Chooses a Capital,' *Geographical Review,* XLVIII (1958), 336-64.

13 Great Britain, Colonial Office, *Report of the Chaguaramas Joint Commission,* Col. No. 338 (London, 1958), p 2

14 Eric Williams, *History of the People of Trinidad and Tobago* (Port-of-Spain, 1962), pp 269-79

15 Taken from Psalm 135: 'Behold how good and pleasant it is for brethren to dwell together in unity.'

16 'The West Indian Experience and Hopes,' in P.A. Lockwood, ed, *Canada and the West Indies,* Mt Allison University Publication No. 2 (Sackville, New Brunswick, 1957), p 24

17 Dudley Seers, 'Federation of the British West Indies: The Economic and Financial Aspects,' *Social and Economic Studies,* VI (June 1957), 204

18 Joseph Bousquet of St Lucia, *Daily Gleaner,* 19 Nov. 1960

19 An interesting discussion of this theme is 'Federation in the British Caribbean: An Exercise in Colonial Administration,' *Round Table,* XXXIX (June 1949), 230-9

20 Peter Abrahams, *Jamaica* (London, 1957), p 197

21 'Labour and Management in the West Indies,' *West Indian Economist,* II (April 1960), 17-20

22 F.W. Dalley, *General Industrial Conditions and Labour Relations in Trinidad* (Port-of-Spain, 1954), pp 7-15, 32-40, 46-9

23 *New Commonwealth,* British Caribbean Supplement, XXX (July-Dec. 1955), 2

NOTES TO CHAPTER 6

1 *Daily Gleaner* (Kingston), 5 April 1957; 21, 22 June 1956

2 Mr Cargill was an unusual type of West Indian politician. A white planter and a

brilliant journalist, under the pseudonym 'Thomas Wright' he long contributed to the Jamaican *Gleaner* a column notable for style, wit, and good sense.

3 *Daily Gleaner*, 13 Jan. 1958; *Trinidad Guardian*, 18 Jan. 1958

4 *The Trumpet* (Kingston), I (Oct. 1957), 12

5 *West Indian Review*, IV (Aug.-Sept. 1959), 11

6 *Daily Gleaner*, 4 June, 13 Sept. 1957; *Sunday Gleaner*, 22 Sept. 1957

7 *Daily Gleaner*, 14 Jan. 1957

8 *Sunday Gleaner*, 22 Sept. 1957

9 *Trinidad Guardian*, 16 Jan. 1958

10 *Sunday Guardian*, 16 March 1958

11 *Sunday Gleaner*, 11 Jan. 1959

12 The Council of State was composed of Sir Grantley Adams (Barbados), Prime Minister; R.L. Bradshaw (St Kitts), Minister of Finance; C.D. La Corbinière (St Lucia), Deputy Prime Minister and Minister of Trade and Industries; F.B. Ricketts (Jamaica), Minister of Natural Resources; W.A. Rose (Trinidad), Minister of Communications; Mrs Phyllis Allfrey (Dominica), Minister of Social Affairs; and V.B. Vaughan (Barbados), N.H. Richards (Antigua), Senator A.G. Byfield (Jamaica), Senator J.W. Liburd (Nevis), and Senator J.J. Charles (St Lucia), ministers without portfolio.

13 In a BBC broadcast at the end of the 1956 London Conference: *Barbados Advocate*, 1 Sept. 1963

14 *Daily Gleaner*, 24, 25 April 1958

15 Ibid, 29 Aug. 1958

16 *Trinidad Guardian*, 26 Sept. 1958

17 Eric Williams, *History of the People of Trinidad and Tobago* (Port-of-Spain, 1962), p 258

18 G. St C. Scotter, 'ToDay,' *Daily Gleaner*, 22 Nov. 1958

19 Handley Powell, 'The Progress of Federation,' *West Indies Federal Review* (Jan. 1959), pp 81-7; *Daily Gleaner*, 31 Oct. 1958

20 *Daily Gleaner*, 5, 9 Nov. 1958

21 Ibid, 30 Nov., 5, 6 Dec. 1958

22 Ibid, 4 Feb. 1959

23 The West Indies, *Report* of the Trade and Tariffs Commission appointed by the Secretary of State for the Colonies (Port-of-Spain, 1958), pp 1-59

24 *Daily Gleaner*, 18 Aug. 1958

25 Sir John Mordecai, *The West Indies: The Federal Negotiations* (London, 1968), pp 124-7; *Trinidad Chronicle*, 29 Aug. 1958; *Trinidad Guardian*, 30 Aug. 1958

26 *Voice of St. Lucia* (Castries), 8 Nov. 1958

27 Mordecai, p 187

28 *West Indies Federal Review* (Oct. 1960), 11

29 Aug. 1958; *Trinidad Guardian*, Service, *The First Year; Six Broadcasts by Ministers of the Federal Government of the West Indies* (Port-of-Spain, 1959), pp 12-14

30 Ibid

31 *Daily Gleaner*, 8, 28 Jan. 1959; *Sunday Gleaner*, 18 Jan. 1959.

32 *Daily Gleaner*, 3 Feb. 1959

33 Government of Trinidad and Tobago, Office of the Premier and Ministry of Finance, *Economics of Nationhood* (Port-of-Spain, 1959), pp 4-11

34 John Pilgrim, 4 Feb. 1959

35 *Report by the Leeward and Windward Islands Constitutional Conference*, held in London in June 1959 (Port-of-Spain, 1959)

36 The West Indies, *Report* of the Inter-Governmental Conference on Review of the Federal Constitution, Sept. 28-Oct. 9 1959 (Port-of-Spain, 1959)

37 Jamaica, House of Representatives, *Proceedings* Session 1959-60, No. 5 (3-5 Nov. 1959), pp 98-105. For a commentary on this debate see S. Walter Washington, 'Crisis in the British West Indies,' *Foreign Affairs*, XXXVIII (July 1960), 645-66.

38 *Sunday Gleaner*, 14 Feb. 1960

39 West Indies Federal Information Service, *The Federal Principle* (Port-of-Spain, n.d.), p 2

NOTES TO CHAPTER 7

1 Joint memorandum by the Colonial Office and the Jamaican delegation, summarizing the London talks on federation; published in the *Daily Gleaner* (Kingston), 29 Feb. 1960

2 Sir John Mordecai, *The West Indies: The Federal Negotiations* (London, 1968), p 202

3 *Daily Gleaner*, 19 Jan. 1960

4 Government of Jamaica, *Ministry Paper No. 3* (Kingston, 1960), also published in the *Daily Gleaner*, 27 Feb. 1960

5 *Sunday Gleaner*, 6 March 1960

6 *Daily Gleaner*, 1 Feb. 1956

7 'Sentimental Campaign on for Federation,' ibid, 3 April 1960

8 *Daily Gleaner*, 12, 14, 15 March 1960

9 Ibid, 23 March 1960

10 Ibid, 27 March 1960

11 Ibid, 28 April 1960

12 *The Nation* (Port-of-Spain), 28 Jan. 1966

13 'Planning and Politics in the British Caribbean,' *West Indian Economist*, II (May-June 1960), 26

14 *Daily Gleaner*, 2, 6 May 1960

15 The West Indies House of Representatives *Parliamentary Debates*, 2nd session (1959-60), 1266-9

16 The West Indies Federal Information Service, *The West Indies Federal Review*, I (June 1960), 10-11

17 *Daily Gleaner*, 9 May 1960

18 Ibid, 17, 18 May 1960

19 *The Democrat* (Port-of-Spain), 14 June 1960

20 *The West Indies Federal Review*, I (June 1960), 6, 7, 15

21 *Daily Gleaner*, 1, 17, 18 June 1960

22 Ibid, 22 July 1960

23 'The West Indies Without Jamaica: Who Killed Cock Robin?' *Sunday Guardian* (Port-of-Spain) 1 Oct. 1961

24 *Trinidad Guardian*, 7, 8, 15 Aug. 1960; *Daily Gleaner*, 11, 13 Aug. 1960. On the Antigua Pact see Sir John Mordecai, *The West Indies: The Federal Negotiations* (London, 1968), pp 245-58.

25 *Trinidad Guardian*, 14 Aug. 1960; *Daily Gleaner*, 13 Aug. 1960

26 *Daily Gleaner*, 6, 20 Feb. 1961

27 *Sunday Guardian*, 11 Feb. 1962; *Christian Science Monitor* (Boston), 30 Sept. 1961; *Daily Gleaner*, 1, 17 Oct. 1961

28 *Daily Gleaner*, 30 April, 4 May 1960

29 Ibid, 17, 20, 21, 24, 25, 28 June, 4, 14 July 1960; *Sunday Advocate*, 7 Aug. 1960

30 *Daily Gleaner*, 13 July 1960

31 *Chronicle of the West India Committee*, LXXV (Aug. 1960), 230

32 *Daily Gleaner*, 15 Oct. 1960

33 *West Indies Federal Review*, I (Oct. 1960), 8-10; Federal Information Service Press Release, 22 Oct. 1960

34 *Daily Gleaner*, 18, 19, 22, 24, 25 Oct. 1960

35 Ibid, 19 Nov. 1960

36 Eric Williams, *History of the People of Trinidad and Tobago* (Port-of-Spain, 1962), 274-5

37 Ibid, 277-8; 'West Indies Bases Conference,' *West Indies Federal Review*, I (Nov.-Dec. 1960), 16-17

38 *Commonwealth Survey,* VI (20 Dec. 1960), 1211-12; VII (3 Jan. 1961), 27-8

39 *Daily Gleaner*, 16 Dec. 1960

40 *Daily Mirror* (Port-of-Spain), 8 Feb. 1966; *Chronicle of the West India Committee*, LXXXII (Jan. 1967), 37

41 *Chronicle of the West India Committee,* LXXVI (April 1961), 91-4

42 *Daily Gleaner*, 23 Jan. 1961

43 Ibid, 19, 20 April 1961

44 Ibid, 14 April 1961

45 Ibid, 7 April 1961

46 *West Indies Federal Review*, II (April 1961), 11-15. The broadcast was on 23 April 1961.

47 Ibid, II (May 1961), 216

48 *Daily Gleaner*, 17 May 1961

49 *The Times* (London), 18, 19 May 1961

50 'Thomas Wright,' *Daily Gleaner*, 18 May 1961

51 *Daily Gleaner*, 22, 25 May, 12 June 1961

52 Editorial on the 'Federal West Indies,' *Manchester Guardian Weekly*, 8 June 1961

53 West Indies Federal Information Service, Press Release, 31 May 1961; *The Times* (London), 1, 6, 7 June 1961

54 *Report* of the West India Royal Commission, Cmd. 8655, 8657, 8667, 8669 (London, 1898). A British journalist commenting on the constitutional conference described Dr Williams as a man who knew that Trinidad was 'far too small for him ... For chilly remoteness and ruthless logic, the veterans of Lancaster House can compare him only to Sir Edgar Whitehead of Southern Rhodesia.' Tom Stacey, 'West Indian Leaders Struggle for Federal Premiership,' *Sunday Times* (London), 11 June 1961

55 *Daily Gleaner*, 8 June 1961

56 Great Britain, *Report of the West Indies Constitutional Conference, 1961*, Cmnd. 1417 (London, 1961), pp 10-13 A detailed discussion of this conference is given in Mordecai, *The West Indies*, chap 21.

57 *Sunday Guardian*, 5 Nov. 1961

58 George John, *Daily Gleaner*, 2, 3 June 1961

59 'Thomas Wright,' *Daily Gleaner*, 8 June 1961

60 *The Times* (London), 2 June 1961

61 *Report of the West Indies Constitutional Conference, 1961*, pp 16-17; *Daily Gleaner*, 7, 8, 9, 12, 16 June 1961

62 The West Indies House of Representatives, *Parliamentary Debates*, II (1959-60), 16 May 1960, col 1269. The importance of this point was emphasized in a letter by Mona Macmillan to *The Times* (London), 15 May 1963. 'I believe,' she wrote, 'that the British Government which had done so much to promote the experiment [of federation], doomed it to failure when it refused the guaranteed income which it had been generally understood in the West Indies would be forthcoming to prime the Federal pump. With funds behind them the new Ministers might have made an immediate impact ... [which] would have fired the West Indian imagination. Greater sums than this were asked for and have been given to colonial territories which have behaved less well.'

63 Great Britain, *Report* by the Leeward Islands and Windward Islands Constitutional Conference, Cmd. 1434 (London, 1961), pp 5-18

64 The West Indies, House of Representatives, *Parliamentary Debates*, (20 July 1961), cols 385ff; (25 July 1961), col. 517

65 *The Times* (London), 20 June 1961; *The Nation* (Port-of-Spain), 23 June 1961. Mr Macleod was reporting on 19 June 1961, to the British House of Commons about the West Indies Constitutional Conference.

NOTES TO CHAPTER 8

1 'Referendum a Fight for Life,' *Sunday Gleaner* (Kingston), 6 Aug. 1961

2 *Daily Gleaner*, 28 July, 22 Aug., 17 Sept. 1961

3 *Federation: What it Will Really Cost Jamaica* (Kingston, 1961); Rex Nettleford, ed, *Manley and the New Jamaica* (London, 1971), p 175

4 *Daily Gleaner*, 17, 19, 29 Aug., 16, 19 Sept. 1961

5 'The End of the Federation: Some Constitutional Implications,' *West Indian Economist*, IV (March 1962), 16

6 *Sunday Guardian* (Port-of-Spain), 17 Sept. 1961

7 *Daily Gleaner*, 10 Oct. 1961

8 J.B. Kelly, 'The Jamaica Independence Constitution,' *West Indian Economist*, IV (Christmas 1962), 9-20, and (March 1962), 11-26

9 *West Indian Economist*, III (Oct. 1961), 3

10 *Weekly Gleaner*, 23 Aug. 1967; Sir John Mordecai, *The West Indies: The*

Federal Negotiations (London, 1968), p 311; *Daily Gleaner*, 25 Aug. 1967

11 *The Times* (London), 21, 22 Sept. 1961; *Daily Gleaner*, 2 Oct. 1961. A thoughtful analysis of the significance of the referendum is given by Brian Chapman, 'Jamaica's Future in Doubt,' *Manchester Guardian Weekly*, 28 Sept. 1961.

12 *The Times* (London), 21 Sept. 1961

13 *The Torchlight* (Grenada), 22 Sept. 1961; *The Voice of St Lucia* (Castries) 30 Sept. 1961; *Daily Gleaner*, 14 Oct., 4 Nov. 1961

14 *Commonwealth Survey*, VII (10 Oct. 1961), 1035; Sir Algernon Aspinall, *The British West Indies* (London, 1912), p 415

15 *The Times* (London), 30 Sept., 6 Oct. 1961: *Daily Gleaner*, 6 Oct. 1961; *Chronicle of the West India Committee*, LXXVI (Oct.-Nov. 1961), 248

16 *Sunday Guardian*, 1, 8 Oct. 1961; *Daily Gleaner*, 9 Oct. 1961

17 Address to a press conference on 4 Nov. 1961; *Weekly Gleaner*, 6 Nov. 1961

18 *The Times* (London), 25 Sept. 1961; *Sunday Guardian*, 5 Nov. 1961

19 'Thomas Wright,' *Daily Gleaner*, 11 Nov. 1961

20 Broadcast on 15 Oct. 1961, published in the *West Indies Federal Review*, II (Oct. 1961), 2-15

21 *West Indies Federal Review*, II (Oct. 1961), 2-15

22 The West Indies Federal Information Service, Press Release, 29 Oct., 21 Dec. 1961

23 *Sunday Guardian*, 24 Sept., 1, 20, 22 Oct. 1961; *Daily Gleaner*, 20 Oct. 1961

24 *Eastern Caribbean Federation*, Report to the Prime Minister by Professor Arthur Lewis (Port-of-Spain, 1961). In Feb. 1962 Professor Lewis presented a second report, *Proposals for an Eastern Caribbean Federation of Eight Territories* (Port-of-Spain, 1962), embodying minor alterations in his original recommendations. See also his *The Agony of the Eight* (Bridgetown, n.d.).

25 *Sunday Guardian*, 5 Nov. 1961; *Daily Gleaner*, 13 Nov. 1961

26 *Sunday Guardian*, 12 Nov. 1961

27 *Daily Gleaner*, 12, 19 Oct. 1961

28 'Behind the Curtain,' *Sunday Guardian*, 8, 22, 29 Oct., 12, 19 Nov., 17 Dec. 1961, 7 Jan. 1962

29 *Weekly Gleaner*, 9 Dec. 1961, 9 Feb. 1962

30 *The Nation* (People's National Movement party organ), IV, 15 Jan. 1962

31 Trinidad and Tobago House of Representatives, *Debates* (12 Jan. 1962), cols 27, 50

32 Leading editorial on 'Fixing our Day of Destiny,' *Sunday Guardian*, 27 May 1962

33 Henry Paul, *Sunday Guardian*, 13 May 1962

34 *Sunday Guardian*, 18, 27 March 1962

35 Albert Gomes and David J. Chin, *Sunday Guardian*, 21, 22 Jan., 4 Feb. 1962

36 *Weekly Gleaner*, 19 Jan. 1962

37 Leigh Richardson, 'Disruption and Confusion in the West Indies,' *Sunday Guardian*, 28 Jan. 1962

38 *Weekly Gleaner*, 2 Feb. 1962

39 *Sunday Guardian*, 21, 28 Jan., 4, 11, 25 Feb. 1962

40 *Weekly Gleaner*, 9 Feb. 1962

41 *Voice of St. Lucia*, 3 Feb. 1962

42 *The Times* (London), 13 Dec. 1962; *Weekly Gleaner*, 2 Feb. 1962

43 *Daily Gleaner*, 31 Jan. 1962

44 *West Indian Economist*, IV (May 1962), 6-7

45 *Weekly Gleaner*, 2 Feb. 1962

46 Ibid

47 Great Britain, *Report of the Jamaica Independence Conference, 1962*, Cmnd. 1638 (London, 1962), 5-14

48 Leading editorial on 'Jamaica Alone?' *Chronicle of the West India Committee*, LXXVII (March 1962), 111-16

49 Great Britain, House of Commons, *Parliamentary Debates*, vol 653, no. 49

(6 Feb. 1962), cols 230-5; Mordecai, *The West Indies*, p 448

50 Great Britain, House of Lords, *Parliamentary Debates*, vol 237 (6 March 1962), cols 1158-90

51 Great Britain, House of Commons *Parliamentary Debates*, vol 656 (26 March 1962), cols 849-941. This long and able debate examined in detail the various reasons for the collapse of The West Indies Federation.

52 *Weekly Gleaner*, 9 Feb. 1962

53 The West Indies, House of Representatives, *Parliamentary Debates*, V (14-22 Feb. 1962), cols 763-1336

54 Ibid, V (22 Feb. 1962), cols. 1369-80

55 *The Times* (London), 15, 21, 26 March 1962

56 *Sunday Guardian*, 3 June 1962

57 Derek Walcott, 'Spiritual Purpose Lacking,' *Sunday Guardian*, 5 Jan. 1964

58 Great Britain, *Report of the Trinidad and Tobago Independence Conference, 1962*, Cmnd. 1757 (London, 1962)

59 *Weekly Gleaner*, 9 Feb. 1962

60 *Sunday Guardian*, 1 April, 27 May 1962

61 Kenneth Hill, 'Trinidad's Need for Tolerance,' *Sunday Guardian*, 3 June 1962

62 *Anti-Slavery Monthly Reporter* (Aug. 1828), pp 284-5, cited by D.J. Murray, *The West Indies and the Development of Colonial Government, 1801-34* (Oxford, 1965), p 155

63 Grenada Legislative Council, *Debates*, 21 June 1960, p 7. The extent to which West Indians participated, at each step of the way, in deciding to federate and in determining the shape of their national constitution is carefully traced in an illuminating article by Jesse H. Proctor, Jr, 'The Framing of the West Indian Federal Constitution: an Adventure in National Self-Determination,' *Revista de Historia de América*, LVII-LVIII (Dec. 1964), 51-119.

64 Barbados House of Assembly, *Debates*, 10 Feb. 1948, p 255; 19 Jan. 1956, p 1957

65 Jamaica House of Representatives, *Proceedings*, 30 Nov. 1955; *Daily Gleaner*, 2 Nov. 1958

66 The West Indies, Federal Information Service Press Release, 31 May 1961

67 *Daily Gleaner*, 22 May 1962

68 Ibid, 17 April 1961

69 *The Times* (London), 9 May 1962

70 The West Indies, House of Representatives, *Debates*, V (19 July 1961), cols 250-1. See also 'Britain, Europe and The West Indies,' *West Indian Economist*, III (June 1961), 10-16.

71 *Weekly Gleaner*, 14 Sept. 1962

72 Ibid, 1 Feb. 1963

73 'Is Jamaica Awakening?' *West Indian Economist*, IV (April 1962), 5

74 Albert Gomes, 'Behind the Headlines,' *Sunday Guardian*, 17 Dec. 1961

75 C.L.R. James, *Party Politics in the West Indies* (San Juan, Trinidad, 1962), p 143

76 *Sunday Guardian*, 4 Feb. 1962

77 *Weekly Gleaner*, 2 Feb. 1962

78 The West Indies, House of Representatives, *Debates*, II (25 May 1960), col. 1645; J.H. Proctor, Jr, 'Constitutional Defects and the Collapse of the West Indian Federation,' *Public Law* (Summer 1964), 131; Sir Arthur Lewis, 'Epilogue' in Mordecai, *The West Indies*, p 461

79 'Overcoming Insularity in Jamaica,' *Weekly Gleaner*, 11 Nov. 1970

80 'Death of a Federation — Epilogue,' *Sunday Advocate*, 2 April 1967

81 Great Britain, Colonial Office, No. 218, *Proceedings* of the Conference on the Closer Association of the British West Indian Colonies, part II (London, 1948), pp 25, 57-62

82 'The West Indian Experience and Hopes,' in P.A. Lockwood, ed, *Canada and the West Indies*, Allison University Publication No. 2 (Sackville, New Brunswick, 1957), p 28

83 'Thomas Wright,' *Weekly Gleaner*, 2 March 1962

84 Dr Patrick Solomon, in an address to the Caribbean Commonwealth

Parliamentary Association, *Weekly Gleaner*, 18 May 1966

85 Great Britain, House of Commons, *Parliamentary Debates*, vol. 656, No. 83 (26 March 1962), col 883. Nigel Fisher was the speaker.

86 Brian Chapman, 'Jamaica's Future in Doubt,' *Manchester Guardian Weekly*, 28 Sept. 1961

87 James, *Party Politics in the West Indies*, p 156

88 Hugh W. Springer, *Reflections on the Failure of the First West Indian Federation*, Occasional Papers in International Affairs No. 4 (Cambridge, 1962), pp 41-2

89 Albert Gomes, 'Behind the Curtain,' *Sunday Guardian*, 11 March 1962

90 'The West Indian Experience and Hopes,' in Lockwood, p 28

91 Epilogue to Mordecai's *The West Indies*.

92 Radio broadcast on 9 June 1960, announcing his intention to hold a referendum. Nettleford, ed, *Manley and the New Jamaica*, p 175

93 Epilogue to Mordecai, p 461

NOTES TO CHAPTER 9

1 Edgar H. Brookes, *Power, Law, Right and Love* (Durham, North Carolina, 1965), pp 7, 68

2 W. Arthur Lewis, *Politics in West Africa* (Toronto, 1965), p 29

3 *Sunday Guardian* (Port-of-Spain), 23 April 1972

4 *Sunday Guardian*, 25 June 1972; *Weekly Gleaner* (Kingston), 28 June 1972

5 *Weekly Gleaner*, 28 June 1972

6 'Quashie,' 'The Times Shaped Us Differently,' *Sunday Guardian*, 12 Jan. 1964

7 David Renwick, 'In Deep Water,' *West Indies Chronicle*, LXXXX (May-June 1975), 4-7

8 Mr Manley's 'citizens of one land' were Jamaicans, to whom he was broadcasting on the eve of his departure for the Jamaica Independence Conference in London: *Weekly Gleaner*, 2 Feb. 1962.

Select bibliography

GOVERNMENT DOCUMENTS

United Kingdom

Report of the Commission of Enquiry into the Recent Disturbances at Port-of-Spain, Trinidad, Cmd. 1662 (London, 1903)
Report by the Hon. E.F.L. Wood, M.P. on his Visit to the West Indies and British Guiana, Cmd. 1679 (London, 1922)
British Guiana Commission *Report*, Cmd. 2841 (London, 1927)
Memorandum prepared by the Elected Members of the Combined Court of British Guiana in reply to the Report of the British Guiana Commission, Cmd. 3047 (London, 1928)
Report of the West Indian Sugar Commission, Cmd. 3517 (London, 1930)
Report of the Closer Union Commission (Leeward Islands, Windward Islands, Trinidad and Tobago), Cmd. 4383 (London, 1933)
West India Royal Commission 1938-39, *Recommendations,* Cmd. 6174 (London, 1940); *Report,* Cmd. 6607 (London, 1945)
Report on Closer Association of the British West Indian Colonies, Cmd. 7120 (London, 1947)
Report of Conference on the Closer Association of the British West Indian Colonies, Montego Bay, 11-19th Sept. 1947, Cmd. 7291 (London, 1948)
Report of the British Guiana and British Honduras Settlement Commission, Cmd. 7533 (London, 1948)
British Dependencies in the Caribbean and North Atlantic, 1929-52 (London, 1952)
Report by the Conference on West Indian Federation held in London in April, 1953, Cmd. 8837 (London, 1953)

The Plan for a British Caribbean Federation agreed by the Conference on West Indian Federation held in London in April, 1953, Cmd. 8895 (London, 1953)
British Honduras, Report of an Inquiry held by Sir Reginald Sharpe, Q.C., into Allegations of Contacts between the People's United Party and Guatemala, Cmd. 9139 (London, 1954.
The Colonial Territories, 1953-54, Cmd. 9169 (London, 1954)
Colonial Development and Welfare Act, Cmd. 9462 (London, 1955)
The Plan for a British Caribbean Federation: Report of the Fiscal Commissioner, Cmd. 9618 (London, 1955)
The Plan for a British Caribbean Federation: Report of the Civil Service Commissioner, Cmd. 9619 (London, 1955)
The Plan for a British Caribbean Federation: Report of the Judicial Commissioner, Cmd. 9620 (London, 1955)
Report by the Conference on British Caribbean Federation, held in London in February, 1956, Cmd. 9733 (London, 1956)
The Colonial Territories, 1955-6, Cmd. 9769 (London, 1956)
Report of the West Indies Constitutional Conference held in London, May-June, 1961, Cmd. 1417 (London, 1961)
Report by the Leeward and Windward Islands Constitutional Conference held in London in June, 1961, Cmnd. 1434 (London, 1961)
Report of the Jamaica Independence Conference, 1962, held in London in February, 1962, Cmnd. 1638 (London, 1962)
Report of the Eastern Caribbean Federation Conference, 1962, Cmnd. 1746 (London, 1962)
Report of the Trinidad and Tobago Independence Conference, 1962, Cmnd. 1757 (London, 1962)

Colonial Office

Report of the Barbados Disturbances Commission, 1937 (London, 1937)
Annual Report on the Social and Economic Progress of the People of British Honduras, 1938, Col. No. 1894 (London, 1939)
Report of the West Indian Conference held in Barbados, March 21-30, 1944, Col. No. 187 (London, 1944)
Proceedings of the Conference on the Closer Association of the British West Indian Colonies, Montego Bay, Jamaica, 11th-19th Sept. 1947, part II (London, 1948)
Report of Conference on the Closer Association of the British West Indian Colonies, part II, Col. No. 218 (London, 1948)
Report of the Commission on the Unification of the Public Services in the British Caribbean Area, 1948-49, Col. No. 254 (London, 1949)

Report of the British Caribbean Standing Closer Association Committee, 1948-9, Col. No. 255 (London, 1950)

Report of the Commission on the Establishment of a Customs Union in the British Caribbean Area, 1948-50, Col. No. 268 (London, 1951)

British Guiana, Report of the Constitutional Commission, 1950-51, Col. No. 280 (London, 1951)

Report of the Conference on Movement of Persons within a British Caribbean Federation, held in Port-of-Spain, 14-17 March, 1955, Col. No. 315 (London, 1955)

British Caribbean Federal Capital Commission Report, Col. No. 328 (London, 1956)

Report of the Chaguaramas Joint Commission, Col. No. 338 (London, 1958)

Jamaica

Report (with appendices) of the Commission appointed to enquire into the disturbances which occurred in Jamaica between the 23rd May and the 8th June, 1938 (Kingston, 1938)

Central Bureau of Statistics. *Trade Unionism in Jamaica: 1918-1946* (Kingston, 1946)

Despatch with Enclosures from the Comptroller for Development and Welfare on Financial Aspects of Federation of the British West Indian Territories (Kingston, 1953)

A National Plan for Jamaica, 1957-67 (Kingston, 1958)

Ministry Paper No. 18 (Kingston, 1959)

Ministry Paper No. 3 (Kingston, 1960)

Trinidad and Tobago

Trinidad Constitutional Reform Committee Report (Port-of-Spain, 1948)

Office of the Premier and Ministry of Finance. *Economics of Nationhood* (Port-of-Spain, 1959)

British Honduras

Report of the Commission of Inquiry on Constitutional Reform (Belize, 1951)

The West Indies

Report of the Trade and Tariffs Commission, appointed by the Secretary of State for the Colonies (Port-of-Spain, 1958)

Federal Information Service. *The First Year: Six Broadcasts by Ministers of the Federal Government of the West Indies* (Port-of-Spain, 1959)

Other West Indian documents

Proceedings of the West Indian Conference, convened by the Dominica Taxpayers' Association (Roseau, 1932)

Minutes of a Conference on Closer Union of the Windward and Leeward Islands held at St. Kitts, 1st February, 1947. Supplement to the Leeward Islands *Gazette*, 3 Feb. 1947

Report by the Leeward and Windward Islands Constitutional Conference, held in London in June, 1959 (Port-of-Spain, 1959)

MONOGRAPHS

Abrahams, Peter. *Jamaica* (London, 1957)

Allen, James G. *Editorial Opinion in the Contemporary British Commonwealth and Empire*, University of Colorado Studies Series C (Boulder, 1946)

Aspinall, Sir Algernon. *The British West Indies* (London, 1912)

Atwood, Thomas. *The History of the Island of Dominica*, Cass Library of West Indian Studies No. 27 (London, 1971)

Augier, F.R. and Gordon, S.C. *Sources of West Indian History* (London, 1962)

Ayearst, Morley. *The British West Indies: The Search for Self-Government* (London, 1960)

Bowen, Walter. *Colonial Trade Unions*, Fabian Research Series No. 167 (London, 1954)

Breen, Henry H. *St. Lucia: Historical, Statistical, and Descriptive,* Cass Library of West Indian Studies No. 9 (London, 1970)

Clementi, Sir Cecil. *A Constitutional History of British Guiana* (London, 1937)

Coleridge, Henry Nelson. *Six Months in the West Indies in 1825*, 2nd ed (London, 1826)

Craig, Hewan. *The Legislative Council of Trinidad and Tobago*, vol VI in Margery Perham, ed, *Studies in Colonial Legislatures* (London, 1952)

Dalley, F.W. *General Industrial Conditions and Labour Relations in Trinidad* (Port-of-Spain, 1954)

Daly, Vere T. *A Short History of the Guyanese People* (Georgetown, 1966)

Despres, Leo A. *Cultural Pluralism and Nationalist Politics in British Guiana* (Chicago, 1967)

Des Voeux, Sir William. *My Colonial Service*, 2 vols (London, 1903)

Farley, Rawle, ed. *Labour Education in the British Caribbean* (Kingston, 1959)

Fortescue, J.W. *A History of the British Army*, 3 vols (London, 1899-1912)

Goldsworthy, David. *Colonial Issues in British Politics, 1945-1961* (Oxford, 1971)

Hall, Douglas. *Free Jamaica, 1838-1865* (New Haven, 1959)

Hamilton, B.L. St J. *Problems of Administration in an Emergent Nation: A Case Study of Jamaica* (New York, 1964)

Hamilton, Bruce. *Barbados and the Confederation Question* (London, 1956)

Hoyos, F.A. *The Rise of West Indian Democracy: The Life and Times of Sir Grantley Adams* (Bridgetown, 1963)

Jagan, Cheddi. *British Guiana's Future: Peaceful or Violent?* (Georgetown, 1963)

Jagan, Cheddi. *Forbidden Freedom: the Story of British Guiana* (New York, 1954)

Jagan, Cheddi. *The West on Trial* (London, 1966)

Jagan, Janet. *History of the P.P.P.* (Georgetown, 1963)

James, C.L.R. *The Life of Captain Cipriani: The Case for West Indian Self-Government* (London, 1932)

James, C.L.R. *Party Politics in the West Indies* (San Juan, Trinidad, 1962)

Kingsley, Charles. *At Last: A Christmas in the West Indies* (London, 1890)

Knowles, William H. *Trade Union Development and Industrial Relations in the British West Indies* (Berkeley, 1959)

Lamont, Norman. *Problems of the Antilles – A Collection of Speeches and Writings on West Indian Questions* (Glasgow, 1912)

Lewis, Gordon K. *The Growth of the Modern West Indies* (New York, 1968)

Lewis, W. Arthur. *The Agony of the Eight* (Bridgetown, n.d.)

Lewis, W. Arthur. *Eastern Caribbean Federation*, Report to the Prime Minister (Port-of-Spain, 1961)

Lewis, W. Arthur. *Labour in the West Indies: The Birth of a Workers' Movement*, Fabian Society Research Series No. 44 (London, 1939)

Lewis, W. Arthur. *Proposals for an Eastern Caribbean Federation of Eight Territories* (Port-of-Spain, 1952)

Listowel, Earl of, et al. *Challenge to the British Caribbean*, Fabian Colonial Bureau Pamphlet, Fabian Research Series No. 152 (London, 1952)

Lockwood, P.A., ed. *Canada and the West Indies Federation* Mount Allison University Publications No. 2 (Sackville, 1957)

Lowenthal, David. *West Indian Societies* (London, 1972)

Lowenthal, David, ed. *The West Indies Federation*, American Geographical Society Research Series No. 23 (New York, 1961)

Manley, Norman. *Federation: What It Will Really Cost Jamaica* (Kingston, 1961)

Matthews, Cedric O.J. *Labour Policies in the West Indies* (Geneva, 1952)

Meikle, Louis S. *Confederation of the British West Indies versus Annexation to the United States of America — A Political Discourse on the West Indies* (London, 1912)

Merivale, Herman. *Lectures on Colonization and Colonies* (London, 1928; first published in 1841)

Mordecai, Sir John. *The West Indies: The Federal Negotiations* (London, 1968)

Munroe, Trevor. *The Politics of Constitutional Decolonization: Jamaica, 1944-62*, Institute of Social and Economic Research, University of the West Indies (Mona, 1972)

Murray, C. Gideon. *A Scheme for the Federation of Certain of the West Indian Colonies* (London, 1911)

Murray, C. Gideon. *A United West Indies* (London, 1912)

Murray, D.J. *The West Indies and the Development of Colonial Government* (Oxford, 1965)

Nath, Dwarka. *A History of East Indians in British Guiana* (London, 1950)

Nettleford, Rex, ed. *Manley and the New Jamaica: Selected Speeches and Writings, 1938-1968* (London, 1971)

Newman, Peter. *British Guiana: Problems of Cohesion in an Immigrant Society* (London, 1964)

Norman, Frank A. *Whitehall to West Indies* (London, 1952)

Norris, Katrin. *Jamaica: The Search for an Identity* (London, 1962)

Olivier, Lord, *Jamaica, the Blessed Island* (London, 1936)

O'Loughlin, Carleen. *Economic and Political Change in the Leewards and Windwards* (New Haven, 1968)

Palmer, Ransford W. *The Jamaican Economy* (New York, 1968)

Poole, Bernard L. *The Caribbean Commission: Background of Co-operation in the West Indies* (Columbia, South Carolina, 1951)

Proudfoot, Mary. *Britain and the United States in the Caribbean: A Comparative Study in Methods of Development* (London, 1954)

Reno, Philip. *The Ordeal of British Guiana* (New York, 1964)

Rickards, Colin. *Caribbean Power* (London, 1963)

Roberts, B.C. *Labour in the Tropical Territories of the Commonwealth* (Durham, North Carolina, 1964)

Roberts, W. Adolphe. *Six Great Jamaicans* (Kingston, 1952)

Salmon, G.S. *The Caribbean Confederation: A Plan for the Union of the Fifteen British West Indian Colonies* (London, 1888)

Sewell, William Grant. *The Ordeal of Free Labour in the British West Indies* (New York, 1861)

Shephard, Charles. *An Historical Account of the Island of St. Vincent*, Cass Library of West Indian Studies No. 23 (London, 1971)

Sherlock, Sir Philip. *West Indies* (London, 1966)

Singham, A.W. *The Hero and the Crowd in a Colonial Polity* (New Haven, 1968)

Smith, Raymond T. *British Guiana* (London, 1962)

Smith, Raymond T. *The Negro Family in British Guiana* (London, 1956)

Springer, Hugh. *Reflections on the Failure of the First West Indian Federation*, Occasional Papers in International Affairs, No. 4 (Cambridge: Harvard Center for International Affairs, 1962)

Sturge, Joseph, and Harvey, Thomas. *The West Indies in 1837* (London, 1838)

Swan, Michael. *British Guiana: The Land of Six Peoples* (London, 1957)

Taylor, Sir Henry. *Autobiography* (London, 1885)

Trollope, Anthony. *The West Indies and the Spanish Main* (New York, 1860)

Tugwell, Rexford G. *The Stricken Land: The Story of Puerto Rico* (New York, 1947)

Underhill, Edward Bean. *The West Indies: Their Social and Religious Conditions* (London, 1862)

Waddell, D.A.G. *British Honduras: A Historical and Contemporary Survey* (London, 1961)

Waddell, D.A.G. *The West Indies and the Guianas* (Englewood Cliffs, New Jersey, 1967)

Waller, John Augustine. *A Voyage in the West Indies* (London, 1820)

Walrond, Theodore, ed. *Letters and Journals of James, Eighth Earl of Elgin* (London, 1873)

Weller, Judith Ann. *The East Indian Indenture in Trinidad,* Caribbean Monograph Series No. 4, Institute of Caribbean Studies, University of Puerto Rico (San Juan, 1968)

Will, H.A. *Constitutional Change in the British West Indies, 1880-1903* (Oxford, 1970)

Williams, Eric. *Capitalism and Slavery* (Chapel Hill, North Carolina, 1944)

Williams, Eric. *Federation: Two Public Lectures* (Port-of-Spain, 1956)

Williams, Eric. *History of the People of Trinidad and Tobago* (Port-of-Spain, 1962)

Williams, Eric. *Inward Hunger: The Education of a Prime Minister* (London, 1969)

Williams, Eric. *The Negro in the Caribbean* (Washington, 1942)

Winks, Robin W. *Canadian-West Indian Union: a Forty Year Minuet* (London, 1968)

Woodcock, Henry Iles. *A History of Tobago*, Cass Library of West Indian Studies No. 28 (London, 1971)

Wrong, Hume. *Government of the West Indies* (Oxford, 1923)

ARTICLES

Aspinall, Algernon E. 'West Indian Federation: Its Historical Aspects,' *United Empire*, X n.s. (Feb. 1919)

Bobb, Lewis E. 'The Federal Principle in the British West Indies,' *Social and Economic Studies*, VI (June 1957)

Bradley, C. Paul. 'Mass Parties in Jamaica: Structure and Organisation,' *Social and Economic Studies*, IX (Dec. 1960)

Braithwaite, Lloyd L. ' "Federal" Associations and Institutions in the West Indies,' *Social and Economic Studies*, VI (June 1957)

Braithwaite, Lloyd L. 'Progress towards Federation, 1938-56,' *Social and Economic Studies*, VI (1957)

Brown, John. 'William Des Voeux: A Portrait of a Crown Colony Governor,' *Chronicle of the West India Committee*, LXXXIX (Jan. 1964)

Burns, Sir Alan. 'Toward a Caribbean Federation,' *Foreign Affairs*, XXXIV (1955-6)

Chapman, Brian. 'Jamaica's Future in Doubt,' *Manchester Guardian Weekly*, 28 Sept. 1961

Comitas, Lambros. 'Metropolitan Influence in the Caribbean,' *Annals of the New York Academy of Sciences*, LXXXIII (1960)

Cumper, G.E. 'The Differentiation of Economic Groups in the West Indies,' *Social and Economic Studies*, XI (Dec. 1962)

Daniel, George T. 'Labour and Nationalism in the British Caribbean,' *Annals of the American Academy of Political and Social Science*, CCCX (March 1957)

Harris, Coleridge. 'Constitutional History of the Windwards,' *Caribbean Quarterly*, VI (May 1960)

Higham, C.S.S. 'The General Assembly of the Leeward Islands,' *English Historical Review*. XLI (April 1926) and (July 1926)

International Commission of Jurists. 'Racial Problems in the Public Service,' *Report of the British Guiana Commission of Enquiry* (Geneva, 1965)

Kelly, J.B. 'The Jamaica Independence Constitution,' *West Indian Economist*, IV (Christmas 1962)

Kelsick, Cecil A. 'Constitutional History of the Leewards,' *Caribbean Quarterly*, VI (May 1960)

Lamont, Norman. 'The West Indian Recovery,' *Contemporary Review*, CI (Feb. 1912)

Lamont, Norman. 'The West Indies: A Warning and a Way,' *Empire Review*, IV (Aug. 1902)

Lewis, Gordon K. 'West Indian Federation: The Constitutional Aspects,' *Social and Economic Studies*, VI (June 1957)

Lowenthal, David. 'The West Indies Chooses a Capital,' *Geographical Review*, XLVIII (1958)

Luke, Sir Harry. 'The West Indies since the Moyne Report,' *Geographical Magazine*, XXII (1949-50)

Mason, G.B. 'The Needs of the West Indies,' *Empire Review*, V (July 1903)

Mordecai, Sir John. 'Federation and After,' *New World*, III (Barbados Independence Issue, 1966)

Olivier, Sydney. 'Mr. Wood on the West Indies,' *Contemporary Review*, CXXII (July-Dec. 1922)

Phelps, O.W. 'Rise of the Labour Movement in Jamaica,' *Social and Economic Studies*, IX (Dec. 1960)

Proctor, Jesse H., Jr. 'Britain's Pro-Federation Policy in the Caribbean: An Inquiry into Motivation,' *Canadian Journal of Economics and Political Science*, XXII (1956)

Proctor, Jesse Harris, Jr. 'British West Indian Society and Government in Transition, 1920-1960,' *Social and Economic Studies*, XI (1962)

Proctor, Jesse H., Jr. 'Constitutional Defects and the Collapse of the West Indian Federation,' *Public Law* (Summer 1964)

Proctor, Jesse H., Jr. 'The Development of the Idea of Federation of the British Caribbean Territories,' *Caribbean Quarterly*, V (June 1957)

Proctor, Jesse H., Jr. 'The Framing of the West Indian Federal Constitution: An Adventure in National Self-Determination,' *Revista de Historia de América*, LVII-LVIII (Dec. 1964)

Proctor, Jesse Harris, Jr. 'The Functional Approach to Political Union: Lessons from the Effort to Federate the British Caribbean Territories,' *International Organization*, X (1956)

Ramphal, S.S. 'Federal Constitution in the West Indies,' *International and Comparative Law Quarterly*, II (April 1953)

Ramphal, S.S. 'Federalism in the West Indies,' *Caribbean Quarterly*, VI (May 1960)

Seers, Dudley. 'Federation of the British West Indies: The Economic and Financial Aspects,' *Social and Economic Studies*, VI (June 1957)

Springer, Hugh W. 'Problems of National Development in the West Indies,' Canadian National Commission for UNESCO, Fourth National Conference, *Dialogue, 1965* (Ottawa, 1965)

Thompson, A.A. 'University Education on Labour-Management Relations,' *Caribbean Quarterly*, III (1954)

Washington, S. Walter. 'Crisis in the British West Indies,' *Foreign Affairs,* XXXVIII (July 1960)

Wicker, E.R. 'Colonial Development and Welfare, 1929-1957: The Evolution of a Policy,' *Social and Economic Studies,* VII (Dec. 1958)

Wooding, H.O.B. 'The Constitutional History of Trinidad and Tobago,' *Caribbean Quarterly,* VI (May 1960)

Zeidenfelt, Alex. 'Political and Constitutional Development in Jamaica,' *Journal of Politics,* XIV (Aug. 1952)

Index